T0306137

Carbon Markets

cø₂logic

What is a 'CO₂ neutral' book?

The carbon emissions resulting from the production of this book have been calculated, reduced and offset to render the book 'carbon neutral'.

The emissions related to the production of this book have been estimated through a detailed analysis of the carbon emissions related to the supply chain. Using research and emission factors compiled by the French agency for the environment and energy management (ADEME) and the UK Carbon Trust, CO2logic has calculated the carbon footprint of this book.

The production of 620g of paper is responsible for 1250g of CO_2 equivalent emissions (forest product manufacturing facilities, the collection and production of the fibres, the sorting and processing of recovered paper before it enters the recycling process). The other processes involved in the production of this book (ink production, transport, printing and the distribution of the book) have an estimated carbon footprint of 352g CO_2 per book. In total the carbon footprint is estimated to be around 1.6kg CO_2 per book. This is equivalent to driving 6 miles with the average British car or to working 12 hours on a desktop using the average electricity emission factor in the UK.

To improve on this result Earthscan uses sustainable FSC paper. Sustainably managed forests act as carbon sinks and can, over time, have a net positive effect on climate change. Additionally Earthscan is currently working to minimize and mitigate its carbon footprint, reducing waste, promoting sourcing of renewable raw materials such as wood fibre and energy, and working with its stakeholders and suppliers towards a closed-loop material and energy cycle.

Carbon footprint of a 620g book (in gCO₂e)

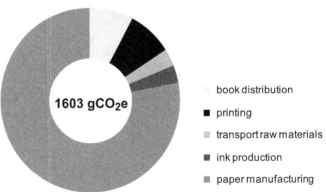

1603 gCO₂e

- book distribution
- ■ printing
- transport raw materials
- ■ ink production
- paper manufacturing

Source: CO2logic, ADEME and the Carbon Trust

Having calculated and analysed the options to reduce its carbon footprint, Earthscan has formed a partnership with CO2logic to offset the remaining emissions related to the production of this book. In practice, a project that uses agricultural waste from farmers in Rajasthan (India) to produce green renewable electricity will be supported and the related carbon credits (CERs) will be cancelled in order to offset the relevant emissions. Through this voluntary and credible action Earthscan and CO2logic hope to contribute towards the protection of our climate.

Carbon Markets

An International Business Guide

ARNAUD BROHÉ,
NICK EYRE AND
NICHOLAS HOWARTH

Routledge
Taylor & Francis Group

LONDON AND NEW YORK

First published 2009 by Earthscan in the UK and USA

Published 2016 by Routledge
For a full list of publications please contact:
Earthscan
2 Park Square, Milton Park, Abingdon, Oxon OX14 4RN
711 Third Avenue, New York, NY 10017, USA

Routledge is an imprint of the Taylor & Francis Group, an informa business

First issued in paperback 2015

ISBN: 978–1–84407–727–4 (hbk)

Typeset by Saxon Graphics Ltd, Derby
Cover design by Clifford Hayes

A catalogue record for this book is available from the British Library

Library of Congress Cataloging-in-Publication Data

Brohé, Arnaud.
    Carbon markets : an international business guide / Arnaud Brohé, Nick Eyre and Nicholas Howarth.
        p. cm.
    Includes bibliographical references and index.
    ISBN 978-1-84407-727-4 (hbk)
    ISBN 978-1-138-88080-1 (pbk)
  1. Carbon offsetting. 2. Emissions trading. I. Eyre, Nick. II. Howarth, Nicholas. III. Title.
    HC79.P55B76 2009
    363.738'746–dc22

                                                    2009014149

Contents

List of Figures, Tables and Boxes

Figures

Tables

Boxes

Acknowledgements

It is in the nature of such a collaborative work that first of all it is necessary to state the obvious and recognize the debt of gratitude that as co-authors we owe to each other. In particular, we wish to recognize Arnaud Brohé for coming up with the early concept of a book encapsulating the full diversity of emissions trading across the globe and for drafting its early chapters, which caught the eye of our publishers at Earthscan. Nicholas Howarth played the role as the project's economist and brought his much appreciated experience as a practitioner in the politics of energy and climate change. The common thread which brought us all together, at the annual workshop of the International Energy Agency in Paris in the summer of 2008, was our connection to the Environmental Change Institute at the University of Oxford, where Nick Eyre leads the Lower Carbon Futures Project. Nick has been a great source of support in the book's early stages and was an invaluable source of editorial guidance as it developed. We would like to particularly thank the Wiener-Anspach Foundation, for financing Arnaud Brohé's Research Fellowship at the University of Oxford, the Jackson Foundation for financially supporting Nick Eyre's post at the University of Oxford and the British Council, the European Investment Bank and Christ Church for their support of Nicholas Howarth's research at Oxford.

We also owe a debt of thanks to the many economists and carbon market experts whose work we have drawn on in the production of this book. Among the many individuals who talked to us and provided support or read over and commented on the draft manuscript, we would especially like to thank (in alphabetical order): Maan Barua, Murray Birt, Amandine Bourmorck, Claire Bramwell, Csaba Burger, Gordon Clark, Quentin d'Huart, Andrew Foxall, Jennifer Helgeson, Samuel Hester, Matt King, Lila McDowell, Lilli Pechey and Dariuz Wojcik.

We are also grateful to CO2logic's founders Tanguy du Monceau and Antoine Geerinckx for their support of the project and valuable comments on earlier versions.

This book also owes its existence to the vision of the staff at Earthscan, who we have been lucky to have as such supportive and professional publishers. In particular we would like to thank Camille Bramall, Alison Kuznets, Claire Lamont and Rob West.

We would like to particularly thank Cameron Hepburn and Lord Nicholas Stern. Their involvement has provided a wealth of inspiration both through their direct participation and through their published work, which continues to set a benchmark in the field.

Finally, the biggest thanks of all go to our families and friends who have put up with our distraction and the mountains of books, journal articles and news reports that have gradually been taking over our homes in its production.

Foreword

As we begin the 21st century, the world faces two challenges which will define our future: the prospect of catastrophic climate change crisis and the battle against world poverty. Furthermore it faces, in the short term, the most severe financial and economic crisis for 80 years. The financial crisis was caused by an inadequate management of risk in the financial sector. Similarly, the severity of the climate crisis will be dependent on our management of the risks from greenhouse gases. The risks however differ fundamentally. Our actions on the financial crisis will shape whether we lose a few or several percentage points of GDP and whether it lasts for a year or two, or a decade. The consequences of mistakes in managing the climate crisis are of an entirely different magnitude, possibly leading to major and irreversible consequences for life on this planet.

Emissions trading has emerged as one of the most important tools for reducing these climate risks. It has the particular advantage over other policies that it can provide finance and technology to assist developing countries towards a clean development path. In doing so, it builds positive incentives into the effort to achieve coordinated action across nations. The market it creates promotes efficiency and the caps on which it is based give greater confidence in quantity reductions than a purely tax-based mechanism. Further, the allocation of caps and how they are auctioned or sold provides for flexibility in industrial strategy and the process of adjustment. Providing a strong, stable carbon price is the single policy action that is likely to have the biggest effect in improving economic efficiency and tackling the climate crisis.

Clarity on policy and prices is all the more important now with companies facing great uncertainty because of the financial crisis: the two risks compound each other, dampening investment, making it all the more important that we take actions now that will markedly reduce uncertainties about future carbon policies and prices.

The stock of greenhouse gases in the atmosphere currently stands at around 430ppm CO_2 equivalent (CO_2e) and is increasing at about 2.5ppm

CO_2e each year. This can be compared to pre-industrial global stocks of greenhouse gases, which were around 280ppm CO_2e in 1850: this has probably increased average global temperatures by around 0.8°C above pre-industrial levels. If humankind were to continue under business-as-usual (the 2.5ppm being added each year is rising), then by 2100 we would have an atmospheric concentration of around or more than 750ppm CO_2e, which would eventually imply approximately a 50 per cent chance that average world temperatures would be 5°C warmer than 1850.

To help understand what this means, we should recall that the last time the world was 5°C cooler than today was 10,000 to 12,000 years ago during the last ice age. At this time, glaciers came down to latitudes as low as London and New York. The last time the world was 5°C higher was when the world was covered in swampy forests in the Eocene period more than 30 million years ago; and remember that *Homo sapiens* is only 100–200,000 years old. A shift upwards in temperature of a similar magnitude, over the course of the 21st century, would see dramatic changes in the physical geography of the world and the redrawing of coasts, rivers and weather patterns. Where people could live, how they could live their lives and the human geography of the world would also be redrawn. Geopolitical stability would be threatened with collapse, as floods trigger mass migration, as cities, even entire nations, disappeared under water and other parts became deserts or battered by hurricanes. For instance, one of the early impacts could be the melting of the Greenland ice cap, which alone could raise sea levels by around 4 to 8 metres globally and spark a chain of destabilizing, unpredictable feedbacks in the global climate system.

In the *Stern Review* on the economics of climate change we estimated that this unmanaged climate change would be equivalent to losing at least 5 per cent of global GDP each year relative to a world without or with relatively small climate change, and up to 20 per cent if a wider range of impacts and risks is taken into account (this is an average over regions, time and possible outcomes). With world GDP currently around US$50 trillion each year[1] this places the costs of climate change at between US$2.5 and US$10 trillion per annum in today's dollars. Looking back at these estimates of the magnitude of losses, we know today with access to the latest science that they are likely to be conservative. More rapid growth of emissions than anticipated and the reduction of the estimated absorptive capacity of oceans imply a faster rise in stocks of the greenhouse gases than estimated. The 'GDP loss' approach has its role to play in understanding the huge costs of inaction but the more direct approach in terms of an examination of possible effects on lives, habitats, ecosystems, location and conflict seems to offer a more direct, transparent and accessible perspective. We can then think of the problem as one of 'risk management' and ask the 'insurance question' of whether the 'insurance payments' are worth the gains in terms of risk reduction. For most people the answer (given costs of action of 1 or 2 per cent of GDP for a few decades[2]) would be a resounding 'yes'.

To manage these risks responsibly, the stock of greenhouse gases in the atmosphere should be held below some target level and brought down from there. Realistically, I believe that it is probably too late to hold below 450ppm (most scientists would look for stabilization below this). We will be there around 2015. But we can hold below 500ppm CO_2e and work to bring concentrations down from there. This would not remove risks but could lead to eventual concentration levels that gave an 'acceptable' probability of holding below 2°C. Certainly the risks would be dramatically lower than business-as-usual.

If we take the 50 per cent target for reductions in annual global emission flows articulated at the 2007 G8 summit at Heiligendamm in Germany and in 2008 at Hokkaido in Japan, then by 2050 annual global emissions will need to be close to $20GtCO_2$e[3] (assuming these reductions are, as they should be, relative to 1990).

Because around two-thirds of the existing stocks of greenhouse gases have been created by industrial countries, equity requires that the rich world should reduce their emissions more than poor countries. Their wealth and stronger technological skills add to the responsibility to lead. Some countries and regions have already recognized this in their long-term 2050 targets. For instance, following his election as President, Barack Obama, proposed that the United States adopt an 80 per cent national target (reductions 1990 to 2050). Canada and the UK also have 80 per cent targets, France 75 per cent and Australia a 60 per cent target.

By 2050 the world's population is expected to increase from 6.7 billion people today to around 9 billion. This growth in population is almost entirely centred in the developing world, where the population is expected to increase from around 5.7 today to around 8 billion by 2050. Per capita emissions (CO_2e) range from over 20 tonnes in countries like the US, Canada and Australia and around 10 to 12 tonnes in the European Union to 5 to 6 tonnes in China, 1.5 tonnes in India and much less than 1 tonne per person in much of Africa. If annual flows of emissions are to be 20GtCO$_2$e in 2050 and there are 9 billion people on the planet, it is a simple calculation to see that per capita emissions will need, on average, to be around 2 tonnes per person.[4] For Europe and Japan an 80 per cent reduction would yield around 2 tonnes per capita (stronger reductions in the US, Australia and Canada would be necessary to reach this level). Of course, quota allocations are not necessarily the same as actual emissions and given historical responsibilities here there is a strong argument for such allocations being lower per capita in rich countries.

If the rich world were to emit zero in 2050, the countries currently seen as 'developing', 8 billion out of the 9 billion, would have to have an average of 2.5 tonnes per capita by 2050, for the 20GtCO$_2$e flow of emissions to be achieved. They are least responsible for the bad starting point and earliest and hardest hit. It is for them to set out the overall terms of a global deal and to place the necessary conditionalities on the rich world: strong targets, early demonstration of low-carbon growth, carbon finance, sharing of technology and strong assistance with funding for adaptation.

So far I have outlined many of the key elements of what realistically might constitute a new Global Deal on climate change. World emissions must fall from around 40GtCO$_2$e to 20GtCO$_2$e per annum by 2050 to have a chance of holding concentrations below 500ppm CO$_2$e. A possible global agreement, its foundations and the challenge of building and sustaining it are set out in my recent book *A Blueprint for a Safer Planet*. All countries must be involved.

We understand the scale of necessary action. We can identify the key areas for action: energy efficiency, low-carbon technologies and halting deforestation. And we know the types of economic instrument necessary; crucially this requires a price for greenhouse gases to correct the market failure of the damage caused by emissions. Of great importance too will be appropriate regulation and support for new technologies. And a major global programme combining development with halting deforestation, shaped by the countries where the trees stand, will be crucial. We will learn greatly along the way but the direction is clear. The challenge now is political will.

Put simply, we have to manage a transition, rapid in historical terms, to low-carbon growth. There will be significant costs over the coming few decades. But the rewards will be still greater than the fundamental returns of managing climate change and protecting the planet. We should see those costs as investments with very high returns in the short, medium and long term.

In the short term a green fiscal stimulus can be a key element in taking us out of the current slowdown. For example, through work on energy efficiency, such as the insulation of houses, we can provide opportunities for unemployed construction workers. And we can do this in a way that lays the foundation for strong growth in the next two or three decades and avoid the mistake, which we made in emerging from the slowdown from the collapse of the dot.com bubble a decade ago, of sowing the seeds for the next bubble as we emerge from the slowdown.

In the medium term, the next few decades, low-carbon technologies will be a major driver of growth, analogous to or stronger than the railways, electricity, motor cars or information technology.

In the longer term we will have low-carbon growth, which will be cleaner, more energy secure, more biodiverse and probably quieter and safer. And it will be growth. High-carbon growth will kill itself, first because of high hydrocarbon prices, and more fundamentally from a very hostile physical environment. Low growth is unacceptable in a world of poverty and aspiration. That does not mean we can propose or envisage perpetual growth; but over the next several decades, only low-carbon growth can overcome world poverty. Thus we will succeed or fail together on the two defining issues of this century. If we do not manage climate change we cannot overcome world poverty and if we try to manage climate change in a way which, over the next few decades, prevents rising living standards in the developing world, we will not be able to construct the necessary global coalition for the management of climate change.

We can and must rise to both these challenges. The arguments concerning what to do and how to do it are clear and overwhelming. Weak or delayed action will be extremely costly. The creation of political will requires strong and powerful arguments. That is the responsibility of us all and an important contribution of this book.

Sir Nicholas Stern
IG Patel Professor
and Chair of the Grantham Research Institute on Climate Change and the Environment
London School of Economics
April 2009

Notes

1   US$50,000,000,000,000.
2   See HM Treasury (2006) *Stern Review on the Economics of Climate Change*, HM Treasury, London, www.hm-treasury.gov.uk/sternreview_index.htm; or Stern, N. (2009) *A Blueprint for a Safer Planet: How to Manage Climate Change and Create a New Era of Progress and Prosperity*, Bodley Head, London.
3   20,000,000,000 tonnes.
4   Remembering that a gigatonne is a billion tonnes.

List of Acronyms and Abbreviations

AAUs	Assigned Amount Units
ACCC	Australian Competition and Consumer Commission
ACPs	Abatement Certificate Providers
ACT	Australian Capital Territory
AIEs	accredited independent entities
AOSIS	Alliance of Small Island States
B&C	baseline and credit
C&T	cap-and-trade
BAU	business as usual
BTU	British thermal unit
C&C	Contraction & Convergence
CAFE	Corporate Average Fuel Economy
CBI	Confederation of British Industry
CCA	Climate Change Agreement
CCAP	Climate Change Action Plan
CCAP	climate change agreement participant
CCL	Climate Change Levy
CCS	carbon capture and sequestration
CDM	Clean Development Mechanism
CDM EB	Clean Development Mechanism Executive Board
CDP	Carbon Disclosure Project
CER	Certified Emission Reduction
CFCs	chlorofluorocarbons
CH_4	methane
CITL	Community Independent Transaction Log
CMP 1	Carbon Market Programme (UNFCCC)
CO_2	carbon dioxide

CO_2e	carbon dioxide equivalent
COP	Conference of the Parties
COP1	1st Conference of the Parties
COP2	2nd Conference of the Parties
COP7	7th Conference of the Parties
COP14	14th Conference of the Parties
COP15	15th Conference of the Parties
CPRS	Carbon Pollution Reduction Scheme
CPTF	Citizen Protection Trust Fund
CRC	Carbon Reduction Commitment
CRF	Common Reporting Format
DNA	designated national authority
DOE	designated operational entity
DP	direct participant
EEA	European Economic Area
ED	Environmental Defense
EFRAG	European Financial Reporting Advisory Group
EPA	Environmental Protection Agency (US)
EPC	Energy Performance Commitment
EPC	UK Energy Performance Certificates
ERT	expert review team
ERU	Emission Reduction Unit
EU ETS	European Union Emissions Trading Scheme
EU15	EU members 1995
EU25	EU members 2004
EU27	EU members 2007
EUA	EU allowances
EV	electric vehicle
FAR	first assessment report
FERC	Federal Energy Regulatory Commission
FIT	feed in tariffs
GDP	gross domestic product
GGAS	Greenhouse Gas Reduction Scheme
GHG	greenhouse gas
GNP	gross national product
GtC	gigatonne of carbon
GtCe	gigatonne of carbon equivalent

$GtCO_2$	gigatonne of carbon dioxide
$GtCO_2e$	gigatonne of carbon dioxide equivalent
GWh	gigawatt hours
GWP	global warming potential
HFC	hydrofluorocarbon
IASB	International Accounting Standards Board
IBRD	International Bank for Reconstruction and Development
ICAO	International Civil Aviation Organization
ICE	InterContinentalExchange
IMO	International Maritime Organization
IPART	Independent Pricing and Regulatory Tribunal
IPCC	Intergovernmental Panel on Climate Change
IPE	International Petroleum Exchange
IRP	integrated resource planning
ISO	International Organization for Standardization
ITL	International Transaction Log
JI	Joint Implementation
JISC	Joint Implementation Supervisory Committee
JVETS	Japan Voluntary Emissions Trading Scheme
LPG	liquified petroleum gas
LUAC	Large User Abatement Certificates
LULUCF	land use, land use change and forestry
MAC	marginal abatement costs
MATTERS	Market, Auction, Trust and Trade Emissions Reduction System
MCD	Marginal Damage Costs
MEP	Member of the European Parliament
MOP	Meeting of the Parties
MOU	memorandum of understanding
MPB	marginal private benefit curve
MPC	marginal private cost curve
MRET	Mandatory Renewable Energy Target
MSB	marginal social benefit curve
MSC	marginal social cost curve
NAP	national allocation plans
NF_3	nitrogen trifluoride
NGAC	NSW Greenhouse Gas Abatement Certificates

NGO	non-governmental organization
NO_x	nitrous oxides
NPV	net present value
NRDC	Natural Resources Defense Council
NSW	New South Wales
NSWETS	New South Wales Emissions Trading Scheme
NZ ETS	New Zealand Emissions Trading Scheme
NZU	New Zealand Unit
OCMO	Office of Carbon Market Oversight
OECD	Organisation for Economic Co-operation and Development
OPEC	Organization of the Petroleum Exporting Countries
PCT	personal carbon trading
PDD	project design document
PFCs	perfluorocarbon
PIN	project idea note
ppm	parts per million
PV	photovoltaic
R&D	research and development
REC	Renewable Energy Certificates
REDD	Reduced Emissions from Deforestation in Developing Countries
REGO	Renewable Energy Guarantee of Origin
RGGI	Regional Greenhouse Gas Initiative
RMU	Removal Unit
RPS	Renewable Portfolio Standards
RTD	research, technology and demonstration
SEC	Securities and Exchange Commission
SF_6	Sulfur hexafluoride
SO_2	sulfur dioxide
SRES	Special Report on Emissions Scenarios
STL	Supplementary Transaction Log
TAP	Technology Accelerator Payment
TEQs	Tradable Energy Quotas
TGC	Tradable Green Certificates
TWC	Tradable White Certificates
UCS	Union of Concerned Scientists

UNEP	United Nations Environment Programme
UNFCCC	United Nations Framework Convention on Climate Change
USCAP	United States Climate Action Partnership
UV	ultraviolet
VER	voluntary (or verified) emissions reductions
WCI	Western Climate Initiative
WMO	World Meterological Organization
WTO	World Trade Organization

Introduction

We have written this book as a practical guide for those interested in the rapidly growing world of carbon markets. Each chapter, whether dealing with the science of climate change, the theory of emissions trading, or the politics and operation of an individual country or region's carbon market, is written to be immediately accessible. No prior understanding of economics or carbon markets is assumed, and we have endeavoured to provide a full explanation of technical terms and concepts before delving into detailed discussion.

The rewards of understanding carbon markets have never been greater. The worst banking crisis and recession since the Great Depression is causing tectonic shifts in our social and economic order as governments seek to put in place more sustainable systems of governance. As a result, old modes of doing business are being challenged, while new opportunities are being created in what can be described as a process of creative destruction (Schumpeter, 1950). At the same time, this process of realignment is being influenced by scientific and popular pressure to take action on climate change. Most recent scientific research shows that we are approaching the critical threshold where average temperatures are likely to rise by 2°C or more above pre-industrial levels. Without significant and immediate action this tipping point stands no more than a decade or two away. Businesses that are responsive to this changing environment are more likely to be successful through the economic crisis and ready to hopefully expand in a world structured around a more sustainable mode of economic growth. One of the reasons we set out to write this book is that we believe it is likely that emissions trading will play a key role in shaping this new economic paradigm.

The success and appeal of emissions trading lies in the way it simultaneously supports innovation, entrepreneurship and the desire of regulators to set tight standards. It has clear goals, easily communicated by politicians to the public, and can provide useful signals in international cooperation.

Perhaps less widely appreciated, it has also created a new class of asset based on the right to use the atmosphere for pollution. For example approximately €50 billion of new atmospheric property rights were generated in Phase I of the European Union Emissions Trading Scheme (EU ETS), and the recent Federal Budget in America estimates potential emissions trading permit auctions to be worth some US$80 billion in 2012, rising to $646 billion by 2019 (Hepburn, et al, 2006; White House, 2009). To date these assets have been mainly used to help purchase support for the introduction of emissions trading in a way that would be impossible with other policy tools. Trading in these new atmospheric property rights has also drawn in the powerful, if currently somewhat tarnished, interests of the financial sector in the effort to curb greenhouse gas emissions. It also allows the costs of emissions mitigation to be minimized across the economy.

This book documents the emerging trend among nations towards the use of emissions trading in managing greenhouse gases. Led by the example of the EU ETS, regional schemes in the US and the New South Wales Emissions Trading Scheme in Australia, we are now witnessing a mushrooming of schemes around the world. In addition to New Zealand and Australia, which will introduce national schemes in 2009 and 2010, President Obama has signalled that America is to implement a national level scheme by 2012, with analysts expecting this market may be up to three times the size of the EU ETS. Furthermore, America's lead will compel many nations that have been on the sidelines of emissions trading such as Japan and Canada to develop their own markets.

The trend towards emissions trading will be driven by market forces – self-interest and fear – as firms and countries position themselves in the new carbon constrained world. First, emissions trading encourages businesses to account for their emissions. Companies that do so may then capture the value that reducing emissions presents. However, firms (and nations) that remain outside the system are likely to leave themselves increasingly exposed to environmental risks as consumers and governments push for the cost of carbon to be accounted for. This has given rise to the prospect of environmental protectionism and border tariffs against those not accounting for carbon.

The growing popularity of emissions trading has not been without controversy or its critics. For example, one view is that nature should be a sacred reserve and by commodifying nature we undermine its inherent value. Extending this theme, some compare greenhouse gas emitters who buy carbon offsets to medieval sinners who sought absolution through buying indulgences. Perhaps more pragmatically, others fear that the right to use the environment will be bought by those who can afford it leaving the poor dispossessed and marginalized. In this book we do not avoid these criticisms, but rather seek to introduce readers to the advantages and disadvantages of using emissions trading and the practical experience so far – what has worked, and where legitimate questions can be raised and improvements made.

A key observation we made as this book developed was that no two emission trading schemes are the same. To start with, they can differ in the stringency of their caps. Some use carbon intensity targets, others absolute emission targets. Allocation methods can differ, with many schemes distributing permits via 'free allocation' while others auction up to 100 per cent. Each system may also use different methodologies in the accounting of greenhouse gases. The oft-quoted saying 'a tonne is a tonne is a tonne' (of CO_2 emissions reductions) – regardless of its source – is not always true. For example, some schemes use broad top-down measurement approaches and others detailed bottom-up ones that more closely reflect actual emissions. The reliability of carbon accounting may also differ across countries, firms and different mitigation technologies. Critically, unless carefully quality assured and verified, these different accounting rules mean that the fundamental property rights in each system may also be different. This has important implications. Firstly, it means so-called 'emission caps' mean different things and might not actually limit emissions as they might suggest. For example, building a large new coal power plant could actually contribute positively to a firm meeting its 'cap' if the scheme uses emissions intensity rules. Secondly, if rules are not consistent then the linking of different schemes will be restricted. Linking is beneficial as it extends the scope for emissions reductions to take place where it is cheapest for them to occur. However, linking also results in the spread of financial capital and mitigation investment between regions or countries. The tendency of some countries to limit such transfers suggests that there is a desire to keep climate investment 'at home'.

While the focus of this book is on emissions trading, we are careful to point out that carbon markets are not a panacea, or a silver bullet solution, to the problem of climate change. If dangerous climate change is to be avoided government and industry must look beyond setting targets and establishing carbon prices towards a full portfolio of environmental measures. This includes tax incentives, greater support for private and public sector research and development, boosting low-carbon education and training in schools, technical colleges and universities, active industry policy through subsidies, reducing regulatory hurdles and increasing community acceptance to low-carbon technologies and lifestyles.

We also suggest that is misguided to claim the general superiority of one policy tool over another, such as carbon trading over taxation. Each tool has its place depending on the task and context. For example the relationship of trust between government and industry in Japan is reflected in the gradualism of their 'voluntary' approach to emissions trading. Eastern Europe has different economic and political priorities to western Europe having recently undergone a structural shift away from heavy industry following the collapse of communism, which has resulted in a large surplus of carbon credits in countries like the former East Germany, Poland, Ukraine and Russia. China must grapple with the paradox of having one of the world's largest economies and being the most significant CO_2 emitter, while still being a developing country. How does Australia reconcile being one of the world's largest coal exporters, fuelling the rapid expansion of coal power in China, while at the same time setting its own 'domestic' carbon targets? Reducing electricity sector emissions is also very different from reducing them in agriculture or forestry, and every country has a different history and existing set of regulations that must be taken into account. What we hope to convey by this, at the outset of this book, is that we should check our arguments in support of emissions trading with a degree of humility regarding the diversity of national and sectoral situations and objectives.

One aspect of the economic crisis has been a fall in the price of emission credits under the EU ETS from as much as €30 per tonne to €10 per tonne. One estimate suggests that the value of the carbon trading market will fall by nearly a third from €92 billion in 2008 to €63 billion in 2009 (*Financial Times*, 2009). Despite this fall in carbon prices the volume of trading for 2009 is set to increase by 20 per cent to 5.9 billion tonnes up from 4.9 in 2008. These volumes will continue to increase as the new emissions trading schemes discussed in this book are implemented.

While some have pointed to the volatility in carbon prices as introducing uncertainty into the carbon market and therefore discouraging investment, others argue that it is no more 'volatile' than other commodity prices and demonstrates the inherent flexibility of a market-driven response – a positive factor when the economy is under pressure. This discussion opens up some interesting debates for the future of emissions trading such as the potential role for price floors and ceilings. Another important factor for the future of emissions trading will be the credibility of carbon policy stretching forward over the next decades. Decisions to invest in major energy infrastructure, for example, are more sensitive to the long-term trend in carbon and energy prices than short-term fluctuations. Long-term prices are fundamentally determined by government processes and thus open to the pressures of the politics of the day. This has led some to argue for the need for greater long-term policy certainty. For example, specific proposals include extending the trajectory of the ETS cap to 2050 (CBI, 2009) and independent institutions modelled on monetary policy and the process of setting interest rates, to oversee carbon markets (Helm et al, 2005).

This book also comes at an important time in the development of international climate policy. In the non-binding 'Washington Declaration' agreed on 16 February 2007, heads of government from the US, China, India, Russia, Japan, Brazil, Germany, the UK, France, Italy, Canada, South Africa and Mexico (the G8+5) agreed in principle on the outline of a successor to the Kyoto Protocol after it expires in 2012. This statement envisioned a cap-and-trade system that would apply to both industrialized and developing countries. While the financial crisis has put many governments on the defensive, areas of consensus still remain. These include the need to articulate long-term climate goals with developed countries enacting significant cuts, enhanced mechanisms for adaption to climate impacts and cooperation on technology. Judging from the proliferation of regional and national mandatory schemes going forward, the continuation of international emissions trading mechanisms in some form is extremely likely. However, as would be expected significant details are yet to be resolved. These include whether the Clean Development Mechanism is to remain only a project-based system, or be opened up to sectoral projects such as envisaged by proposals to slow deforestation in Brazil, Southeast Asia and Africa and how carbon capture and storage can be built into the international framework.

Worldwide, as of March 2009 around US$429 billion had already been earmarked for 'green initiatives' as part of government stimulus packages totalling $U2451 billion (HSBC, 2009). As part of the response to climate change an increasing number of countries are forming mandatory emissions trading schemes, and many more are participating in markets through the Kyoto mechanisms. In preparing this book, we foresee that emissions trading will be a central part of what some are now calling the 'New Green Deal' – the 21st century's equivalent of Franklin D. Roosevelt's history-making response to the Great Depression of the 1920s. However, we are still moving through this turning point and the success of our ability to grasp this opportunity for change will depend on our understanding and use of the options available to us.

References

CBI (2009) 'Confederation of British industry position on ETS price floors' email from Murray Birt, Senior Policy Advisor – Energy

Financial Times (2009) 'Carbon trading poised to decline', *Financial Times,* 24 February

Helm, D., Hepburn, C. and Marsh, R. (2005) 'Credible carbon policy', *Climate Change Policy*, Oxford University Press, Oxford

Hepburn, C., Grubb, M., Neuhoff, K., Matthes, F. and Tse, M. (2006) 'Auctioning of EU ETS phase II allowances: How and why?' *Climate Policy*, no 6, pp137–160

HSBC (2009) 'Which country has the greenest bailout', *Financial Times*, 2 March

Schumpeter, J. A. (1950) *Capitalism, Socialism and Democracy*, Third Edition, Harper Colophon edition (published 1975), New York

White House (2009) 'Budget of the United States Government', Presidential Budget, Office of Management and Budget, Washington DC, see www.whitehouse.gov/omb/assets/fy2010_new_era/Summary_Tables2.pdf

Chapter 1

Climate Change

Introduction

Climate change is now established as a major problem for governments and the international community to address. The bulk of this book is devoted to carbon markets – market-based solutions designed to address the problem. However, to understand the context within which these markets operate, it is necessary to have a basic knowledge of the science and likely impacts of climate change.

Climate change is a relatively new phrase in day-to-day language. It joins a number of others in the same field – 'the greenhouse effect', 'global warming', 'carbon', 'carbon dioxide' and 'greenhouse gases' to name a few. This chapter seeks to provide a layperson's guide. It explains the basic scientific process involved, where the relevant emissions come from, how they are changing and what the impacts are on the natural environment and human society. These issues are inevitably more complex than we can explain here in great detail. For a fuller explanation interested readers should refer elsewhere, most notably to the reports that set out the consensus of world scientific opinion – the 'Fourth Assessment Report of the Intergovernmental Panel on Climate Change'. With climate change at the top of the international agenda, understanding both the basics of the science and the context is a prerequisite to acting wisely in a carbon-constrained 21st century.

A brief overview of the science

The greenhouse effect is a natural phenomenon that maintains an average temperature of 15°C on Earth, allowing life to exist. It is caused by the natural presence of gases, the so-called greenhouse gases (GHGs), which trap part of the sun's heat in the atmosphere. On the following page is a brief description of the natural phenomenon.

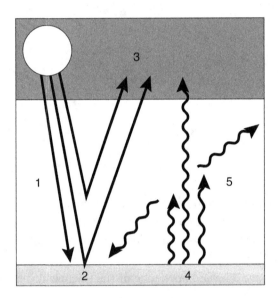

Figure 1.1 Greenhouse effect

The main GHG is water vapour. But if one limits consideration to the anthropogenic greenhouse effect (i.e. additional to the natural greenhouse effect), human emissions of water vapour have virtually no impact. Because the planet is two thirds covered by water, the average water vapour content of the atmosphere depends largely on temperature. The average residence time of water in the atmosphere is only of the order of a week and therefore anthropogenic emissions of water vapour do not significantly alter the global water cycle, although higher temperatures caused by anthropogenic climate change are amplified by a positive feedback from increased atmospheric water vapour (Jancovici, 2002).

Carbon dioxide (CO_2) is the primary cause of the human-induced greenhouse effect. Its average lifetime in the atmosphere is approximately 125 years, which means that the effect of emissions reduction measures taken today on future concentrations are slowed by this significant inertia. This CO_2 released by human activities (83 per cent of emissions of the European Union (EU) in 2005) comes mainly from burning fossil fuels and deforestation. Methane (7 per cent of EU emissions in 2005) from the burning of forests, ruminant livestock, rice paddies, farms and landfill gas, nitrous oxide (NO_x) (8 per cent of EU emissions in 2005) from fertilizers and some chemical processes, halocarbons (1 per cent of EU emissions in 2005) for example from refrigerant gases, and tropospheric ozone (from the combustion of hydrocarbons) are the main other GHGs.[1]

The development of human activities has significantly altered the concentration of GHGs in the atmosphere. This change in concentration is a phenomenon that has been identified for a long time. In 1896, chemist Svante Arrhenius had already found that the concentration of CO_2 into the atmosphere had increased considerably since the beginning of the Industrial Revolution (Arrhenius, 1896). Understanding that this increase would grow in parallel with the growth in consumption of fossil energy, and knowing the role of CO_2 in the augmentation of temperature, the Swedish scholar concluded that if the concentration of CO_2 doubled, the temperature would rise by several degrees Celsius.[2]

The strong growth of our fossil fuel consumption is inevitably accompanied by release of GHGs into the atmosphere. Indeed, by burning oil, natural gas and coal that are the results of slow decomposition of plant residue layers that had captured atmospheric carbon for millions of years, we emit into the atmosphere an additional quantity of GHGs that disturbs the carbon cycle through photosynthesis and respiration in the natural world. In a few decades we release CO_2 that was emitted and captured by ecosystems over millions of years.

Although the quantity of CO_2 emissions resulting from anthropogenic activities is small compared with those in the natural carbon cycle (involving forests, soils and oceans), these additional quantities are not completely recycled by ecosystems. The Intergovernmental Panel on Climate Change (IPCC) estimates that, of the 7 billion tonnes of carbon equivalents (7GtCe, roughly 26GtCO$_2$e)[3] released yearly by human activities, about 4GtCe remain in the atmosphere without being recycled, causing an increase in GHG concentration from 280 parts per million (ppm) since pre-industrial times to 430ppm today (including all GHGs (IPCC, 2007). At the current level of anthropogenic emissions, the concentration increases by about 4ppm each and every year. This increasing concentration is consistent with the observed average atmospheric warming of +0.7°C since the pre-industrial era, with significant spatial variability (greater warming at the poles with less warming at the equator and mid-latitudes).

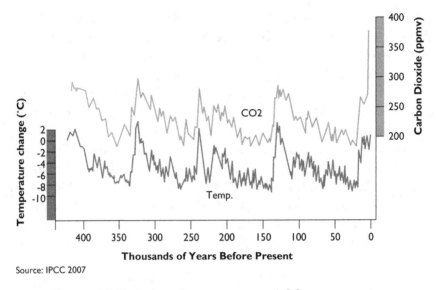

Source: IPCC 2007

Figure 1.2 Evolution of temperature and CO_2 concentration

Today, the concentration of GHGs is higher than at any time during the last 450,000 years and the IPCC projections indicate that it will continue to increase. The concentration of CO_2 alone has already increased by 35 per cent (from 280ppm to 380ppm) in the atmosphere since the Industrial Revolution, and the IPCC predicts that this concentration could triple (Special Report on Emissions Scenarios (SRES) A2 scenario[4]) by 2100 if no action is taken, given its current progress.

In its Fourth Assessment Report (2007), the IPCC felt it was 'very likely' (90 per cent chance of occurrence) that man is responsible for the warming observed in the 20th century. The IPCC considered it 'very likely' that the continuation of anthropogenic emissions will lead in the 21st century to a further warming greater than that of the 20th century. The climate sensitivity (i.e. the equilibrium change in global mean surface temperature following a doubling of the atmospheric equivalent CO_2 concentration [CO_2e]) is probably between 2 and 4.5°C, with a best estimate of about 3°C.

Distribution and evolution of GHG emissions

GHG emissions by country

The United States of America (US) was the biggest emitter of GHGs in the world in 2005. With just over 5 per cent of the world population, the US is responsible for more than a quarter of global GHG emissions. Since 1990, its carbon emissions have increased by an average of 1 per cent per annum. China, which has more than 20 per cent of the world's population, was the second largest emitter of GHGs. Due to a high growth rate, it is estimated that emissions from China exceeded those from the US in late 2007. The EU15 countries (EU countries that were already members upon ratification of the Kyoto Protocol) come in third place. The case of Indonesia and Brazil is special. Although these countries directly emit fewer GHGs than Russia, they occupy the top five places when one takes into account the emission/absorption balance of GHGs from deforestation. The case of Indonesia is particularly worrying because its annual growth rate has reached 12.7 per cent due to the combined effect of increased direct emissions and extended deforestation (part of which is palm oil production, responding to the growing demand for biofuels). In absolute terms, the annual growth of Indonesian emissions corresponds to the total emissions of Benelux, and is comparable to that of the annual growth from China. Among the major polluters, only the EU15 (collectively), Russia and Germany have experienced a decline in their emissions since 1990. The decreases in emissions in Russia and Germany are mainly due to transition periods following the fall of communist regimes, when many heavy industries collapsed.

As well as absolute emissions per country, it is interesting to be aware of average per capita emissions by country. Global emissions of anthropogenic GHGs were around $26GtCO_2e$ in 2005 for approximately 6.5 billion people, making the world average 4 tonnes of CO_2e per capita. We have seen that ecosystems are able to absorb about $3GtC$ ($11GtCO_2e$). This means that the Earth can absorb a release of 1.7 tonnes of CO_2 per capita. Taking into account expected population growth, average per capita emissions need to be below this level if we are to stabilize the global climate.

The chart below (Figure 1.3) shows the values for a dozen countries. Citizens from Australia, Canada and the US are the biggest emitters with emissions of GHGs per capita of more than 24 tonnes of CO_2e. These high emissions are partly explained by the lifestyle in these countries (widespread

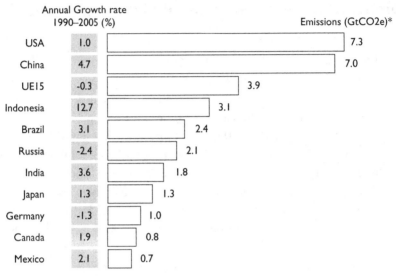

*Including deforestation (LULUCF)
Sources: IEA, EPA, WRI, UNFCCC, EEA and McKinsey

Figure 1.3 Emissions and annual growth for main GHG emitters

use of air conditioning, high meat consumption) and also by their electricity industry (mainly coal in the US and Australia) and transport systems, which focus on private cars and domestic airlines (which unlike international flights are included in national emissions inventories). Oil and gas extraction (Canada and US) and mining (Canada and Australia) are also important sources. High emissions in the Netherlands (in comparison with the EU15 average) are partly explained by the importance of chemical and refining industries in Holland. In China, a country often stigmatized since it exceeded the emissions of the US, average per capita emissions are just above the average global per capita value. The figure for India, comparable to many countries in sub-Saharan Africa, illustrates the state of underdevelopment in a large part of the subcontinent. However, this low level is the emission level we should strive for if we want to stabilize the concentration of GHGs in the atmosphere.

What can we learn from these figures? On the one hand that significant differences exist between developed countries and developing countries (e.g. all countries in sub-Saharan Africa, excluding South Africa, lie

Per capita GHG emissions – 2005

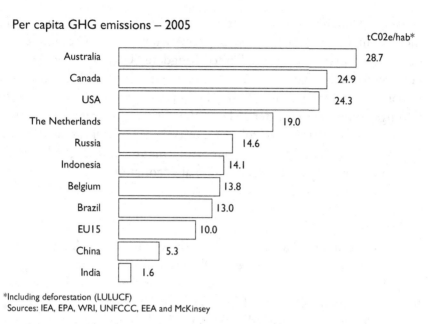

tC02e/hab*

Australia	28.7
Canada	24.9
USA	24.3
The Netherlands	19.0
Russia	14.6
Indonesia	14.1
Belgium	13.8
Brazil	13.0
EU15	10.0
China	5.3
India	1.6

*Including deforestation (LULUCF)
Sources: IEA, EPA, WRI, UNFCCC, EEA and McKinsey

Figure 1.4 Per capita GHG emissions

between 1 and 4 tonnes of CO_2e per capita). On the other hand there is a significant difference among Organisation for Economic Co-operation and Development (OECD) countries. For the pessimists, the figures from the top three indicate that emissions of GHGs have a very important growth potential if we all adopt an 'American way of life'. For the optimists, the difference between the emission of GHGs per capita in Europe (10 tonnes) and North America (more than 24 tonnes) suggests that the correlation between well-being and emissions is far from complete and it is possible to have a good quality of life with emissions 60 per cent lower than those of the US. Note that a country such as Switzerland, with an economy largely dependent on the services sector, reached a very high standard of living with per capita emissions of 7 tonnes of CO_2e. Moreover, the lower use of fossil fuel in Europe could increase its competitiveness, while oil dependency in the US is already a burden for the American trade balance. Finally, it is worth clarifying that per capita figures are an imprecise measure of consumption effects because of industry relocation and embodied carbon of imported goods. Where emissions from European countries have fallen this is partly due to the increase in imports of finished products from Asia. For example, the decline in emissions from the United Kingdom (UK) in recent years has been more than offset by rising emissions effectively embedded in UK imports (Wiedmann et al, 2008). The implications for the UK (but the findings could well be extended to other European countries) are that global GHG emissions control needs to consider consumption effects as well as production. Countries importing manufactured goods should therefore consider in future international negotiations their influence on rising emissions in a country such as China.

GHG emissions by sector

Globally, anthropogenic emissions of GHGs can be divided into seven broad categories. Nearly a quarter of all GHG emissions (a little over 30 per cent of CO_2 emissions) are due to the production of electricity and heat.[5] Industry is responsible for one fifth of global GHG emissions, a proportion comparable to the combined emissions of transport (13 per cent) and heating of buildings (8 per cent). Deforestation at a rapid pace in developing countries is responsible for almost one fifth of emissions (17 per cent). Agriculture (primarily methane and NO_x) represents 13 per cent of global emissions, and waste (mostly methane) just 3 per cent.

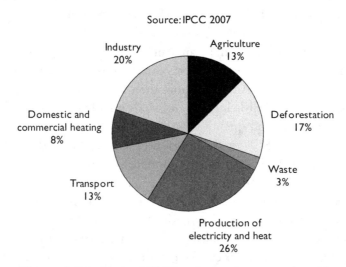

Figure 1.5 Sources of GHG emissions by sector (world)

At the European level, we find the same general pattern, with the exception of deforestation, which is no longer an issue in Europe, where even a little reforestation has occurred since 1990. Transport and heating are proportionately greater in the EU15 (more than one third of GHG emissions) than globally (only one fifth).

In most European countries, use of electricity is split approximately equally between three sectors: industry, commerce and households. Energy use in the transport, buildings and industry sectors are each responsible for approximately a quarter of EU emissions.

GHG emissions by source

All fossil fuels contribute to GHG emissions through the formation of CO_2 from the carbon contained in the fuel. The extent to which different fuels contribute depends upon both the quantity of fuel used and its specific carbon content, that is, the amount of carbon per unit of energy in the fuel. The major fossils fuels – coal, oil and gas – contribute approximately 3GtC, 3GtC and 1.5GtC respectively to global emissions (Oak Ridge National Laboratory, 2008). The lower emissions of natural gas are partly because it

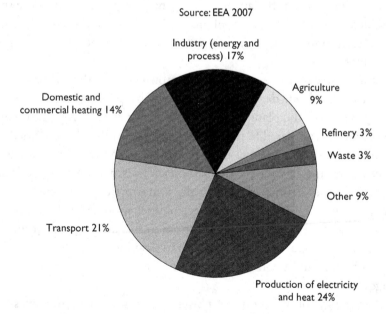

Source: EEA 2007

Industry (energy and process) 17%

Agriculture 9%

Domestic and commercial heating 14%

Refinery 3%

Waste 3%

Other 9%

Transport 21%

Production of electricity and heat 24%

Figure 1.6 Sources of GHG emissions by sector (EU15)

remains the least used fossil fuel, but partly because it has the lowest specific carbon content.

The exact specific carbon content depends on the precise fuel grade. As a general rule, coal, oil and gas contribute in the ratio 5: 4: 3, so that coal is the 'dirtiest' fossil fuel and natural gas the 'cleanest'. In essence, combustion of natural gas provides a greater fraction of its energy from hydrogen than other fossil fuels, because of its chemical composition (it is predominantly methane, CH_4).

The carbon contributions of different energy sources also depend on the efficiency with which energy is converted into different forms in the fuel supply chain. This is particularly important for electricity, where the power generation stage is quite inefficient, so that fossil-generated electricity is a very carbon-intensive fuel, particularly coal-generated electricity, which uses the highest carbon fuel and is less efficient than modern natural gas technologies.

For the purposes of GHG emissions estimates it is often assumed that all of the carbon contained in the fuel is completely converted to CO_2 in the combustion process. In practice there is usually some incomplete combustion, resulting in some of the carbon being emitted as carbon monoxide or hydrocarbons. These are also GHGs, but are usually converted into CO_2 in the atmosphere by natural processes on quite short timescales. Moreover, the extent of incomplete combustion is usually small. So an assumption of complete conversion of fossil carbon to CO_2 implies only a small error.

Biofuels also derive energy from the combustion of hydrocarbons. This is energy that has been derived from sunlight by photosynthesis over the growing period of the plant – typically a year for energy crops and tens of years for wood, compared to millions of years for fossil fuels.[6] Provided that the production of the biofuel is sustainable (i.e. the harvested plants are replaced), the net impact on the carbon cycle is neutral over timescales shorter than the lifetime of CO_2 in the atmosphere and biofuels can be treated as carbon neutral. In practice, biofuel production is not always sustainable and GHG emissions result from unsustainable production. The convention developed to deal with this is to treat biofuels as 'zero carbon' at the point of combustion and to account for emissions from land-use changes directly.

Other energy sources – nuclear power and non-biofuel renewables – do not directly emit CO_2 and therefore are also treated as zero carbon fuels. Of course, there may be appreciable GHG emissions associated with other stages of the life cycle of these technologies (e.g. steel and cement production), but full life cycle analyses tend to show these GHG emissions per unit of useful energy output are a least a factor of ten lower than the direct emissions from fossil fuels.

Emissions of other greenhouse gas are not, in most cases, directly associated with energy use. There are exceptions – e.g. methane from coal mining and natural gas leakage and tropospheric ozone production from the complex chemistry of reactions between oxides of nitrogen and hydrocarbons, especially in strong sunlight. However, in general these effects are not as significant as the direct effects of CO_2.

The only significant exception is the combustion of aviation fuel at high altitudes. In general, airplanes fly at altitudes above 10km to benefit from the reduced air resistance at the much lower air pressure at this height. This produces some fuel efficiency benefits but means that aviation emissions are at the top of the troposphere where the atmospheric physics and chemistry are significantly different from ground level.

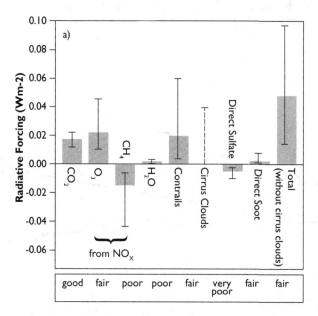

Figure 1.7 Radiative forcing from aircraft in 1992

However, emissions in the high troposphere have different effects. Emissions of oxides of nitrogen (NO_x), which are highly oxidizing, contribute to increase concentrations of ozone and reduced concentrations of methane. Emissions of water vapour have a longer lifetime if they reach the lower stratosphere, but more importantly they condense to form contrails and promote the formation of high altitude cirrus, which adds to greenhouse warming. Lastly, there are small emissions of sooty and sulfate aerosols that have opposite effects. The combined effect of all these emissions is shown in Figure 1.7 (IPCC, 1999). Not all the effects are well understood or accurately quantified, and therefore the uncertainty in the total effect is large, but the best estimate of the overall effect is that aviation GHG emissions have approximately double the impact of the same emissions at ground level.

Evolution of GHG emissions

Globally, GHG emissions have almost doubled since 1970. The growth is especially important in the electricity sector.

Within the EU (EU15), emissions have stabilized since 1990, with a slight increase in emissions of CO_2, which was offset by a decrease in emissions of methane and N_2O. For the EU27, the decrease is a bit more pronounced, because of the transition experienced by countries of the former Eastern bloc.

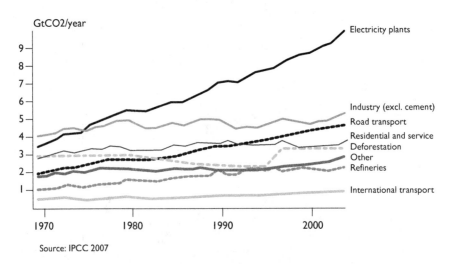

Source: IPCC 2007

Figure 1.8 Sources of global CO_2 emissions since 1970 (world)

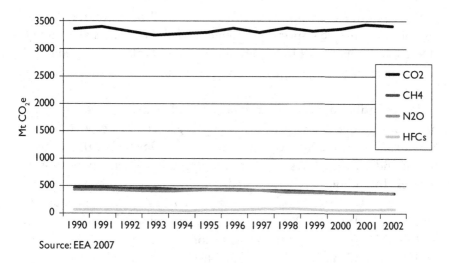

Source: EEA 2007

Figure 1.9 Evolution of greenhouse gas emissions since 1990 (EU15)

Natural consequences of climate change

Ongoing climate changes have already affected many physical systems and have an impact on biodiversity. The impacts of climate change occur not just through a rise in average temperatures. The changes are expected to be different in different regions. And the increased energy in weather systems will increase both the magnitude and frequency of extreme weather events.

IPCC models project a rise in sea levels between 19 and 58cm by 2100, but the melting of ice, the importance of which is suggested by recent observations, is not taken into account (IPCC, 2007). So these models give a lower estimate of the rise in sea level for the 21st century. This rise threatens coastal areas (Church et al, 2006). The rise in water level, coupled with predictions of storms of increased frequency and intensity, will be particularly problematic for small island states[7] and countries such as Bangladesh and Egypt (Nile Delta), where millions of people may be displaced.

There is a 'probable' increase in the intensity of tropical cyclones (with greater certainty for the North Atlantic than for other basins). During the 21st century, it is 'likely' that the intensity of hurricanes will also increase.

It is 'very likely' that some extreme events will become more frequent and/or more intense (especially extreme rainfall, heat waves and droughts (Dore, 2005, pp1167–1181). Periods of extreme cold will be reduced by the rise in average temperature, although winter temperature variation may be at least as great.

The scientific community recognizes the vulnerability to climate change of various unique ecosystems, for example, glaciers (Gregory et al, 2004; Silviero and Jaquet, 2005), coral reefs and atolls (Obura, 2005), mangroves, boreal and tropical forests, polar and alpine ecosystems, wetlands and prairies. In addition, scientists predict that climate change will threaten some species with greater risk of extinction. For example, a study published by *Nature* in January 2004 suggests that a warming of 1.8–2°C between 1990 and 2050 could lead to the extinction of one quarter of living species by 2050 (Pounds and Puschendorf, 2004; Thomas et al, 2004).

The social and economic consequences of climate change

Changes to temperature and rainfall patterns have potentially important implications for agriculture, forestry and water. Some cool temperate zones will experience increased crop productivity due to longer growing seasons. But reduced rainfall and increased rates of evaporation will lead to greater risk to food production in lower latitudes where rainfall is already limited for productive agriculture. Water supply will also be negatively affected, with implications for settlement and agriculture.

Higher temperatures reduce the need for space heating and risk of cold-related health impacts. On the other hand, they will increase energy use in air conditioning. The net effect will be strongly regionally dependent. The increase in extreme weather – heat waves, floods, storms and droughts – has a negative impact on human health (Haines et al, 2006). In Europe, the heat wave in the summer of 2003 (Schär and Jendritzky, 2004) led to increases in mortality, especially in France (Poumadere et al, 2005). Record-breaking temperatures occurred again in June and July 2006. Higher temperatures also increase risks from tropical diseases, notably the spread of malaria. Overall, the negative health impacts will be strongest in low-income countries, which are less able to take the necessary adaptation measures (Monirul Oader Mirza, 2003).

The implications of climate change that are the most difficult to predict are those relating to social and political reactions to change, especially where there are multiple impacts and limited capacity to adapt. For example, the implications of the combined impacts of reduced water supply, loss of agricultural production and extreme weather in a resilient society might be limited to higher food and water prices, but where vulnerability is higher could potentially result in desertification, hunger, mortality risk and even migration and conflict.

For these reasons assessing the aggregate consequences of climate change is subject to high levels of uncertainty. Placing a reliable monetary value on these consequences has been even more difficult, as it involves monetizing impacts that are normally outside the market (notably mortality risk, biodiversity and ecosystem loss) and doing so across different generations and long time periods.

Monetary assessments of biodiversity and ecosystems (Farber et al, 2002) are notoriously complex as they involve the key life support systems (e.g. clean air, clean water, genetic diversity and climate control) within which economic activity occurs. In addition, these assessments must take into account ethical concerns such as the evaluation of losses in human life or quality of life. For example, valuing the loss of life that would be caused by an increase in temperature, using the most conventional economic technique for non-market values ('willingness to pay'), the value of a resident of a high-income country is several times that of a resident of a developing country (Spash, 2002). This type of problem has been controversial within international negotiations.

Another major problem that affects economic analysis is the choice of discount rate, i.e. how economic values at different points in time are compared. Using the conventional approach of discount rates based on market, or even central banks', interest rates makes even very significant damage in 2100 have little economic value today. It correctly reflects market-based economic decision making that neglects the far future, but is based on an assumption of 'business as usual' economic growth and an ethic of personal impatience for consumption. Neither of these seems a sound basis on which to make decisions about intergenerational sustainability.

Early attempts to place a money value on climate change tended to produce quite low values (Nordhaus, 1991; Fankhauser, 1994), because they underestimated the importance of extreme events and strongly discounted the future. Later estimates, including that used by the UK Government in its first estimate of a shadow price for carbon (Eyre et al, 1999), have addressed these issues, resulting in higher values. The publication of Sir Nicholas Stern's *Review* on the economics of climate change in October 2006 brought these issues to a mainstream audience and under the media spotlight (Stern, 2006). It is interesting to note that this 700-page report on climate change is the first of this scale to be led by an economist and not a climatologist. The report combines recent scientific understanding and economic expertise, and its legitimacy derives from its major review of the academic literature.

The overall assessment of the potential annual cost of climate change in 2100 is estimated by Stern at 20 per cent of global gross national product (GNP) (or about 5500 billion euros) (Stern, 2006, p144). This figure led to a great deal of media attention. However, given the uncertainties and ethical choices implicit in valuing climate change damage, not too much weight should be placed on the exact number, as the Stern Report itself acknowledges. This does not diminish the substance of the message of the Stern Review: climate change poses serious risks to our societies and economies; these risks justify early actions to limit them. In fact, the main message delivered by the Stern Review is that the total cost of the action to counter climate change and stabilize emissions of GHGs to below 550ppm is 5–20 times less than the cost of inaction. This message is rather optimistic as it implies that development of the economy and environmental protection are consistent goals. It has been very well received by governments and private companies and has increased awareness of the need for actions to tackle climate change.

Conclusion

The fundamental science of climate change has been known for over 100 years and is not disputed by any reputable scientist. It is known beyond any reasonable doubt that CO_2 emissions and other gases (GHGs) cause the Earth's atmosphere and surface to warm. And it is known that human activities lead to increased emissions of these gases and that this results in increased concentrations of them in the atmosphere.

The largest source of emissions is combustion of fossil fuels – coal, oil and natural gas – and our knowledge of the sources of these emissions by process and by country of origin is very well established. The predominant use of fossil fuels is for energy – heating our buildings and industrial processes, fuelling our transport systems and providing the energy input for most electricity generation. The currently industrialized countries have been responsible for most emissions historically and their per capita emissions remain far higher than those of developing countries, although some of the latter now have rapidly increasing emissions.

The future impacts of climate change are more uncertain for various reasons, including the trajectory of future emissions, the regional variation in projected climate change, the physical impacts these will have on natural systems and how effectively society will respond to these. However, these issues have all been researched extensively and are better understood than a few years ago. Impacts on natural systems are extremely likely to include sea-level rise – resulting in inundation of unprotected low-lying areas, increased frequency of extreme weather events – including droughts and storms – and loss of some natural ecosystems.

Impacts on humans will depend on how effectively society responds to these changes in the natural environment. There will certainly be impacts on human health, agriculture, forestry and water supply and, in aggregate, these are very likely to be damaging, with risks especially high in the most vulnerable tropical countries.

Placing economic values on the impacts is difficult. Standard economic practice is not designed to deal with such large-scale, uncertain outcomes into the far future, and placing monetary values on generally unpriced goods, such as human health and natural ecosystems, is inevitably contentious. However, the risk of very serious outcomes from unabated growth in emissions is now generally understood to be so high that there is broad agreement that the costs of reducing emissions to very significantly below 'business as usual levels' are lower than the costs of inaction. This forms the basis for the international political and economic responses, including carbon markets.

Notes

1   To be distinguished from stratospheric ozone that forms the ozone layer and protects the Earth from solar ultraviolet (UV) radiation.
2   This phenomenon has been known since the first half of the 19th century. The natural greenhouse effect was first described by Joseph Fourier, who gave the name greenhouse effect to this phenomenon (Fourier, 1824). The role of water vapour and CO_2 was identified later by Claude Pouillet (Pouillet, 1838).

3    $1tC = 3.6667tCO_2$.
4   The A2 scenario family is used in IPCC models. 'The A2 scenario family represents a differentiated world. It is characterized by lower trade flows, relatively slow capital stock turnover, and slower technological change. The A2 world "consolidates" into a series of economic regions. Self-reliance in terms of resources and less emphasis on economic, social, and cultural interactions between regions are characteristic for this future. Economic growth is uneven and the income gap between now-industrialized and developing parts of the world does not narrow' (IPCC, 2007).
5   In this sense 'heat' is heat energy produced as a commodity usually co-produced with electricity in a combined heat power (cogeneration) plant, rather than heat produced for 'own use' in industry and buildings.
6   Peat is intermediate with typical formation lifetimes of thousands of years.
7   The Alliance of Small Island States (AOSIS) is a coalition of 43 small islands and low-lying coastal countries that share similar development challenges and concerns about climate change.

References

Arrhenius, S. (1896) 'On the influence of carbonic acid in the air upon the temperature of the ground', *Philosophical Magazine*, vol 41, pp237–276
Church, J. A., White, N. J. and Hunter, J. R. (2006) 'Sea-level rise at tropical Pacific and Indian Ocean islands', *Global and Planetary Change*, vol 53, no 3, pp155–168
Dore, M. H. I. (2005) 'Climate change and changes in global precipitation patterns: What do we know?', *Environment International*, vol 31, pp1167–1181
Eyre, N. J., Downing, T., Hoekstra, R. and Rennings, K. (1999) 'ExternE – Externalities of energy', *Global Warming Damages*, vol 8, European Commission, Brussels
Fankhauser, S. (1994) 'The social costs of greenhouse gas emissions: An expected value approach', *Energy Journal*, vol 15, no 2, pp157–184
Farber, S. C., Costanza, R. and Wilson, M. A. (2002) 'Economic and ecological concepts for valuing ecosystem services', *Ecological Economics*, vol 41, pp375–392
Fourier, J. (1824) 'Remarques générales sur les températures du globe terrestre et des espaces planétaires', *Annales de chimie et de physique*, vol 27, pp136–167
Gregory J. M., Hsuybrecht, P. and Raper, S. C. B. (2004) 'Threatened loss of the Greenland ice sheet', *Nature*, vol 428, p616
Haines, A., Kovats, R. S., Campbell-Lendrum, D. and Corvalan, C. (2006) 'Climate change and human health: Impacts, vulnerability, and mitigation', *The Lancet*, 24 June
IPCC (1999) *Aviation and the Global Atmosphere*, Cambridge University Press, Cambridge
IPCC (2007) Working group II contribution to the fourth assessment report, *Climate Change 2007: Climate Change Impacts, Adaptation and Vulnerability*, summary for policymakers, IPCC, Geneva
Jancovici, J. M. (2002) *L'avenir climatique: Quel temps ferons nous?*, Seuil, Paris
Monirul Oader Mirza, M. (2003) 'Climate change and extreme weather events: Can developing countries adapt?', *Climate Policy*, vol 3, no 3, pp233–248
Nordhaus, W. D. (1991) 'To slow or not to slow: The economics of the greenhouse effect', *Economic Journal*, vol 101, no 407, pp920–937
Oak Ridge National Laboratory, Carbon Dioxide Information Analysis Center (2008) http://cdiac.ornl.gov/

Obura, D. O.(2005) 'Resilience and climate: Lessons from coral reefs and bleaching in the western Indian Ocean', *Estuarine, Coastal and Shelf Science*, vol 63, no 3, p353

Pouillet, C. (1838) 'Mémoire sur la chaleur solaire', *Comptes rendus de l'Académie des Sciences*, vol 7, pp24–65

Poumadere, M. C., Mays, C., Le Mer, S. and Blong, R. (2005) 'The 2003 heat wave in France: Dangerous climate change here and now', *Risk Analysis*, vol 25, no 6, pp1483–1494

Pounds, J. A. and Puschendorf, R. (2004) 'Clouded futures', *Nature*, vol 427, p107

Schär, C. and Jendritzky, G. (2004) 'Climate change: Hot news from summer 2003', *Nature*, vol 432, pp559–560

Silveiro, W. and Jaquet, J. M. (2005) 'Glacial cover mapping (1987–1996) of the Cordillera Blanca (Peru) using satellite imagery', *Remote Sensing of Environment*, vol 95, no 3, p342

Spash, C. (2002) *Greenhouse Economics: Value and Ethics*, Routledge, London

Stern, N. (2006) *The Economics of Climate Change*, The Stern Review, Cambridge University Press, UK

Thomas, C. D., Cameron, A., Green, R. E., Bakkenes, M., Beaumont, L. J. and 14 others (2004) 'Extinction risk from climate change', *Nature*, vol 427, pp145–148

Wiedmann, T., Wood, R., Lenzen, M., Minx, J., Guan, D. and Barrett, J. (2008) *Development of an Embedded Carbon Emissions Indicator – Producing a Time Series of Input-Output Tables and Embedded Carbon Dioxide Emissions for the UK by Using a MRIO Data Optimisation System*, UK Department for Environment, Food and Rural Affairs http://randd.defra.gov.uk/Document.aspx?Document=EV02033_7331_FRP.pdf

Chapter 2

Emissions Trading: A New Tool for Environmental Management

Why create a 'market' for pollution?

At first glance, people concerned about the environment might greet the idea to use markets to *protect* nature with a degree of scepticism. After all, was it not markets and the economic system that created our environmental woes, polluting waterways and the atmosphere, driving deforestation and overexploiting the oceans and causing species decline in the first place?

Somewhat understandably then, hearing economists speaking of 'unleashing' market forces to cut carbon emissions can elicit conflicting emotions. How can these economic forces, which were so destructive, be transformed into environmental champions?

To understand how the forces of the economy play out on the environment and the relatively new role of carbon markets, it is useful to go back to first principles and define what exactly we mean by such terms as 'the economy' and 'the market'.

Much more than the acts of buying and selling, markets are the interrelated systems of human interaction by which we organize our lives and the things we value. Together, these systems constitute the economy. Stemming from the ancient Greek *oikos* and *nomos* literally meaning 'house' and 'law' respectively, economics at its most elemental is the study of the forces that govern the human world.

Today we can say modern economics is concerned with the nature and governance of the social systems that make up our world. Having placed economics in this context we can more clearly see that far from being exclusively about how money is made, economics can be more accurately described as being concerned with what humans value and how society organizes and apportions this value, given limited time, money and other resources.

Amartya Sen, for example, has focused his research on the capabilities and freedoms of individuals to live a life they have reason to value, rather than narrowly on the bundles of goods and services they consume (Sen, 1999). In the climate change context, we can think of 'a stable climate' as one of the key sources of value for individuals and society alongside quality of life factors such as access to education, health care, a rewarding job, time with the family – and money, which of course has a significant bearing on the opportunities we have.

This means that in addition to the economics of the various commodities, the things we buy and sell, interest rates, housing, unemployment and the measurement of gross domestic product, there is also the economics of environment, happiness and elements of behaviour extending to encapsulate this broader term *value*.

Saying this, in order to compare different options to support informed decision making – say between a pristine river catchment and increased agricultural production and employment – economics does attempt to quantify this broader sense of value in monetary terms and, for some, this can raise ethical objections.

Box 2.1 Commodifying the environment – whose ethics?

Steven Kelman asks the question: Is it ethical to put a price on the environment and to use incentive programmes to solve environmental problems (Kelman, 1981)? His argument is that by placing a monetary value on the environment we are undermining its intrinsic value and transforming it from being a sanctified preserve to a marketable commodity. He argues that the use of economic incentives changes our attitude towards the environment and cheapens traditional values by legitimizing polluting activities by allowing those who can afford it to continue polluting while the poor are disadvantaged. Kelman argues that regulatory controls are more desirable as they send a powerful moral signal that the polluting activity is socially wrong and through such controls the state can better handle the equity dimensions around the use of the environment (Kelman, 1981).

Economist Nicholas Stern states, 'if we do not act, the overall costs and risks of climate change will be equivalent to losing at least 5 per cent of global

GDP each year, now and forever... If a wider range of risks and impacts is taken into account, the estimates of damage could rise to 20 per cent of GDP or more... In contrast the costs of action – reducing greenhouse gas emissions to avoid the worst impacts of climate change – can be limited to around 1 per cent of global GDP each year' (Stern, 2006). Stern argues how the use of emissions trading will allow these emissions reductions to occur in the most cost-effective way, potentially solving problems such as deforestation and providing much needed financial support to developing countries for projects to increase (clean) energy production and offer more sustainable income sources than (often illegal) deforestation.

It is how this broad concept of value is translated into everyday decisions that is the focus of economics, and with respect to the subject of this book – emissions trading – how the value we place on preventing catastrophic climate change is translated into low-carbon lifestyles, technologies and infrastructure.

Even with this broader appreciation for markets and economics it is easy to see that, even though many people are worried about the risk of climate change and value a stable climate, individuals, companies and governments are still not taking action to reduce harmful emissions. What has gone wrong?

Market failure

When society values something more highly than the sum of the amount that the individual or company value it, economists call this an *externality* (i.e. the value is external to the decisions made by the individual agent). These can be positive, as in the case of education or research and development (RBD), or negative as in the case of GHG pollution.

In the case of the positive externality, society demands more of the good or service in question than will be provided naturally by market interactions. However, in the case of the negative externality, society demands less of the goods or services produced (in our case high-carbon energy from fossil fuels, or products from land that has been subject to tropical deforestation) than what will naturally be provided by the market. These externalities can therefore be described as leading to *market failure*: failure to adequately protect the environment; failure to support education or R&D; and failure to supply adequate health care – all these are good examples of (bad) market failures.

Diagrammatically the negative externality associated with climate change and fossil-fuel energy production is shown in Figure 2.1 by the deviation of the marginal private cost curve (MPC) from the marginal social cost curve (MSC). However, energy production also has a positive externality associated with it because of the large public benefit of having continuous, uninterrupted energy supplies; this requires producers to maintain a surplus capacity above what they would provide as normal profit-maximizers. Thus in addition, a marginal social benefit curve (MSB) lies above the marginal private benefit (MPB) curve of energy production.[1]

This theory of externalities helps explain the evolution of energy provision. Historically, governments have subsidized energy production to ensure that a stable supply is guaranteed. This has shifted the 'free market' equilibrium from 1 to 2 in Figure 2.1. For example, the Global Subsidies Initiative has estimated that the size of global energy subsidies for fossil fuels could be in the order of US$600 billion per annum in 2006 (Doornbosch and Knight, 2008).[2]

Now that society has become aware of the climate change problem associated with the burning of fossil fuels (the MSC moves outwards with time

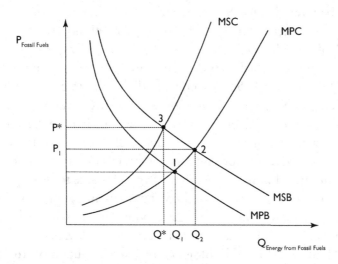

Figure 2.1 The externalities of energy production from fossil fuels

as our understanding of the higher costs of climate change increases), the socially desirable level of production moves from Q_2 to Q^*. Note that moving to this point requires imposing a higher price on fossil fuels *and/or* lowering the existing subsidies used in the first place to ensure a stable and secure energy supply.[3]

Note that the socially desirable, or optimal, level of pollution is positive. This means that society is prepared, in this case, to tolerate some pollution in exchange for the benefits of the energy provided. However, this need not be the case. The optimal level of pollution would be zero when the MSC curve was above all points on the MSB curve. This would become the case in the event that costs of climate change become larger and more immediate than currently understood.

Market failure, policy choice and socio-economic organization

How society chooses to deal with market failures shapes, not just the environmental quality, level of innovation or life expectancy in a country, but also, because of the pervasiveness of the market as broadly defined as our mode of social and economic organization, the politics of a country. It is for this reason – for good or bad – that regulatory approaches can become closely tied in with political ideology.

If we believe Nicholas Stern's assertion that climate change represents the biggest market failure in the history of mankind,[4] we must also be mindful of the changes to socio-economic organization that climate change has the potential to precipitate through new regulatory environments. Until the late 1950s opinion was divided as to how to most effectively deal with the regulation of externalities, such as industrial pollution. At the time, in the post-World War Two environment, the dominant view of policy makers was that pollution should be controlled by a series of legal regulations such as the special zoning of polluting activities, quantitative limits on the physical volumes able to be disposed into rivers and the atmosphere, technology standards and so on. This involved the public sector working closely with polluters to establish how much pollution could be emitted by individual firms and industry as a whole, setting standards for technologies, and setting up monitoring and enforcement agencies.

An alternative view was put forward by the economists of the time, influenced predominantly by the Standard Welfare Economics of Professor A. C. Pigou, which suggested that a better approach would be to impose a unitary tax on the polluting activity.[5]

Economists argued that the outcomes of the traditional regulatory or what they termed a 'command-and-control' approach could be achieved at a lower cost to society and with a smaller government bureaucracy through a tax. Taxes, they argued, would also provide incentives to continuously improve environmental performance as firms were always looking to minimize costs if they could, whereas there was no reason for a firm to exceed the pollution abatement beyond what was expected by the standard.

This tax could be set at the marginal external damage (the difference between the MPC and MSC curves in Figure 2.1) caused by the pollution at the optimal (Q*) level of pollution. This would therefore cause polluters to *internalize* the externality by imposing extra costs on production. Faced with higher costs, the polluting firm produces less ($Q_1 \rightarrow Q^*$).

Officials in the public service, who perhaps saw these proposals as a direct threat to their jobs (and they were: economists also generally modelled the public service as trying to maximize their budgets, rather than social welfare, in the same way as a private firm seeks to maximize profits), responded that the information burden to achieve the optimal tax rate for a given pollution level was unrealistic and would require just as many resources to do properly as using the traditional regulatory command-and-control approach.

The result of this debate was an acrimonious stand-off, with market-based mechanisms such as taxes remaining unpopular. This situation persisted until Ronald Coase, from the University of Chicago, launched an attack on the Standard Welfare Economics of Pigou and reframed pollution control as a problem of poorly defined property rights. In arguing his case, Coase applied basic logic to synthetic or imaginary examples of people and firms to show that:

If factors of production are thought of as rights, it becomes easier to understand that the right to do something that has a harmful effect (such as the creation of smoke, noise, smell, etc.) is also a factor of production... The cost of exercising a right (of using a factor of production) is always the

loss that is suffered elsewhere in consequence of the exercise of that right
– the inability to cross land, to park a car, to build a house, to enjoy a view,
to have peace and quiet or to breathe clean air. (Coase, 1960)

Government regulation of the environment had in many cases already created a set of de facto property rights by controlling how much and where pollution was allowed to occur. Therefore, it was already established that once a certain standard of water or air quality was breached the offending individuals or firms (or the government) could be accountable to the legal system that would enforce the pollution control with fines or injunctions.

Coase went on to argue that this regulatory system could be improved by making these rights more transparent (by allocating pollution rights to individual firms) and transferable (allowing them to trade in these rights). In this model the role of government involved setting the appropriate standard for protection, allocating the initial rights and then stepping back to let the market decide over time where and how the pollution rights would be used between different firms. Critically, Coase showed that this would allow property rights to flow to their highest-value use.

For example, a new firm that wants to enter the market to produce the commodity that generates pollution needs to obtain the required 'pollution rights' in order to operate. Assuming the market for emissions rights is already fully allocated, the new entrant will need to buy these rights from an existing firm. To do this it must offer the existing firm a price high enough to entice it to sell its pollution rights. The vendor of pollution rights must reduce its production, increase efficiency or leave the market entirely. In order to offer a price high enough to induce a sale, the new entrant must be more profitable than the existing firm. The end result, in theory, is that across the regulated sector emissions rights will go to those who are able to pay the most for them. Therefore only the highest-value users will continue operating.

While this is a very powerful result, we shall see in the following chapters that it also raises equity concerns around the ability to pay for rights, especially if pollution rights are being traded across countries with vastly different economic means. Furthermore, in addition to encouraging pollution to move towards the highest value (albeit polluting) activities, emissions trading also promotes 'least cost' emissions control. By this we mean that the trading of emissions rights encourages the firms, countries or sectors with the lowest costs of abatement to do most of the pollution control. In theory, the firms, countries or sectors with higher abatement costs utilize the emissions market to buy this cheaper abatement up until the point where the marginal costs of abatement are equal across all firms, sectors and countries.

A good example of this principle at work can be found in the operation of the Clean Development Mechanism (CDM) of the Kyoto Protocol. This allows cheap emissions credits to be bought from projects in countries such as China and Brazil and imported to countries where the costs of abatement are higher, such as the European Union and Japan. To see how this works, consider Figure 2.2 below.

The costs of abatement at each additional unit of pollution control in each firm, sector or country 'A' (from now on denoted as firm A) is described by the MAC_A curve and the same for firm B. As the MAC_B curve lies beneath the MAC_A curve the costs of abatement are lower for firm B. Suppose the combined total of emissions reductions required are described by Q*, which is the sum of the allowed emissions of each firm set by the regulator (the emissions cap).

Simply allocating pollution rights by regulating emissions at Q* with no trading,[6] would result in each firm (country) abating pollution at point 1 on their respective MAC curves (this would be their level of pollution at the

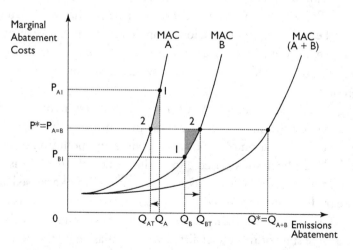

Figure 2.2 The economic benefits of emissions trading

start of the scheme minus some adjustment to reduce emissions to a required standard). Observe it costs more for firm A to control pollution at this point – with each additional unit of abatement costing P_{A1} – whereas firm B abates much more at a lower price of P_{B1}.

To 'unleash the power of markets', or move towards the Coasian solution, let us now consider the introduction of emissions trading. Firm B realizes that it can carry out extra abatement beyond what is strictly required by it at a cheaper price than it costs firm A to do abatement itself. It pays for firm A to increase its emissions (decrease abatement) from Q_A to Q_{AT} and buy permits from firm B which increases its abatement from Q_B to Q_{BT}. Q^* remains the same.

Firm A will decrease its emissions abatement from Q_B to Q_{BT} up until the point that it costs the same to buy rights off firm B or do the abatement itself. This will occur when the marginal abatement costs (MAC) for firms A and B are equalized at P^*. The benefit to society is that emissions reductions are carried out in a *least cost* manner, by the most efficient polluter. Graphically, this economic benefit to society is represented by the shaded segments of the figure. At Q_{BT} and Q_{AT} neither firm has any incentive to trade and the model is in equilibrium.[7]

Emissions trading in context

Above we saw how Coase applied his property rights theory to 'The Problem of Social Cost' or externalities to offer an alternative logic to policy makers and economists who were locked in an argument between two ends of what can be described as an ideological or policy spectrum with 'command-and-control' one end and market-based approaches such as taxation on the other.

In Figure 2.3 command-and-control policy instruments are characterized as having the state or government in control of the key decisions relating to the production of goods and services and pollution abatement. Alternatively, at the market-based end of the spectrum, these decisions are taken by individuals and firms. For these reasons, market-based mechanisms are traditionally supported by the champions of free markets or libertarians, whereas command-and-control approaches are favoured by those who see a large state or more socialist government as being the best form of social and economic organization.

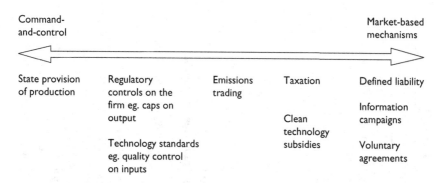

Figure 2.3 A spectrum of policy instruments

It is important to keep these institutional and political considerations in mind when evaluating policy instruments as in practice different policies will be more or less effective depending on the context in which they are applied. For example, as pointed out by Stern, regulation may be more effective in countries with a culture of using command-and-control methods, or where there are political or administrative problems with raising taxes or with tax collection (Stern, 2006). Policies that work in one sector, such as stationary energy, maybe less appropriate for others, such as transportation or agriculture.

In addition, any decision to implement a new policy instrument should be taken in the context of policies already in place that impact on the problem. For example, it is more efficient to first dismantle existing subsidies that encourage fossil fuel use than to implement a new tax or an emissions trading scheme, and it is necessary to be mindful of the geopolitics of energy security regarding sovereign autonomy.

Contingent on these broader geographical, cultural and political contextual considerations, policy instruments may vary in their environmental effectiveness, distributional impact, cost-effectiveness in achieving emissions reductions and in their institutional feasibility. As a rule of thumb, these four considerations are useful starting points for evaluating policy. With these caveats in mind, let us now consider the advantages and disadvantages of the main policy instruments for CO_2 emissions control, which are summarized in Table 2.1.

Within economics there is a vigorous debate around the question 'to tax or to trade?'[8] That is, should governments be aiming to impose a

Table 2.1 The relative strengths and weakness of regulatory standards, emissions trading schemes and taxation

	Regulatory Standards	Emissions Trading Schemes	Taxation
Principle	The state sets mandatory rules or imposes technology standards	**Cap-and-trade (C&T)** The firm receives a quota of emissions. To comply it either reduces its emissions or buys additional quota from another company directly **Baseline and credit (B&C)** No cap on overall emissions. A baseline is established and emissions credits or allowances are earned once participants reduce emissions under the baseline	The producer pays a fee proportional to its emissions of pollutants
Example of Main Application	Emissions standards for car manufacturers Standard on NO_x emissions from boilers	Kyoto Protocol (C&T+B&C) EU ETS (EU) (C&T) RGGI (US) (C&T) NSWETS (Australia) (B&C) Voluntary Carbon Market (B&C)	Fuel taxes Registration fees for cars based on engine size Proposed tariffs on high-carbon goods
Strengths	Simple Can have low transaction costs Very appropriate where there are high damages from pollution, e.g. nuclear meltdown Transparent	Dynamically efficient, by encouraging innovation and investment in new abatement technologies Emissions cap provides an attractive political signal Cap focuses on achieving a specific quantity of abatement Auctioning permits under cap-and-trade	Dynamically efficient, by encouraging innovation and investment in new abatement technologies Creates a flow of revenue for government that can be used to lower other taxes (the 'double dividend')

	Can be easy to implement	can raise revenue for government and produce a 'double dividend'	Arguably less open to political lobbying than C&T
	Can send a powerful moral signal	Cap and trade achieves least cost abatement between firms	Keeps investment in low-carbon solutions local
	Does not involve operating through behavioural response to price signals	If MAC uncertain better than tax if MDC is steep	If MAC is uncertain better than ETS if MDC is flat
	Low transaction costs	Engages the banking and finance sector in abatement innovation	Sets a clear carbon price that investors in infrastructure can use to plan with greater certainty
		Can be used as a tool to combat global inequity	Low transaction costs if integrated into existing tax systems
		Carbon pricing is hidden behind CO_2 cap, increasing political acceptability	
Weaknesses	Not dynamically efficient – provides little incentive to improve beyond the standard	Open to political gaming (e.g. limited auctioning and preference to incumbent firms vs new entrants)	Politically very difficult to bring in as adverse equity effects on poor citizens very transparent
	Can dampen technological innovation	Information requirements initially high to set cap for each firm	Difficult to control the quantity of pollution with a price instrument under uncertainty
	Abatement is unlikely to be achieved in a least cost manner	Resources for abatement can be dispersed geographically	Behaviour is not always sensitive to price signals
		Can introduce uncertainty over price, therefore undermines long-term investment planning	
		High transaction costs	
		Baseline and Credit Schemes can lack enviro. effectiveness	
		Behaviour not always sensitive to price signal	

Notes: RGGI = Regional Greenhouse Gas Initiative; NSWETS = New South Wales Emissions Trading Scheme; MDC = Marginal Damage Costs.

carbon price through taxes on fossil fuels such as oil and coal? or through setting emissions quotas on firms and countries and then allowing trading à la Coase? In each case the policy objective is to establish a carbon price sufficient to shift the economy away from GHG-producing activity, but one operates through the price mechanism and the other through the quantity mechanism.

William Nordhaus represents the canonical perspective of economic theory applying the insights from Martin Weitzman that under different types of uncertainty price instruments (taxes) should be preferred over quantity instruments (quotas and emissions trading) and vice versa (Weitzman, 1974 and Nordhaus, 2007). This follows a simple and powerful logic.

Using a pure price instrument, such as taxation, while achieving certainty on what the price of carbon will be (in theory optimality at P*) the policy maker is unsure exactly what the final quantity of emissions will be. The carbon price is set and the quantity of pollution emerges through the market. It may take several years and changes in taxes to achieve the optimal tax rate (P*) and the desired level of emissions at Q*. However, what it does guarantee is what the cost of pollution abatement will be – thus providing certainty for polluters to plan their investment.

Alternatively, by using a quantity instrument, the policy maker provides certainty around the level of pollution that will be emitted (Q*) and allows the price of carbon to emerge in the market. However, this can mean that the polluting industry faces greater uncertainty around the costs of abatement than under the taxation system.

Whether taxes or trading is to be preferred in this simple model depends on the policy priority of the regulator and the relative costs of the damage from pollution and cost of abatement in the event of uncertainty and the position of the marginal damage curve (see Figure 2.4).

If the marginal damage costs are high (steeply sloping) – that is if not hitting the emissions target results in catastrophic events (such as melting of the Greenland ice sheet, or release of methane from the permafrost, leading to a positive feedback cycle that rapidly accelerates global warming) – then clearly ensuring that Q* is achieved is highly desirable: the policy maker should use a quantity instrument.

If on the other hand, if the damage costs are low (i.e. a flat curve) and the marginal abatement costs are high – for example, it may be extremely

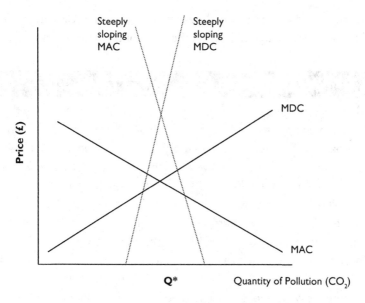

Figure 2.4 Balancing pollution and abatement costs under uncertainty

expensive to decommission long-lived, high-carbon energy infrastructure and expensive to scale up renewable energy – then it would be preferable to set the carbon price to allow people and industry flexibility around how much abatement needs to be achieved.

Under these circumstances, the choice of instrument depends on the view that the policy maker takes on the costs of abatement versus the risk of a catastrophic event occurring. If they are very worried about the risk of a climate catastrophe (steep MDC curve) they should use a quota and emissions trading; if they are more worried about the costs of mitigation, such as higher fuel prices, inflationary pressures, higher long-term interest rates, slower economic growth, higher unemployment and so on, then the use of taxes would, in theory, be preferred.

Discount rates and policy choice

This highlights one reason why the somewhat esoteric debate around discount rates is so important. As most of the costs of dangerous climate change occur 20 years and more into the future, but the costs of mitigation are incurred in the short term, how we account for these far off costs in *today's* terms is critical to our view on the slope of the marginal damage curve.

Box 2.2 Why discount?

Discount rates are implicit in dozens of decisions we make every day, though most people do not usually think about it in these terms. The reason why most people discount is due to the simple reason that humans are impatient by nature and generally speaking we value things more, the sooner we can get them. This form of discounting is known as pure time discounting.

An additional reason why we discount the future is because we assume we will be better off in the future, combined with the general belief that an extra pound is generally worth less the better off you are.

On a practical level, this is reflected by interest rates. One pound invested today would accumulate to $£(1 + r)$ in year 2 if the interest rate was r per cent, where r is typically expressed as a decimal point, e.g. 6 per cent would be 0.06, 10 per cent is 0.10, and so on.

Turning this logic around, we can ask, 'How much is £1 in year 2 worth to us today in year 1?' The answer is that it is worth $£1/(1 + r)$ for the reason that this is the amount you would have to invest in year 1 to obtain £1 in year two.

For example, using a relatively high discount rate of say 6 per cent or more (approximately what is used for long-term commercial decision making) would mean that the policy maker perceives the marginal damage function today as quite flat, as the costs of climate change occurring in the future would be worth a lot less in today's terms. Therefore according to the logic above, taxes should be preferred.

Using a low or declining discount rate over time (such as used in the Stern Review) of say 4 per cent or less would mean the policy maker would weight the long-term costs of climate change more relative to the short-term costs of mitigation, and (according to theory) should lean towards a cap-and-trade scheme.

It is an implicit argument of the Stern Review that it is appropriate for governments to use lower discount rates than in the private sector as they must make decisions both in the public interest and for the benefit of future generations just as much as for current citizens; whereas the private sector is focused on the interests of current shareholders and must weigh investments against opportunity cost of capital (the interest rate).

The Stern Review attracted considerable criticism for adopting a low discount rate and somewhat less criticism for favouring emissions trading over taxation.[9] At the centre of the controversy was that the Review only discounted based on the assumption that future generations will be richer in the future and the chance (about 1 in 1000 each year) that we will be extinct as a society due to meteor strike or some other catastrophe. On the matter of pure time preference (see Box 2.2) the Review assumed a discount rate of zero; meaning that the 'government' should hold no bias between the welfare of current and future citizens on the basis that society as a whole is impatient.[10] It is for this reason that Stern is frequently characterized as taking a stronger ethical stance than other economic studies, such as that by Nordhaus, who favours higher discount rates and also taxation over emissions trading.

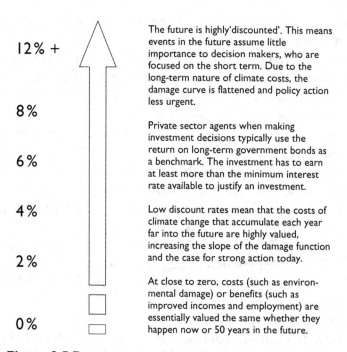

12% +

    The future is highly 'discounted'. This means events in the future assume little importance to decision makers, who are focused on the short term. Due to the long-term nature of climate costs, the damage curve is flattened and policy action less urgent.

8%

6%

    Private sector agents when making investment decisions typically use the return on long-term government bonds as a benchmark. The investment has to earn at least more than the minimum interest rate available to justify an investment.

4%

    Low discount rates mean that the costs of climate change that accumulate each year far into the future are highly valued, increasing the slope of the damage function and the case for strong action today.

2%

    At close to zero, costs (such as environmental damage) or benefits (such as improved incomes and employment) are essentially valued the same whether they happen now or 50 years in the future.

0%

Figure 2.5 Discount rates, decision making and policy choice

Indeed, if the policy maker takes a very low discount rate (assuming marginal damage from CO_2 is very high) and is concerned about whether the price signal will be able to change behaviour in time, then it might become efficient to impose regulatory standards or bans on high-carbon technologies. For example, in the UK the idea of a ban on new coal power plants is being debated and worldwide fuel efficiency standards are already in place for car manufacturers.

Such policies have the advantage of not working all through the slow process of changing behaviour through the price system. However, if not carefully designed, such standards could result in high electricity prices or disruptions to power if new generating capacity was not able to be brought on at a price consumers were willing to pay for. A further disadvantage of such strong regulatory action is that it could act as a disincentive on investment in energy supply, leading to shortages or high prices for consumers.

Theory and practice and the case for 'silver buckshot'

In Figure 2.1 above the simple case of a negative pollution externality was presented in the context of energy production, which we also noted has important positive production externalities. Theoretically we created a framework for looking at the costs and benefits of alternative policy approaches, placing emissions trading in the context of alternative policies such as taxation and regulatory bans standards.

In practice, climate change is a far more complicated externality involving multiple sectors and jurisdictions each with their own economic, cultural and political realities and histories. For example, while it does not matter where CO_2 is emitted when assessing a firm or nation's contribution to global warming, the impacts in terms of storms, floods and droughts *are* distributed differently. Low-lying areas are most at risk from sea-level rise (e.g. Bangladesh, The Netherlands and various small island states) and temperatures will rise most in the Arctic and Antarctic regions, which may in the long run actually be positive for some (Russians in Siberia) but negative for other reasons (for wildlife such as polar bears). This means the slope of the MDC curve varies across geographic regions.

Perversely, the wealthier states most responsible for the historical stock of greenhouse gases are the ones most able to adapt through sea defences, new technologies for growing drought-resistant crops and so on, whereas poorer states will have trouble in accessing adaptation capital and technologies, thus exacerbating damage costs in those regions.

There are also many, many more externalities at play, in addition to the negative pollution externality and those around energy security. For instance one of the most important is due to oil supply being set by the collusive behaviour of the Organization of Petroleum Exporting Countries (OPEC). This leads to tighter supply and higher prices than would otherwise be the case and makes it difficult to assess how 'the market' will respond to higher carbon prices. It is also interesting to note that this oligopolistic behaviour by OPEC reduces supply (Q) and pushes up prices, in a manner similar to a carbon tax (Tietenberg, 2004).

On the one hand, OPEC may decide to increase production and cut prices in response to higher carbon prices in order to maintain market share and slow technological change away from fossil fuels, thus negating the net change in the price of fuel at the pump and any change in emissions. Alternatively, OPEC may tighten supply, pushing up prices even further to maintain profits, so creating political and economic instability in the face of extraordinarily high fuel costs and hoping that democratically elected governments will lose their appetite for imposing higher carbon prices.

Note that the outcome of this struggle between OPEC and the oil-consuming nations (mainly the OECD states) largely comes down to who gets the economic rents from higher fuel prices – the OECD taxpayer in the carbon-pricing scenario, or the OPEC member states in the higher price and collusion scenario. In each case the implicit carbon price could be the same, but the distribution of income from higher fuel prices drastically different.

Table 2.2 shows us that every US$20 increase in the price of a barrel of oil has the same impact on producer prices as a $50 increase in carbon price. Furthermore, an interesting presentation given by the Oxford Institute of Energy Studies showed the results of an investigation into the impact of the recent record oil price on the world economy. What they found was that even though oil prices were at a record high, there was surprisingly little feedback to the economy and underlying inflation. They suggested that this empirical evidence may show that the economy is much more resilient in the face of higher energy prices than is commonly thought. Oil prices, unlike previous shocks, this time was 'the dog that didn't bark' in precipitating the current economic recession. This is good news for those who argue in favour of a

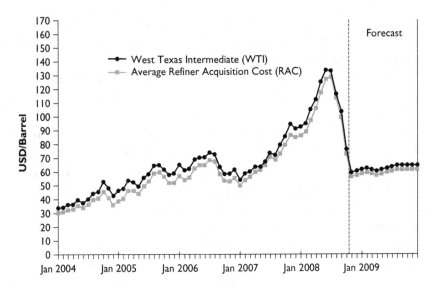

Figure 2.6 Recent oil price movements and forecast

Table 2.2 *Oil prices and the carbon price equivalent*

Oil Price ($/barrel)	Carbon Price ($/tonne CO_2)
20	50
40	100
60	150
80	200
100	250
120	300
140	350
160	400

Source: Stern (2006, p287) assuming a proportionate gas price increase to oil price increase

strong government action to set high carbon prices: if the economy can withstand high oil prices driven by OPEC and demand, then it suggests it may be well placed to absorb the costs of high carbon permit prices (Allsopp, 2009).

The presence of these and other market failures and barriers to change means that while carbon pricing is necessary it is unlikely to be sufficient to effectively reduce emissions.

These practical problems have prompted Steve Rayner at the James Martin 21st Century School at Oxford University to argue that there is no silver bullet solution to carbon policy and that what is needed in practice is 'silver buckshot'. Such an approach would integrate the different carbon pricing strategies with industry policy, research and development in clean technologies through to technological demonstration experiments and early market support with targeted subsidies.

By integrating active *industry policy*, this approach attempts to address concerns that households and firms, especially in the short term, do not always respond to price signals. Reasons for this include system complexity and lack of information about low-carbon technologies, the long-term nature of energy investments, difficulty financing projects with large upfront costs, and the slow pace of cultural change that is required to underpin a low-carbon economy. These problems result in what is called path dependency (see Box 2.3), that is once a particular technology or process (such as energy from fossil fuels) is entrenched it takes a concerted effort beyond just sending price signals to shift the system, for example to a world based on renewables.

Box 2.3 Path dependency and energy investment[11]

According to Brian Arthur, small past decisions can lead to path dependency or the notion that technologies become 'locked in' even though better alternatives exist, simply because once investments are made it makes similar, supportive investments more attractive. There are five main forces that Arthur identifies as driving this process of 'increasing returns to adoption' (Arthur, 1994).

First, learning by doing suggests that the more often a technology is used the more it is developed and improved (Rosenberg, 1982). For example, the use of petroleum-based fuels in the internal combustion engines of cars has led to large improvements in performance of those engines and fuels, compared to the competing technologies of electric-battery or hydrogen motors. Second, network externalities mean that often technologies are advantaged by the number of adopters (Katz and Shapiro, 1985). For example, the vast number of petrol cars limits the diffusion possibility of electric-battery or biofuel cars due to the lack of alternative refuelling infrastructure in the case of the former, and the ability of the engine to handle ethanol or biodiesel in the latter. Third, economies of scale mean the more a technology is used, the lower its cost. Electricity production is one of the classic examples of natural monopoly where the average costs of a large power plant fall with the amount of electricity produced, making them competitive, but only at very large outputs (and levels of market concentration). Fourth, increasing returns in information mean that often the more a technology is adopted, the more it enjoys the advantage of being better known and understood. This means that the risk of adopting a new technology falls as it becomes more widespread. Finally, technological interrelatedness suggests that as technologies become diffused, other subtechnologies and products become part of its infrastructure and help bring down its costs (Frankel, 1955). For example, petroleum-based technologies have a huge infrastructure of refineries, distribution systems, filling stations, car manufacturers and so on that rely on them, further underpinned by an education system that trains engineers, geologists and chemists in the required skills for the industry, in addition to political organizations that have grown up in order to secure the legislative and subsidy frameworks that support the industry.

However, proponents of market-based solutions to climate change may argue that the industry policy elements of the 'silver buckshot' approach constitute 'picking winners' as the government may be put into a position of having to choose one technology over another. For example, the decision around significant new investment in nuclear energy is one such case. While a high carbon price helps the economics of nuclear energy, without substantial additional state support such as an efficient and supportive planning and approval process and the state insurance or subsidization of nuclear waste disposal, it would be very difficult for nuclear investments to take place.

Michael Grubb (2004) outlines a useful framework to consider these competing schools of thought on climate policy (illustrated in Figure 2.7 below).

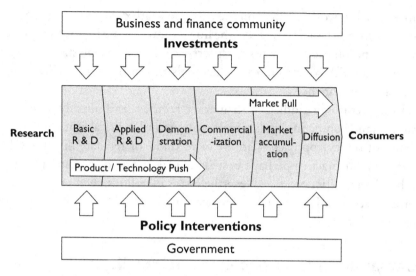

Figure 2.7 Main steps in the innovation chain

Here technological change is mapped as a series of 'steps in the innovation chain'. Accelerating this process for low-carbon technologies requires not only well designed policies and investments on the supply side (technology-push) but also on the demand side (technology-pull) policies. For technology-push the focus is on research and development programmes and demonstration projects of new technology, while technology-pull policies rely mainly on the use of economic incentives such as carbon pricing (Doornbosch and Knight, 2008).

The alternative to 'picking winners' is to set the carbon price high and let 'the market' 'choose' the winners, rather than politicians. In theory, this choice emerges out of a competition between new clean technologies and fossil fuels, as the costs of new mitigation techniques come down due to learning and carbon prices rise, penalizing the old fossil fuel systems. It is argued that such market approaches help avoid the danger of political decisions being captured by vested interests through lobbying.

When considering the nexus between 'picking winners' (technology-push) and letting solutions to CO_2 mitigation emerge through the price signal (technology-pull) there is a trade-off between the danger of political capture (and a bad decision) on the one hand and the time it takes for the price signal to work its effect on the other, for path dependency and behavioural reasons. In practice, where the line is drawn in the innovation process will depend on each country's perspective of the role of the state in organizing economic activity and the policy tools and institutions available to it, such as public finance.

In an economy riddled with market failures, and already subject to various (and competing) policy interventions and political rent seeking, the choice of policy approach – 'to tax or to trade' or regulate in some other manner is in practice perhaps best described as one of guiding principle rather than of strict practice. Nevertheless, as in politics, such principles can form a useful basis to signal a general approach in the face of complexity and uncertainty.

Cap-and-trade vs. baseline and credit

There are two basic types of emissions trading scheme: cap-and-trade and baseline and credit.

Cap-and-trade sets out a system where the government defines a new set of property rights to use the atmosphere based on an emissions limit or cap. Then, after the distribution of the allowances between actors involved in the scheme, it allows trade in these allowances so that actors can choose to conduct abatement or by additional allowances. Finally, at particular times, actors covered by the scheme are required to surrender the allowances that correspond to their level of emissions – this may be above or below what they were originally allocated, depending on the costs of CO_2 abatement they are faced with. The European Emissions Trading Scheme and Sulfur Dioxide Trading Schemes in the US are examples of cap-and-trade schemes.

The baseline and credit schemes involve establishing a baseline level of emissions for a sector (such as proposed plans for deforestation) or a project or company (e.g. the Clean Development Mechanism or the New South Wales (NSW) Emissions Trading Scheme). Under this scheme no overall emissions cap is set: however, actors are encouraged to reduce their emissions below this baseline (usually defined as the business as usual scenario) to generate emissions credits that can then be traded – although some baseline and credit schemes have no, or limited, trading. This approach is the basis for 'White Certificate' schemes that governments are using to encourage energy-efficiency measures such as those in Connecticut, US,[12] Flanders,[13] the UK,[14] France[15] and Italy.[16]

Cap-and-trade schemes

As a first step, the establishment of a cap-and-trade emissions trading scheme involves the definition of a cap on emissions in a specific area. The definition of the scope is based on several parameters including geographical coverage, temporal range and the gases covered. This is usually referred to as the scheme's coverage.

The carbon price, or price of emissions in an emissions trading scheme is shaped by the forces of demand and supply.[17] On the supply side, the legislator sets the desired level of pollution (the cap) *ex ante* – that is before the emissions occur, at the fixed amount Q^*. This cap is generally made a carbon reduction target for that sector.

Demand is driven by the polluters who must operate within the proportion of the cap that has been allocated to them. As each unit of pollution from their business must be offset by an equivalent emissions right, as soon as they exceed the amount they have initially been allocated, they have to enter the market to buy emissions permits, thus creating demand for permits.

Demand for allowances will depend on the severity of the cap but also on the level of actual emissions from involved agents. If the reduction target is small, demand for emissions rights will be weak. Similarly, if the involved agents (states or companies) are able to significantly reduce their emissions, thus remaining within their cap, then demand for permits on the ETS will also be weak and prices will remain low to moderate. This can occur either because of the employment of mitigation technologies, such as improving energy efficiency, or due to a fall in demand for the firms' actual output (as in the case of the economic recession in former communist bloc countries following the collapse of communism and during their transition towards market economies in the 1990s and early 2000s).

The monitoring and reporting of emissions is the next critical element. The precise achievement of the environmental target is known only after the calculation of actual emissions at the end of the commitment period. Therefore, the definition of clear rules and standardized methods for calculating emissions are a prerequisite for the credibility of any emissions trading system.

Emissions are fungible (i.e. transferable); therefore it is important that these measurement methods are reliable and consistent so that a tonne of CO_2 means the same thing between different agents, potentially across different sectors and from different countries. For example, in the US, industry is required to use continuous measurement equipment to monitor flue gases to account for CO_2 to a high degree of accuracy.

Reliable registries are also needed to ensure that emissions and corresponding emissions rights (allowances) can be traced. Registries ensure the booking of transactions of emissions rights. They are similar to a general ledger where all accounting transactions are posted.

In existing schemes, such transfers of ownership take place in real time. This means that registries do not account for future transactions (futures or forward) and only spot transactions can be registered. Registries only provide an inventory of traded quantities; therefore they do not contain any information on agreed prices. Their function is to ensure traceability of the allowances, thereby guaranteeing the environmental integrity of the system. At the end of the accounting period reconciliation between actual emissions and emissions rights held by the participants is performed using the data booked in the registry.

Finally, in order to ensure environmental integrity of the system regarding the cap, the regulator must set sanctions to penalize agents who cannot offset their emissions by an equivalent number of allowances. A system of fines encourages polluting entities not to emit more than the number of allowances they hold. For instance, under the first emissions trading scheme, the US sulfur dioxide market, the government established a penalty scheme in case of shortage of allowances: if a company did not have enough allowances to cover its emissions at the annual reconciliation, it was liable to pay a fine of $2,000 per uncovered tonne.

However, fines alone are not always enough to ensure environmental integrity. Take for example the case where there is a substantial over-demand for permits due to an unusually cold and long winter that meant more energy was used to heat homes than the regulators might have expected when they set the cap. The price of emissions permits in these circumstances may rise so high that the polluter may choose to pay the fine, rather than attempt to buy emissions permits.

To avoid this pitfall, governments may declare that the payment of a penalty does not release the agent from the obligation to reduce emissions.

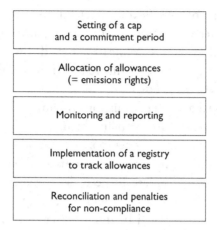

Figure 2.8 Constitutive elements of a cap-and-trade emissions trading scheme

Therefore the entity in default must also redeem the rights missing during periods of subsequent compliance. This approach was chosen under the EU Emissions Trading Scheme.

Setting the cap and commitment period

As discussed above, the setting of the cap (establishing Q*) is the foundation of any emissions trading scheme. The cap establishes the level of scarcity of emissions allowances and therefore the supply side of setting the carbon price in the regulated sectors. To provide environmental integrity, the cap should be set consistently with national, regional or multilateral emissions targets and be clearly below 'business as usual' (BAU) emissions. In practice this process is complicated due to uncertainty around what future emissions will be (Grubb and Neuhoff, 2006).

An important element in setting the cap and emissions rights scarcity is the establishment of rules around the use of emissions credits generated from areas outside the regulated emissions market, such as through the Clean Development Mechanism (CDM). By allowing these outside emissions credits to be imported into the scheme the policy maker allows emissions to rise above the cap within the geographical area that is regulated.

In practice the use of such flexible mechanisms is controlled in order to ensure that investments in domestic emissions reductions are made rather than the purchase of emissions credits from outside the regulated system. In theory, provided the purchased credits represent real emissions reductions, there is no reason why such restrictions should be imposed as it limits one of the most beneficial aspects of emissions trading – that emissions reductions occur where it costs least to obtain them.

The commitment period is the temporal aspect of the cap. It sets out the time period for obtaining emissions reductions at the company level. If the benefits of emissions trading are to be realized the system must balance predictability in its shape and rules with flexibility to take advantage of changing circumstances. As will be discussed later in this chapter, a long commitment period, with banking and borrowing of emissions credits between periods, can provide greater certainty for investors and reduce policy risk (Helm et al, 2005).

Allocation methods

As discussed earlier in the chapter, the creation of a new market for greenhouse gases requires property rights to be identified and made transferable where previously there were none. In practice this amounts to establishing 'rights' to use the atmosphere. This allocation process should not be confused with the buying and selling of these rights within an emissions trading scheme and the resultant price for emission credits that rises and falls once the system has been established.

There are two main allocation approaches: either selling these rights to the atmosphere or giving them away. A hybrid system can also be used that incorporates a combination of the two. There is a vigorous debate around this allocation process and at its core lies an assumption about who initially should own the property right to the environment – the polluter, or the public at large (i.e. the taxpayer and the government).

Under ideal theoretical conditions of perfect information and competition and in a static analysis each allocation method should be equally efficient as the agents involved face the same marginal costs of abatement (set through the market price of emissions credits). In practice, where there are firms entering and exiting a market full of market failures and externalities, selling permits (usually by auction) presents significant efficiency advantages, although on the other hand giving permits away for free increases the acceptance of the scheme. To understand this, let us first examine the case of 'free allocation'.

Free allocation involves giving pollution rights away free of charge under some predefined rule such as 'grandfathering'. This simply means that the property rights to the environment are allocated on the basis of *prior use*. This allocation method is usually strongly advocated by polluters as it recognizes their implicit right to use the environment as they always have, albeit now under the constraint of a cap.

By sheltering industry from the full potential costs of implementing the emissions trading scheme, free allocation seeks to avoid the problem of stranded assets, that is investments made at a time when emissions of GHGs were regarded as harmless and which lose value following the introduction of an emissions market. For example, investment in a coal power plant becomes less profitable after the implementation of a CO_2 emissions trading scheme.

Alternatively, if the government elects to sell permits to industry it assumes that polluters had no prior *right* to the environment and that the atmosphere is a commons effectively owned by all citizens. Under this approach agents covered by the scheme face the upfront cost of participation as they have to bid for the right to use the atmosphere. Once they have this right it is recognized as an asset and can be sold on if the firm decides to stop operating. The value of these permits can be substantial, so their free allocation can be represented as a considerable 'windfall' to the firm (Sijm et al, 2006).

Box 2.4 'Free allocation' of emissions rights to soften negative competitiveness effects

The UK's peak industry group, the Confederation of British Industry (CBI) argues that any plan to auction permits under the European Emissions Trading Scheme (EU ETS) must take into account the competitiveness pressures that auctioning brings to bear on vulnerable sectors. They warn that energy-intensive sectors including aluminium and steel production face a significant risk. Risk is defined as the nexus between international trade exposure and the impact of energy price increases on the final product.

Firms which are unable to pass on costs due to competition from firms in non-EU ETS countries face declining profitability and market share. This then can lead to carbon leakage – the propensity for CO_2 pollution to merely shift from a regulated to a non-regulated country. The result is that the regulated country loses its polluting industry (and the economic activity it produces) but there is no environmental gain, or even worse emissions increase as emissions may be even less regulated than they were before. As a result of this, the CBI argues for 'free allocation' and will only support the full auctioning of permits if an international agreement can be achieved that sets similar standards for all major competitors of energy-intensive British and EU industry.

Free allocations, based on rules such as grandfathering, also raise dynamic competitiveness concerns by implicitly favouring incumbent firms at the expense of new firms wishing to enter the market, who may not receive a free allocation but have to 'buy in'. If there are no reserves for new entrants and all allowances have been granted to existing businesses, newcomers are penalized by having to buy all their allowances on the market.

This may be less of an issue when capital markets work perfectly and take the opportunity costs of emissions into account when assessing the value of existing firms. This is because when an inefficient firm receives sufficient allowances to cover its existing emissions, it should be economically advantageous to close or scale down operations and sell surplus emissions rights to an efficient new entrant (Bosquet, 2000). However, in practice this mechanism does not work perfectly, so states set aside a small quantity of unallocated rights for new entrants under free allocation systems.

In addition free allocation rules have the possible disadvantage of encouraging a 'use it or lose it' mentality among firms and discourage the closure of old or inefficient firms, which are kept operational to secure valuable permits.

Auctioning also avoids the difficulty of defining rules for the sharing of available allowances between states or industries. In other words, no allocation rule needs to be defined. In a free allocation process, the allocation is political and is therefore influenced by various forms of lobbying and can be very laborious (Joskow and Schmalensee, 1998). This also often results in over-allocation.

Finally, auctioning raises funds that can be used for other purposes, for example to address market imperfections in the labour market. Many environmental economists have advanced the hypothesis of a double dividend associated with environmental taxes or levies. The first dividend is an improvement in the quality of the environment. The second is the positive effect on employment and gross domestic product (GDP) resulting from the reduction of other more distorting taxes such as labour taxes (which penalize the incentive to work) thanks to the new funds collected through environmental taxation.

Box 2.5 The advantages of auctioning

Allocative efficiency – a well designed auction system channels permits to those who value them the most, which allows resources to flow to their highest value use.

Efficient price discovery – important price information is provided by the interaction of bidders at an auction. This facilitates price discovery, which has a major role in stimulating behavioural change. For example, the revealing of each emitter's willingness to pay for the right to pollute helps entities manage their emissions obligations and make investment decisions more clearly than if permits are provided by free allocation.

Auction revenue – the sale of permits at auction generates revenue that can be used by the government for difference purposes.

It should be noted that as the secondary emissions market matures the benefits from the first two advantages diminish.

Bosquet analysed practical experiences and studies on the double dividend (Bosquet, 2000). His conclusion is rather mixed. In the short or medium term, benefits are significant in reducing pollution, but weak in terms of job creation. The fundraising aspect is an argument often advanced against auctioning because by creating a transfer of private funds to the state, auctioning tends to harm the competitiveness and profitability of businesses, compared to those outside the emissions trading scheme. In general, environmentalists argue that funds collected should be used for environmental protection while companies consider that funds should be used to compensate businesses, including by research and development support. In both cases, Bosquet found that such requests from pressure groups (green non-governmental organizations (NGOs) or industrial lobbies) prevent the realization of a double dividend.

An alternative method that can be integrated with free allocation or auctioning is benchmarking. If regulators decide to reward emissions reduction before the beginning of the scheme, governments can consider allocating emissions based on energy efficiency or a similar indicator. Such an allocation method uses a comparison of environmental performance across time.

While benchmarking is effective for the allocation of allowances to sectors producing well-defined products (for example megawatt hours of electricity per tonne of steel or cement) benchmarking is more complicated for sectors with differentiated products (for example, defining a CO_2 benchmark for car manufacturers is less than straightforward, given the wide variety of models). When considering allocations between nations, a benchmark could be per capita emissions in the country (an option favoured by some developing countries), or emissions released per unit of gross domestic product.

Governments can also allocate allowances based on projections of future emissions in order to avoid excessive restrictions on expanding industries. However, such an approach requires a considerable amount of information that is often confidential. In practice, industries will tend to overestimate their forecasts for fear of not receiving sufficient allowances. Such an approach can lead to over-allocation, as has been the case during the first phase of the EU ETS (Ellerman and Buchner, 2007).

Another option might be to allocate more allowances to industries that are more vulnerable to international competition. Companies that have to compete with other corporations not involved in an emissions trading system are more vulnerable because they cannot pass on the allowances costs to their customers. This has been claimed for steel, cement and chemicals industries, although analysis in the UK indicates that auctioning EU ETS permits would only affect companies producing less than 1 per cent of GDP (Carbon Trust, 2008). In the case of the power industry, the price of allowances can easily be reflected in the price of electricity (at least in a fully liberalized market), since electricity is not transported in large amounts over very long distances.

In practice, governments sometimes develop a hybrid allocation method. Today with the development of emissions trading platforms, access to allowances is open and prices are publicly available. Indeed, auctioning can be open to all and interest groups (e.g. environmental or health promotion NGOs) may be able to buy allowances in order to further reduce the emissions cap to reflect their members' interests. The extent to which auctioning is allowed will have a significant bearing on the perceived strength of the emissions trading scheme in question. While 'free allocation' offers scope to provide a subsidy to carbon-intensive industry, therefore increasing acceptance of carbon reduction proposals (relative to say a carbon tax), such a subsidy should be carefully evaluated in terms of other competitiveness measures that might be taken, such as border tariff adjustments.

Management of price volatility

As discussed earlier, a system such as an emissions trading scheme that sets a limit on quantities is less able to deliver certainty on prices. A cap-and-trade system can therefore lead to significant price variability. Such volatility potentially poses a significant threat to industries and economies in a carbon-constrained world. There are, however, various mechanisms to control volatility. The common characteristic of the different mechanisms presented here is that they reduce the potential price range for allowances over the course of the commitment period.

The first option is to allow banking of allowances for future use. This allows governments to encourage companies to further reduce their emissions now by allowing them to establish a reserve of allowances for the future. This can limit price volatility between trading periods and smooth prices (Amundsen et al, 2006).

Another approach, still theoretical at present, would be to allow agents to borrow allowances from future periods (Mavrakis and Konidari, 2003). This would help limit the volatility in the short term but could lead to shocks between periods. In addition, borrowing would tend to allow increased short-term emissions that would be detrimental to climate change abatement.

Setting price floors and/or ceilings is another method that could be also used. These would aim to provide a mechanism of safety valves to reduce the risk to investments in emissions reductions (Jacoby and Ellerman, 2004). The price floor would insure the regulator against the emissions market collapsing due to either an over-allocation of permits or a fall in demand for permits. The price ceiling would insure industry against extremely high costs of abatement; however, this would need to be weighed against the loss in environmental integrity induced by the addition of permits to the system.

A minimum price can guarantee a minimum level of profitability for investments in emissions reduction technologies. If a project avoids the release of 10 tonnes CO_2e and costs £100, then setting a minimum price at £10 would help guarantee a safe investment. However, because this requires the regulator to buy emissions rights this mechanism would be expensive for the regulator if the equilibrium price of allowances stabilized below the minimum price.

Despite this drawback, in practice such hybrid systems involving a combination of instruments based on quantity and price are quite popular. For instance, most mandated green certificates markets, that is, markets that have been established to support electricity from renewable energy, include both price controls and quantity targets.[18]

A second method used to limit price volatility is to link cap-and-trade schemes to baseline and credits projects outside the capped system. With a baseline and credits project, an investor can generate additional emissions credits by investing in emissions reductions in other sectors or areas. These credits can then be used for compliance purposes in a cap-and-trade scheme. Emissions savings need to be defined relative to a counterfactual (a baseline without the investment, e.g. BAU). For instance, if it is too expensive for a British company to reduce its emissions, it can decide to invest in a country (e.g. China) where investment can avoid emissions more cost-effectively. The emissions saving achieved through this investment (i.e. the difference between emissions after investment and emissions under the BAU scenario), after monitoring by an accredited external auditor, gives the right for emissions credits. These emissions credits are fungible with the allowances in the cap-and-trade scheme and therefore allow additional emissions.

Finally, in order to avoid fluctuations in a market, a government can link its system to another scheme. The linking mechanism is a way to improve market liquidity by increasing its size and the number of involved parties. In practice linking emissions markets is complex because of varying definitions. Some countries may have more severe monitoring and reporting guidelines, higher penalties for non-compliance and so on. Linking with a less reliable system can harm the effectiveness and credibility of a scheme and actually increase volatility, so should be approached with caution.

Baseline and credit schemes

Baseline and credit schemes also rely on the creation of tradable permits. However, under these schemes no cap is set on overall emissions. Rather, a baseline is established and emissions credits or allowances are earned once actors involved in the scheme reduce emissions under this baseline. This baseline could be set at a project level (as in the case of the CDM), at a firm level (as in the case of the NSW Emissions Trading Scheme), at the sectoral level (see Box 2.4) or at the national level.

An environmentally stronger variant on this is where the baseline is also used to provide emitters with a level of entitlement to emit. If actual emissions are below this entitlement then the actor has allowances it can sell. However, if emissions exceed the entitlement, then allowances must be purchased to account for emissions above the baseline. There are several ways baselines can be set, depending on the policy objective and desired environmental effectiveness of the scheme (Garnaut, 2008). For example, options include:

- setting the baseline as emissions in a particular year;
- average emissions per unit of production based on installed technology in a base year;
- average emissions per unit of production based on best practice technology, or any combination of these or other approaches.

Box 2.6 Reduced emissions from deforestation in developing countries

Land-use change in the tropics accounts for around 20 per cent of global emissions and represents the largest source of developing country emissions, being the second largest source of emissions worldwide after fossil fuel use.[19]

However, in spite of the 'Australia clause' that allows developed countries to claim credits for slowing land clearing, 'avoiding deforestation' is excluded as a way for developing countries to generate emissions credits under the Kyoto Protocol, although afforestation and reforestation are eligible for credit generation.

This exclusion has led to the formation of the Coalition of Rainforest Nations and separately for Brazil to launch what has become know as the Reduced Emissions from Deforestation in Developing Countries (REDD) proposals.[20]

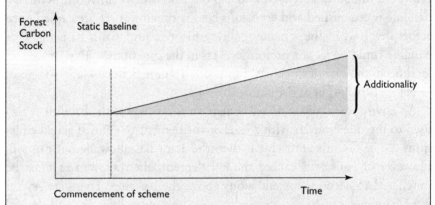

Figure 2.9.1 Static baseline

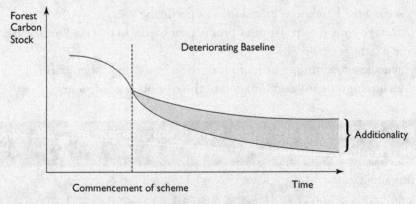

Figure 2.9.2 Deteriorating baseline

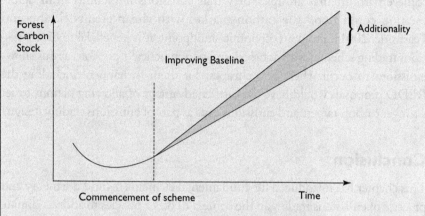

Figure 2.9.3 Improving baseline

The basis of these proposals centres around variants on baseline and credit forms of emissions trading, and have also been termed 'sectoral CDM' as opposed to the project-based CDM.

The structure of the proposed baseline and credit schemes is illustrated in Figures 2.9.1–2.9.3 in the case of nations where the forest carbon stock has stabilized, is deteriorating and is improving. In each case, the establishment of the baseline would require the determination of some historical average of emissions supported by satellite imagery to monitor forest cover and on-the-ground studies to evaluate the CO_2 effects of deforestation.

Such baseline and credit schemes can be used as a 'no regrets' climate policy, where once countries participate they are only exposed to the positive incentive side of achieving and exceeding the baseline. Emissions credits are generated according to the amount of additionality achieved and can be sold into other carbon markets, such as the EU ETS.

However, some developing countries are cautious about such programmes as once established the baseline can easily be transformed into a binding target and penalties imposed for non-compliance. REDD measures may also lead to landholders without political power being dispossessed of their land, and expose developed countries to criticism of 'climate colonialism'. Furthermore, some environmental groups worry that emissions reductions from defor-estation could flood the carbon market with cheap credits (Philip and Fearnside, 2001). From an economic standpoint, it is beneficial to have emis-sions trading schemes with as broad a scope as practically possible, as this allows emissions to occur where it is cheapest for them to happen. Including the REDD proposals would have the further advantage of allowing nations to set stronger carbon targets and emissions caps as part of emissions trading design.

Conclusion

This chapter has introduced the fundamental elements behind the theory and practice of emissions trading in the context of other policies to address climate change. While conceptually it can be useful to debate the pros and cons of emissions trading vis-à-vis other policies, the reality of an economy riddled with market failure and the diversity of economic and political systems make it impossible to conclude that there is any one silver bullet policy mechanism to climate change. Instead, a 'silver buckshot' approach, incorporating emissions trading, may offer the best and fastest solution to manage CO_2 reduction.

As concern and understanding of the damage costs of climate change escalate and the costs of CO_2 mitigation fall, emissions trading becomes increasingly attractive from a theoretical perspective. This is because it can provide greater certainty around the physical quantity of emissions to be reduced as well as providing the economic incentive for companies in the highest value sectors to focus on pollution and to minimize the cost of abatement by fostering continuous innovation in low-carbon technology.

Emissions trading schemes are also politically more attractive than other policies such as taxation, which makes it harder to cushion the competi-tiveness impact of implementing a carbon constraint and can elicit rapid opposition such as increasing petrol pump prices. However, there is still a gap to be bridged between the theoretical benefits that emissions trading offers and its practical implementation – for instance sectors such as transport and emissions from deforestation have been left outside the scope of most emissions trading schemes.

Despite the practical challenges of implementing a new market system for the control of complex pollutants such as GHGs, emissions trading schemes offer a powerful and efficient logic for policy makers, organizations and indi-viduals of all political persuasions. Emissions trading simultaneously satisfies the statist view of taking a tight regulatory approach while allowing for the application of incentive arrangements that provide for continuous innovation, favoured by market libertarians. It is perhaps this Coasian logic that bridges the old conceptual debate around how to manage environmental problems that best explains the growing popularity of emissions trading.

Notes

1   For a full discussion see Helm, 2007.
2   www.globalsubsidies.org/en
3   For a full discussion of the provision of fossil fuel subsidies and climate policy see Myres and Kent, 2001.
4   To appreciate this statement consider the social benefits of improving general levels of education or health in a population above what the market would naturally provide without state support.
5   Pigou, 1912. For examples of application with regard to air pollution, see Baumol, 1972.
6   For example, this might be on the basis of 'grandfathering' (rights allocated according to prior use).
7   Note that this result requires rational, profit-maximizing decision making by firms (countries) and perfect information, i.e. a well functioning market. For simplicity, the model has been restricted to two agents; however, the same logic can be applied to a model with many agents. Indeed the potential gains from emissions trading increases the more firms and countries involved.
8   See for example Hepburn, 2006.
9   An argument based on an ethics or philosophy of Rawlsian equivalence – that is political leaders should make decisions on the basis that when they die they would come back reincarnated randomly as a member of any section of society.
10 Bearing in mind that, as this is a global study, it assumes there is one authority or 'government' that exists to make global decisions and that 'government' continues eternally as opposed to the short lifespans of different administrations in the political cycle. Also see Stern's rationale outlined on page 35 of the Review.
11 For a full discussion see Howarth, 2008.
12 See George et al, 2006.
13 See D'haeseleer et al, 2007.
14 See Defra, 2007.
15 Monjon, 2006.
16 Pavan, 2005.
17 However, in practice, the law of demand and supply does not always work smoothly and if a few large polluters are in surplus they can collude to maintain high prices (as OPEC does with oil).
18 This is the case in the UK and Belgium.
19 www.eci.ox.ac.uk/news/events/amazon/ebeling.pdf
20 Information available at www.rainforestcoalition.org/eng and www.unfccc.int/files/meetings/dialogue/application/pdf/wp_21_braz.pdf

References

Allsopp, C. (2009) 'The financial crisis world recession and energy', Presentation as part of the OEIS Geopolitics of Energy Seminar Series, St Antony's College, Oxford

Amundsen, E. S., Baldursson, F. M. and Morensen, J. B. (2006) 'Price volatility and banking in green certificate markets', *Environmental & Resource Economics*, vol 35, pp259–287

Arthur, W. B. (1994) *Increasing Returns and Path Dependence in the Economy*, University of Michigan Press, Ann Arbor, MI

Baumol, W. (1972) 'On taxation and the control of externalities', *American Economic Review*, vol 62, pp307–321

Bosquet, B. (2000) 'Environmental tax reform: Does it work? A survey of the empirical evidence', *Ecological Economics*, vol 34, pp19–32

Carbon Trust (2008) 'EU ETS impacts on profitability and trade – a sector by sector analysis', Carbon Trust, London

Coase, R.H. (1960) 'The problem of social cost', *Journal of Law and Economics*, vol 3, no 1, pp1–44

Defra (2007) 'Carbon Emissions Reduction Target April 2008 to March 2011', Consultation Proposals, May, Department of Environment, Food and Rural Affairs, UK Government

D'haeseleer, W., Klees, P., Streydio, J.-M., Belmans-Luc, R. and Chevalier-Wolfgang, J.-M. (2007) 'Belgium's Energy Challenges Towards 2030—Final Report', Commission ENERGY 2030, Belgian Energy Commission, Brussels

Doornbosch, R. and Knight, E. (2008) 'What Role for Public Finance in International Climate Change Mitigation?', *Round Table on Sustainable Development*, OECD, Paris

Ellerman, A. D. and Buchner, B. K. (2007) 'The European Union Emissions Trading Scheme: Origins, allocation and early results', *Review of Environmental Economics and Policy*, vol 1, pp66–86

Frankel, M. (1955) 'Obsolescence and technological change in a maturing economy,' *American Economic Review*, vol 45, pp296–319

Garnaut, R. (2008) 'Climate Change Review', *Final Report*, Commonwealth of Australia, Canberra and Melbourne, pp309–310

George, A. C., Betkoski, J. W. and Goldberg, J. R. (2006) 'DPUC proceeding to develop a new distributed resources portfolio standard', State of Connecticut Department of Public Utility Control, 16 February, Docket No. 05–07–19

Grubb, M. (2004) 'Technology innovation and climate change policies: An overview of issues and options', *Keio Economic Studies*, vol 41, no 2, pp103–132

Grubb, M. and Neuhoff, K. (2006) 'Allocation and competitiveness in the EU Emissions Trading Scheme: Policy overview', *Climate Policy*, vol 6, pp7–30

Helm, D. R. (2007) 'European energy policy: Meeting the security of supply and climate change challenges', *European Investment Bank Papers*, vol 12

Helm, D., Hepburn, C. and Marsh, R. (2005) 'Credible Carbon Policy' *Climate Change Policy*, Oxford, Oxford University Press

Hepburn, C. (2006) 'Regulation by prices, quantities, or both: A review of instrument choice', *Oxford Review of Economic Policy*, vol 22, no 2, pp226–247

Howarth, N. (2008) 'Inducing Socio-technological Revolution in Energy Network Investment: An Institutional Evolutionary Economics Model of Agent Behaviour', OUCE Working Paper Series, Oxford University, Oxford

Jacoby, H. D. and Ellerman A. D. (2004) 'The safety valve and climate policy', *Energy Policy*, vol 32, 4, pp481–491

Joskow, P. and Schmalensee, R. (1998) 'The political economy of market-based environmental policy: The US acid rain program', *Journal of Law and Economics*, vol 41, no 1

Katz, M. and Shapiro, C. (1985) 'Network externalities, competition and compatibility', *American Economic Review*, vol 75, pp424–440

Kelman, S. (1981) *What Price Incentives? Economists and the Environment*, Greenwood Publishing Group, Westport, CT

Mavrakis, D. and Konidari, P. (2003) 'Classification of emissions trading scheme design characteristics', *European Environment*, vol 13, pp48–63

Monjon, S. (2006) The French Energy Savings Certificates System, ADEME Economics Department

Myres, N. and Kent, J. (2001) *Perverse Subsidies, How Tax Dollars Can Undercut the Environment and the Economy*, Island Press, Washington DC

Nordhaus, W. (2007) 'To tax or not to tax: Alternative approaches to slowing global warming', *Review of Environmental Economics and Policy*, vol 1, no 1, pp26–44

Pavan, M. (2005) 'The Italian energy efficiency certificates (EECs) scheme', The Italian Regulatory Authority for Electricity and Gas, presentation given to the Ministere de l'Economie des Finances et de l'Industrie, ADEME, Paris, 8 November

Philip, M. and Fearnside, P. M. (2001) 'Environmentalists split over Kyoto and Amazonian deforestation', *Environmental Conservation*, vol 28, pp295–299

Pigou, A. C. (1912) *Wealth and Welfare*, Macmillan, New York

Rosenberg, N. (1982) *Inside the Black Box: Technology and Economics*, Cambridge University Press, Cambridge

Sen, A. (1999) *Development as Freedom*, Anchor Books, London

Sijm, J., Neuhoff, K. and Chen, Y. (2006) 'CO_2 cost pass-through and windfall profits in the power sector', *Climate Policy*, vol 6, pp49–72

Stern, N. (2006) *The Economics of Climate Change*, The Stern Review, Cambridge University Press, Cambridge

Tietenberg, T. (2004) *Environmental Economics and Policy*, Pearson Addison Wesley, Upper Saddle River, NJ, pp69–70

Weitzman, M. L. (1974) 'Prices versus quantities', *Review of Economic Studies*, vol 41, no 4, pp477–491

Chapter 3

The Kyoto Protocol

Introduction

The Kyoto Protocol and the subsequent decisions agreed during the Conference of the Parties to the United Nations Framework Convention on Climate Change set the foundations for the first emissions trading scheme between nations. This chapter sets out the international political context within which this market was established. It goes on to describe the principle elements of the market – the cap that establishes a value for carbon, how the emissions rights have been defined and distributed, and how emissions are reported and enforced.

This is followed by a section that summarizes the issues associated with the two baseline and credits schemes implemented by the Kyoto Protocol, namely the Clean Development Mechanism and the Joint Implementation. We then provide a short description of the way in which supply and demand for allowances operate in this original market.

Political context

The establishment of the IPCC

At the end of the 1980s, scientific evidence of anthropogenic influence on the climate system and the public's growing interest in environmental issues put climate change on the political agenda. In 1988, the Intergovernmental Panel on Climate Change (IPCC) was established by the World Meteorological Organization (WMO) and the United Nations Environment Programme (UNEP). The objective of this organization is to provide comprehensive reports and updates on the state of scientific knowledge to guide policy makers. Twenty years after its foundation, the IPCC remains the source of the most reliable information and its work has been rewarded with a Nobel Peace Prize received jointly with former US Vice President Al Gore in December 2007.

In 1990, the IPCC published its first assessment report (FAR), confirming that climate change was a threat and stimulating the international community to act. The General Assembly of the United Nations responded in December 1990 by commencing formal negotiations on the Framework Convention on Climate Change with resolution 45/212 and by establishing the Intergovernmental Negotiating Committee for conducting these negotiations (UN General Assembly, 1990).

The Clean Air Act

The Clean Air Act, passed in the United States in 1990, was the first legal document establishing a mandatory emissions trading scheme. The issue addressed by this environmental legislation was not climate change, but the problem of tackling acid rain. As part of the Acid Rain Program, the US government set a maximum emissions level for sulfur dioxide (SO_2) and nitrogen oxides (NO_x).[1]

The US objective is to reduce SO_2 emissions by 10 million tons (50 per cent reduction)[2] by 2010 compared to 1980 levels and those of NO_x by 2 million tons (27 per cent reduction) compared to 1990 levels. For NO_x, the regulator first chose conventional measures (taxes along with strict standards for the burners),[3] while the solution chosen for SO_2 was the establishment of an emissions market (Joskow et al, 1998).

The programme currently covers all installations with a power capacity greater than 25MW and all new power plants. In all, in 2008, more than 2300 facilities are covered. Emissions banking is permitted and the Environmental Protection Agency annually auctions 3 per cent of the allowances, with most allowances grandfathered (i.e. based on historical emissions). The system provides penalties for infringement. If a company does not have enough allowances to cover its emissions at the annual reconciliation, it must pay a $2000 fine per uncovered ton. The establishment of a register (Allowance Tracking System) has facilitated trading of allowances and thus liquidity and market transparency. Price volatility on this market was quite important. Starting at $140 per ton in January 1995, the price has risen from $70 in 1996 to $1550 in late 2005. In March 2007 the price had dropped to around $460 per ton. The environmental success of this experiment and socially acceptable costs for American firms inspired the negotiators of the Kyoto Protocol in 1997.

The **UNFCCC**

On 9 May 1992, the United Nations Framework Convention on Climate Change (UNFCCC) was adopted.[4] The Convention was opened for signature at the United Nations Conference on Environment and Development, also known as the 'Earth Summit' in Rio de Janeiro, 4 June 1992 and came into force on 21 March 1994 after having been ratified by 50 states. The ultimate objective of the Convention (Article 2) is to stabilize concentrations of GHGs in the atmosphere at a level that would prevent dangerous anthropogenic interference with the climate system. Such a level – not defined by the Convention – should allow ecosystems to adapt naturally to climate change, maintain food production and make economic development meet the criteria for sustainability. Such non-quantitative objectives help create a consensus among nations, however they rely on nations to follow through with individual action to actually reduce emissions.

The Convention divided countries into two groups: those listed in Annex I (Annex I Parties) and those not listed (Non-Annex I Parties). Annex I Parties are industrialized countries that have historically emitted the most GHGs. Their per capita emissions are higher than those of most developing countries and they have more financial and institutional resources to address the problem. The principles of equity and of 'common but differentiated responsibilities' set out in the Convention require these parties to take the lead in changing emissions trends. To this end, the Annex I Parties agreed to adopt policies and measures with the (legally non-binding) objective of stabilizing their emissions at 1990 levels in 2000.

Annex I Parties that are members of the OECD are included in Annex II. These countries have an obligation to provide new and additional financial resources to developing countries to help them combat climate change. In addition they must facilitate the transfer of low-emitting technologies to developing countries and Annex I Parties that were not members of the OECD in 1990.

Non-Annex I countries are mainly developing countries. However, there are also some that would now be categorized as newly industrialized countries, such as South Korea, China, Mexico and South Africa.

The Convention recognizes that financial assistance and technology transfer are essential to enable developing countries to cope with global warming and adapt to its effects.

The management of activities related to the implementation of the Convention and its protocols is provided by a Secretariat whose headquarters are based in Bonn. In 2007, the Secretariat's budget was US$27 million. This budget is used primarily to pay for the international officials, experts and infrastructure (including information technology) necessary for the operation of the Convention and its Protocol (Kyoto).

In 2008, 192 governments and the European Community were parties to the Convention. The parties meet annually at the Conference of Parties (COP), the supreme body of the Convention. At these meetings, the parties make the necessary decisions to promote the effective implementation of the Convention and pursue dialogue on the best measures to fight global warming.

The Kyoto Protocol

At the first Conference of the Parties, which took place in Berlin in 1995, the parties agreed that the specific commitments of the Convention for the Annex I Parties were not adequate because they were too vague. The parties then launched a new round of discussions in order to achieve tougher and more specific targets for Annex I Parties. After two and a half years of intense negotiations, the Kyoto Protocol was adopted at the Third Conference of the Parties on 11 December 1997 in Japan.[5]

Under international law, this Protocol is original for several reasons. First, inspired by the success of the Montreal Protocol,[6] the negotiators decided to define measurable and binding targets, moving away from declarations of intent that often characterize international environmental law. Furthermore, this Protocol is the first international implementation of a cap-and-trade scheme. Articles of the Protocol related to emissions trading are:

- Article 3.1: countries can meet their objectives jointly (bubble policy, i.e. one form of flexibility mechanisms in which differentiated commitments are taken between a group of countries with the goal of achieving a common reduction goal). These countries can allocate national commitments in a different ways. We will see that this was chosen by the European Union (EU15 in 1997).
- Article 3.13: countries have the option to set aside emissions unused during the period 2008–2012 (recognition of the banking).

- Article 6: emissions credits can be earned using emissions reductions projects in other countries subject to binding targets (Annex B countries). Annex B countries are authorized to exchange these credits. They may also authorize legal entities to participate in activities relating to the acquisition and transfer of emissions reductions achieved through these projects. This mechanism was later called Joint Implementation (JI).
- Article 12: the Clean Development Mechanism (CDM) allows Annex I countries to achieve 'additional' emissions reductions in non-Annex I countries.
- Article 17: emissions trading between parties of Annex B is permitted.

The European Union approved the Protocol through the Council Decision 2002/358/EC of 25 April 2002 and the Member States ratified it in the months that followed.[7]

The Kyoto Protocol to the UNFCCC entered into force on 16 February 2005, or 90 days after the date of deposition of the instrument of ratification by Russia. Russian participation was essential (following the refusal to ratify by the US) as a prerequisite for the entry into force of the Protocol is that ratifying parties cover at least 55 per cent of the total CO_2 emissions of all Annex I Parties of the Convention. In practice, Russia's target is relatively easy to meet as its emissions have declined substantially through deindustrialization since 1990. Some analysts fear this will create trade in 'hot air', i.e. Russia will sell emissions rights that require no additional abatement action.

On 3 December 2007, the new Prime Minister of Australia Kevin Rudd signed the instruments of ratification of Australia, making the US the only Annex B country that has not deposited its instrument of ratification (the Senate vote was rejected overwhelmingly by both Republicans and Democrats).

The following Conferences of Parties (COPs)

At the time the Protocol was signed, negotiators believed that the commitments of the post-2012 period would be a continuation of the Kyoto period (2008–2012). They had planned to start in 2005 examining commitments for the Annex B countries for the period after 2012 (Article 3.9 of the Protocol).[8] In 2009 commitments after 2012 are still unknown. The 13th

Conference of the Parties (held in Bali in December 2007) ended with an agreement on a roadmap, which sets the agenda for negotiations in the next two years. The timescale is as follows:

- December 2008: climate conference in Poznan, Poland (COP14) – the middle of negotiations (little progress was observed).
- Beginning–mid-2009: A change in government in the United States has signalled a structural shift in US climate policy. However, US support for a Kyoto-style post-2012 agreement remains uncertain.
- December 2009: climate conference in Copenhagen (COP15) – scheduled date for the conclusion of UNFCCC negotiations for a post-2012 framework.
- 2012: deadline for the ratification of a new agreement on climate.

The following sections describe in detail the characteristics of the GHG market as established by the Kyoto Protocol and the subsequent Conferences of Parties.

The characteristics of the emissions market

Cap and period

General principles

The Kyoto Protocol commits the Annex B Parties to a binding target for reducing or limiting their emissions of GHGs. The commitment period extends from 2008 to 2012 (the parties who have ratified the Protocol have to meet their commitments relating to this five-year period). It is important to measure the emissions target over several years because there may be variations from one year to another, for example, severe winters or hot summers directly influence the consumption of fossil fuels and thus emissions of GHGs.

Reduction targets vary from an 8 per cent reduction in some countries to a 10 per cent increase in others (generally compared to 1990 as the base year).

The European bubble

Parties that agree to fulfil their commitments jointly through the bubble mechanism have to share their joint target among themselves. The

European Union is the only group of countries that has used this option to implement an EU-wide 8 per cent reduction compared to 1996 levels. The burden-sharing agreement was originally founded on a methodology developed by a team from the University of Utrecht and based on population growth and energy efficiency. 'But this approach was soon washed away by political compromises' (Bonduelle, 2002). The sharing agreement was approved on 16 June 1998 (EU Council, 1998).

Intuitively, it might seem that countries with high reduction percentages have to take tougher action than countries with low reduction percentages or countries that are authorized to increase their emissions. In practice, this is too simplistic, as the difficulty in reaching an emissions target also depends on the 'business as usual' trend in emissions.

For instance, a country that had many coal-fired power stations in 1990 (for example the UK or eastern Germany), and since then has replaced some of them with lower emissions technologies (e.g. gas power stations) will already have achieved some emissions reductions. Similarly, a country

Table 3.1 *Commitments under the Kyoto Protocol*

Percentage of the reference level					
Australia	108	Greece	92	Norway	101
Austria	92	Hungary	94	Poland	94
Belgium	92	Iceland	110	Portugal	92
Bulgaria	92	Ireland	92	Romania	92
Canada	94	Italy	92	Russian Federation	100
Croatia	95	Japan	94	Slovakia	92
Czech Republic	92	Latvia	92	Slovenia	92
Denmark	92	Liechtenstein	92	Spain	92
Estonia	92	Lithuania	92	Sweden	92
European Community	92	Luxembourg	92	Switzerland	92
Finland	92	Monaco	92	Ukraine	100
France	92	Netherlands	92	UK	92
Germany	92	New Zealand	100	US	93

where heavy industries closed since 1990 (e.g. Luxembourg) will have a lower baseline trend than a country that continued to industrialize after 1990 (e.g. Greece, Ireland and Portugal). These examples help to explain the wide differences between Member States' emissions targets.

In January 2008, the EU announced a second sharing agreement, which should lead to overall emissions reductions of 20 per cent by 2020 compared to the baseline of the Kyoto Protocol. The section above sets out the reductions targets for the first Kyoto period; the Kyoto baseline needs further explanation. The best approximation is the level of emissions in 1990 for the six gases or families of gases addressed in the Protocol. However, there are quite a few exceptions and the determination of the baseline is not as straightforward as one might expect. The following sections present different aspects that influence the baseline and therefore the number of allocated allowances.

Afforestation, reforestation and deforestation

The definition of the cap and the actual extent of reductions is also complex because some activities related to change of land use (e.g. deforestation or reforestation), which emit or capture CO_2 in the atmosphere, are also covered (using the acronym LULUCF). These changes are accounted for within the emissions of GHGs. The estimate of these changes in land use and the impact of CO_2 equivalent (CO_2e) is complex, but it can have significant consequences for national targets and has therefore been a controversial issue within Kyoto negotiations (see Chapter 6 on Australia).

Emissions caused or prevented by land use, land use change, and forestry (LULUCF) are accounted for as part of the national inventories to

Table 3.2 *Burden sharing among EU15's Member States*

Percentage of the reference level					
Austria	87.0	Germany	79.0	Netherlands	94.0
Belgium	92.5	Greece	125.0	Portugal	127.0
Denmark	79.0	Ireland	113.0	Spain	115.0
Finland	100.0	Italy	93.5	Sweden	104.0
France	100.0	Luxembourg	72.0	UK	87.5

the UNFCCC. However, under the Kyoto Protocol flexibility mechanisms (Joint Implementation and the CDM), such emissions are only accounted for if they result from human activities. The reason for this non-inclusion is twofold. First, understanding of the carbon cycle is not sufficiently precise to permit quantification in 'Kyoto' units (i.e. tonnes of CO_2e), and second it is arguably unfair to financially reward or penalize a country if changes in land use are not human-induced (e.g. penalizing a country where warming harms forests and increases the desertification would be counter productive).

Article 3.3 states that 'net changes in GHG emissions by sources and removals by sinks resulting from direct human-induced land use, land use change and forestry activities, limited to afforestation, reforestation and deforestation since 1990 shall be used by Parties to meet their commitments'.

It was only in 2005, in Montreal, that the decision 16/CMP.1 confirmed that land-use change from human activities could be included in the accounting of emissions under the Protocol and set limits on the emissions that could then be recorded.[9]

The comparison of different GHGs

The Protocol recognizes six gases: CO_2, CH_4, N_2O, hydrofluorocarbons (HFCs), perfluorocarbons (PFCs) and sulfur hexafluoride (SF_6). However, aggregate targets and emissions trading make it necessary to define a common currency, or at least a conversion rate between these gases.

In order to compare the impact of different GHGs, the concept of global warming potential (GWP) is used. GWP is a measure of how much a given mass of GHG is estimated to contribute to global warming. It is a relative scale that compares the gas in question to that of the same mass of CO_2 (whose GWP is by definition 1). A GWP is calculated over a specific time interval and the value of this must be stated whenever a GWP is quoted or else the value is meaningless. Usually the time interval chosen is 100 years, so the GWP is defined as the radiative forcing, i.e. the effect of emissions now of a unit of each GHG on aggregate radiation from the atmosphere over a 100-year period. For instance, the GWP for CH_4, according to the latest estimates, is 25. In other words we can say that over 100 years the release of one tonne of CH_4 is equivalent to the release of 25 tonnes of CO_2 (1t CH_4 = 25tCO_2e). The residence time of most GHGs in the atmosphere is determined by atmospheric chemistry. For CO_2 the situation is more complex as it is influenced by the ecosystem and oceanic removal mecha-nisms: i.e. when CO_2 sinks approach saturation, the lifetime of CO_2 in the atmosphere increases. As a result, the GWP might have to be evaluated according to the saturation of sinks. The determination of the GWP of different GHGs is a complex and still evolving science. Note that according to decision 2/CP.3, GWPs used under UNFCCC and Kyoto accounting are from the IPCC Second Assessment Report (1995). Consequently, on the international emissions market, one tonne of CH_4 is considered equiv-alent to 21 tonnes of CO_2.

No GWP is calculated for water vapour. Although water vapour has a significant influence with regard to absorbing infrared radiation, its concentration in the atmosphere mainly depends on air temperature. Anthropogenic emissions of water vapour (at ground level) do not signifi-cantly perturb atmospheric water vapour concentration. However, the dependence of water vapour concentration on temperature means that water vapour is a positive feedback to emissions of other GHGs.

Flexibility in the choice of the reference year

Articles 3.5 and 3.8 were drafted to enable countries whose emissions from some GHGs greatly varied around 1990 to choose a less penalizing baseline.

Article 3.5 allows Annex I Parties with economies in transition to choose another baseline year to meet their commitments. For CO_2, CH_4 and N_2O emissions, Bulgaria chose 1988 as the reference year; Hungary chose the average emissions between 1985 and 1987; Poland chose 1988; Slovenia chose 1986 and Romania 1989. This flexibility was granted to facilitate the participation of countries whose economies (and emissions) fell sharply just before 1990. In many cases this was due to the decline of heavy industry following the collapse of the former Soviet Union.

Article 3.8 allows the possibility of choosing 1995 as the reference year for the calculation of emissions from hydrofluorocarbons (HFCs), perfluo-rocarbons (PFCs) and sulfur hexafluoride (instead of 1990 for other gases and forestry activities). This flexibility increases the baseline and helps facil-itate the achievement of the target. Indeed, following the Montreal Protocol (1987), a range of substances that deplete the ozone layer (including CFCs) have been progressively banned and replaced by other substances, not harmful to the ozone layer but highly potent GHGs, including HFCs. This explains the increase in emissions between 1990 and

Table 3.3 *GWP for different GHGs according to the IPCC Assessment Reports*

Gas	GWP IPCC 1995	GWP IPCC 2001	GWP IPCC 2007
Carbon dioxide	1	1	1
Methane	21	23	25
N_2O	310	296	298
HFC-23	11,700	12,000	14,800
HFC-125	2800	3400	3500
HFC-134a	1300	1300	1430
HFC-143a	3800	4300	4470
HFC-152a	140	120	124
HFC-227ea	2900	3500	3220
HFC-236fa	6300	9400	9810
Tetrafluoromethane (CF_4)	6500	5700	7390
Hexafluoroethane (C_2F_6)	9200	11,900	12,200
Sulfur hexafluoride (SF_6)	23,900	22,200	22,800

1995 and why some countries, including Japan (Den Elzen and De Moor, 2002), have called for this exception for the calculation of the baseline emissions. Twelve of the EU15 Member States chose 1995 as reference year for fluorinated gases. France, Austria and Italy kept 1990 as reference year. Slovakia chose 1990 for fluorinated gases and Romania 1989. All other 'new' Member States (i.e. Member States that joined the EU after the ratification of the Kyoto Protocol) chose 1995.

Exclusion of international aviation and maritime transport emissions

GHG emissions from fuels used in international aviation and marine transportation are not accounted for within the targets of the Kyoto Protocol. This is partly due to accounting difficulties. To better understand the technical difficulties of accounting, consider the example of an aeroplane from an American company that flies to Dubai with passengers of different nationalities on board. The aircraft stopped in Zurich to fill its tanks with kerosene. Which country is responsible for the GHG emissions? No clear answer could satisfy parties during the Kyoto negotiations and as a consequence the Protocol limited itself to asking (in Article 2.2) the International Civil Aviation Organization (ICAO) and the International Maritime Organization (IMO) to work on this issue. More than ten years later little progress has been made. Note that in the context of road transport, the accounting procedure implies that the country responsible for the release of emissions is the country where the fuel was sold. This decision has a significant impact for a country like Luxembourg, famous for fuel tourism due to lower taxation.

The exclusion of international aviation and maritime emissions is widely recognized as a weakness of the Kyoto Protocol, although the national target-based approach of the Protocol makes the problem difficult to address within the existing framework. International aviation and maritime emissions currently form only a small percentage of total GHG emissions, even accounting for the greater potency of aviation emissions at altitude (estimated between 5 and 7 per cent). However, the scope for addressing these emissions technologically is relatively limited, as airplanes are already efficient and the scope for fuel substitution is limited due to the tight specification placed on aviation fuel.[10] Using a biologically sourced fuel (bio-kerosene) could address CO_2 emissions but would not affect the impact of water vapour described in Chapter 1.

Moreover, GHG emissions from international transport, in particular aviation, are growing more rapidly than those from other sectors. Some scenarios undertaken at national level, and assuming major action to reduce CO_2 emissions from other sectors, indicate that aviation emissions alone could form a very high share of emissions by 2050.[11] Concerns about the treatment of aviation within the international regime relate principally to this issue of future trends.

Defining emissions rights

The Kyoto Protocol and subsequent decisions under the Conferences/Meetings of the Parties (COP/MOP) recognize four types of emissions allowances or credits.

First Assigned Amount Units (AAUs) are the allowances allocated to parties (based on historical emissions and emissions targets as explained in the previous section). An AAU is equal to one metric tonne of CO_2e. According to Article 17 of the Kyoto Protocol, emissions trading is an option for countries to fulfil their GHG targets. These obligations require Annex B Parties to remain within their Assigned Amount Units set out in the Protocol. Emissions trading leads to a change in allocation from the initial allocation of allowances between parties. Any assigned amount that a Party acquires from another Party through emissions trading is added to the assigned amount for the acquiring Party (Article 3, §10 of the Kyoto Protocol). Similarly, any assigned amount that a Party transfers to another Party is subtracted from the assigned amount of the transferring Party (Article 3, §11 of the Kyoto Protocol).

The Kyoto Protocol recognizes three other types of credits that can be used instead of AAUs, provided they observe the supplementarity principle. This principle, also referred to as the supplementary principle, is one of the principles of the Kyoto Protocol. Its objective is to limit the application of the Protocol's flexibility mechanisms and establishes that each should be supplemental to domestic action in meeting the emissions reductions targets of the parties to the Protocol. However, the Protocol provides no quantification of the required level of domestic action on which to base a judgement of supplementarity.

- A Certified Emission Reduction (CER) is a unit issued pursuant to Article 12 of the Protocol and subsequent COP/MOP decisions, including the provisions from the appendix to decision 3/CMP.1.[12] Specifically, it is a credit issued under the Clean Development Mechanism (see below).
- An Emission Reduction Unit (ERU) is a unit issued pursuant to the provisions of Article 6 of the Protocol. Specifically it is a credit issued under Joint Implementation.
- A Removal Unit (RMU) is a unit issued pursuant to the relevant provisions of the modalities concerning increasing the capacities of sinks. It represents one metric tonne of CO_2e.

Allocation

The allocation of emission rights between countries was made on the basis of historical emissions (grandfathering). Such an approach favours industrialized over developing countries since it generally leads to the allocation of more allowances to big emitters.

For the sake of fairness, some people have advocated an allocation of allowances based on per capita emissions (i.e. national allocations based on the number of inhabitants). Indeed, the atmosphere being a public good that benefits humanity as a whole, it may seem more equitable to award the rights to pollute equally among all people. During Kyoto Protocol negotiations, the Brazilians advanced the idea of an allocation based on historical contribution to climate change (Höhne and Blok, 2005; Den Elzen et al, 2005). The rich industrialized countries that emitted large amounts of GHGs during their industrialization would be penalized while developing countries or newly industrialized countries would get more allowances to sustain their growth. Both approaches proposed by the developing countries, and based on ideas of equity, pose practical issues and would be detrimental to the interests of developed countries. It is very unlikely that these proposals, unamended, will lead to a consensus during the post-Kyoto (post-2012) negotiations. However, a hybrid approach with different methods of allocation for developing and developed countries would have a better chance of securing an agreement between Annex I and Non-Annex I countries (Müller, 1999). We can also imagine maintaining a comparison with historical emissions but allowing countries with growing economies to increase their emissions and requiring more efforts from OECD countries. This is closer to the contraction and convergence framework (see Box 3.1).

Box 3.1 Contraction and Convergence

Contraction & Convergence's (C&C) principles require reductions from rich countries in order to allow developing countries to increase their emissions and economic growth, ending in convergence on a (globally) similar per capita level of emissions (Meyer, 2000). This alternative approach would represent a major shift from the current Kyoto Protocol approach. Instead of focusing on the question of how to share the emissions reduction burden as in the present Kyoto Protocol, this approach starts from the assumption that the atmosphere is a global common to which all are equally entitled, and focuses on sharing the use of the atmosphere (resource sharing). The approach defines emissions rights on the basis of a convergence of per capita emissions under a contracting global emission profile. With this approach, all parties would participate immediately after 2012, with per capita emission permits (rights) converging towards equal levels over time. More specifically, over time, all shares converge from actual proportions in emissions to shares based on the distribution of population in the convergence year. For an ethical discussion of the fairness or otherwise of the equal per capita allocation underlying C&C, see Starkey (2008).

Monitoring and reporting of emissions

The Kyoto Protocol's effectiveness will depend upon two critical factors: whether parties follow the Protocol's rule book and comply with their commitments; and whether the emissions data used to assess compliance is reliable. Recognizing this, the Kyoto Protocol and Marrakesh Accords, adopted by the Carbon Market Programme (CMP 1) in Montreal, Canada, in December 2005, include a set of monitoring and compliance procedures to enforce the Protocol's rules, address any compliance problems, and avoid any error in calculating emissions data and accounting for transactions under the three Kyoto mechanisms (emissions trading, Clean Development Mechanism and Joint Implementation) and activities related to land use, land use change and forestry (LULUCF).

Each Annex I Party must submit an annual inventory of its GHG emissions and removals to the UNFCCC Secretariat, calculated using standard guidelines based on IPCC methodologies. This inventory also includes other information that must be submitted annually, for example, on total annual transactions (for the previous year) in AAUs, CERs, ERUs and RMUs and on action taken to minimize adverse impacts on developing countries. As they will be more detailed, these annual inventories will supersede those currently required under the Convention. The emissions are reported in Common Reporting Format (CRF).

Expert review teams (ERT) check annual inventories to make sure they are complete, accurate and conform to the guidelines. The annual inventory review will generally be conducted as a desk or centralized review. However, each Annex I Party will be subject to at least one in-country visit during the commitment period. If any problems are found, the expert review team may recommend adjusting the data to make sure that emissions during any year of the commitment period are not underestimated. If there is disagreement between a party and the expert review team about the adjustment that should be made, the Compliance Committee will adjudicate. Aside from recommending data adjustments, the expert review team has a mandate to raise any apparent implementation problems with the Compliance Committee. Once the compliance procedures have been finalized, the compilation and accounting database will be updated with a record of the party's emissions for that year.

Annex I Parties must also provide national communications on activities they undertake to implement the Protocol. Each communication is subject to a detailed review by the ERT. The ERTs also prepare a report that identifies potential implementation problems. The ERTs for annual inventories and national communications are coordinated by the Secretariat of the UNFCCC. These teams are composed of four to twelve individual experts selected by the parties. Each team is composed of two 'lead reviewers', one from an Annex I Party and the other from a non-Annex I Party.

The annual reports must be submitted by 15 April. The ERT must perform their audit mission within one year after receipt of the initial annual report by the UNFCCC Secretariat.

National registries and the International Transaction Log (ITL)

Registries record the holdings of Kyoto units, and any transactions involving them, through a structure of accounts. They record and monitor all transactions in AAUs, ERUs, CERs and RMUs. This is similar to the way that banks record balances and movements in money using accounts allocated to individuals or other entities. Accounting under the Kyoto Protocol framework is organized on two parallel flows of information: on the one hand the inventories of GHG emissions, on the other hand information on the allocated allowances (assigned amounts). The ultimate objective is to ensure that emissions of the parties are covered by Kyoto equivalent units (compliance test with Article 3.1). The following diagram shows the two data streams.

The equivalence between the allowances side and the emissions side is illustrated in the following figure. First, a country must implement an action plan to ensure that its actual emissions are lower than expected emissions. If these domestic measures to reduce emissions are not sufficient to obtain the amount of AAUs, the country may – under certain conditions – take action to increase the capacity of its sinks and thus benefit from RMU

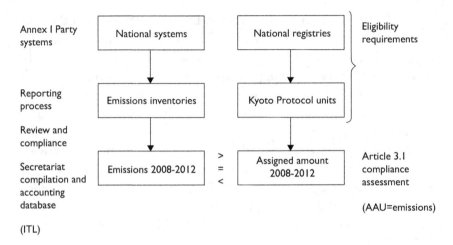

Figure 3.1 Monitoring of emissions data and emissions rights

to cover its excess emissions. Finally, the country can buy credits from CDM and JI projects (CER or ERU) or buy AAU from countries that have a surplus of allowances.

We have seen that the accounting of emissions and AAUs allocated at the national level begins with the annual inventory of GHG emissions. Regarding accounting of emissions rights (AAUs, CERs, ERUs or RMUs), each party shall, in compliance with the Marrakesh Accords, set up a national registry to ensure the traceability of transactions of Kyoto units. Inventory data and information on the number of allowances are listed in the national reports. They are subject to review procedures and compliance audit. The purpose of these procedures is to check emissions levels and the number of allowances held by the parties, as well as compliance with the eligibility criteria of the Kyoto mechanisms.

In addition, the parties can implement Supplementary Transaction Logs (STL) to track and monitor the validity of transactions proposed by national registries where such transactions occur in national or regional trading systems that are consistent with Kyoto units accounting. The Community Independent Transaction Log (CITL), managed by the European Commission to support the EU ETS, is an example of an STL.

As an added monitoring tool, the UNFCCC Secretariat manages an Independent Transaction Log, which will automatically check the validity

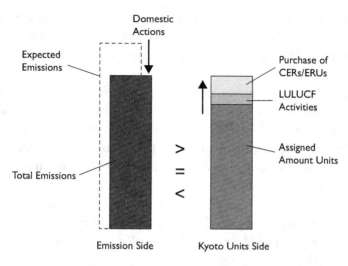

Figure 3.2 Kyoto compliance test with Article 3.1

of transactions under the flexibility mechanisms and LULUCF activities. Every year, the Secretariat will publish a compilation and accounting report for each Annex I Party, based on the information contained in its database. The final Secretariat report published at the end of the commitment period will form the basis for assessing whether Annex I Parties have complied with their emissions targets.

The technical requirements of national registries have been developed in partnership with the UNFCCC Secretariat to ensure that national registries use common procedures and technical specifications that are compatible with the International Transaction Log (ITL). Prior to the start of the commitment period, each Annex I Party was asked to submit a report to the Secretariat describing its national system and registry, and providing the emissions data necessary to formally establish its assigned amount.

Developed by the Belgian IT consultant Trasys and administered by the UNFCCC Secretariat, the ITL tracks all transactions in Kyoto units by the parties and in the CDM registry. Whenever a national registry undertakes a transaction that affects the number of units held by a Kyoto Party, the register communicates with the ITL. The ITL then verifies the compliance of the transaction in accordance with the general rules of accounting for Kyoto units and specific rules for the type of transaction in question. The transactions are approved after successful tests. The CDM registry records all transactions with CERs. The ITL also manages information on ERU transfers under the Joint Implementation (for the procedures in 'Track 2', see below).

In April 2008 only the registers from Japan, New Zealand, Switzerland and the CDM registry were connected to the ITL. The first transactions were carried out from the CDM registry to these three countries. The 25 EU countries participating in emissions trading under the Kyoto Protocol (Cyprus and Malta are not listed in Annex B of the Kyoto Protocol) joined together in October 2008.

The bookings in the registers or the ITL are only related to the number of units. Each unit is regarded as fungible. The financial aspects of the transactions are handled by private trading platforms or contracts when the sale is agreed over the counter.

Sanctions

At the COP7 in Marrakesh, the Parties to the Kyoto Protocol agreed on the design of the enforcement mechanisms, and created two bodies responsible for the implementation of these mechanisms: a Facilitative Branch and an Enforcement Branch. The objective of the Facilitative Branch is to promote compliance by providing advice and assistance to the parties of the Protocol. The Enforcement Branch has the authority to decide whether or not a country is in compliance. Once the Enforcement Branch has determined that a party has failed to comply with its emission targets, the following sanctions apply:

1   A number of tonnes equal to 1.3 times the amount of excess emissions is deducted from the party's assigned amount for the second commitment period.
2   The non-compliant party must develop a compliance action plan.
3   The non-compliant party's eligibility to sell permits must be suspended.

In the event of non-compliance by a party to Annex 1 of the Convention with its obligations relating to its inventory and its national communication, this is made public and the Secretariat requires the Party to correct this failure within one year. Finally, in the event of non-compliance with the eligibility criteria for the flexible mechanisms as adopted in Marrakesh, eligibility for the three mechanisms is suspended. While there are no immediate financial penalties, the multiplier applied to emissions in excess of targets could be very expensive. In addition, the diplomatic consequences of breaching international obligations are potentially significant.

The Clean Development Mechanism

Introduction

The Clean Development Mechanism (CDM) is a flexibility mechanism by which an Annex I Party invests in a non-Annex I Party for the purpose of reducing GHG emissions along with the promotion of sustainability principles in developing countries. For every tonne of CO_2 reduced or absorbed through the project, the investor will receive a Certified Emission Reduction (CER). As shown in the following figure the calculation of the emission reduction is based on a comparison with a baseline scenario without project.

The Kyoto Protocol itself gives very little guidance on the practical implementation of this mechanism. This was clarified in the Marrakesh Accords (COP7 held in November 2001), which defined the practical features of the CDM. These agreements include the establishment of a CDM Executive Board (CDM EB) and detailed the different steps leading to the issuing of certified emission reductions (CERs). They also set a limit

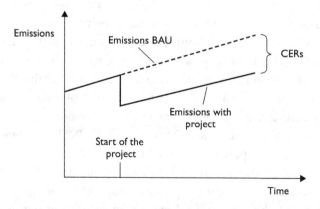

Figure 3.3 Baseline for a CDM project

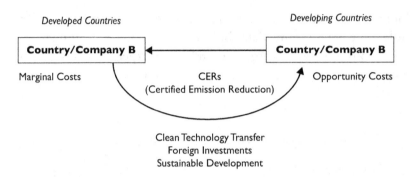

Figure 3.4 Diagram of the operation of the CDM

to the acquisition of CERs generated by forestry activities: a maximum of 5 per cent of the reference year GHG emissions can be offset through CERs from forestry activities.

The CDM EB is responsible for implementing the methodologies and guidelines. This is a committee composed of ten members from the parties to the Kyoto Protocol. This Committee is accountable to the Conference of the Parties for issues related to the implementation of the CDM. Specifically the CDM EB is responsible for approving baseline method-ologies, monitoring plans, accrediting operational entities, and maintaining a CDM registry. The CDM EB is assisted in this task by the fieldwork performed by designated operational entities (DOEs). DOEs are respon-sible for the validation, verification and certification of CDM projects (see below the stages of a CDM project). The designated operational entities are accredited by the EB. They can be public or private, national or interna-tional. They are contractually bound to CDM project participants. Despite their commercial relationship with the participants, they are an integral part of the institutional structure and operate under the direct control of the EB. Their responsibility is comparable to that of a corporate auditor. This is to ensure that the emissions reductions reported by the project developer are real and accurate. DNV, Veritas, SGS, TÜV, PwC, KPMG and Deloitte are examples of accredited DOEs.

The COP/MOP oversees the CDM EB, the standards for accreditation for the DOEs, as well as their designation. It also examines the sectoral and geographical distribution of CDM projects to ensure that they are fair.

The development of a CDM project can be unilateral, bilateral or multi-lateral. Originally it was seen as an instrument with a bi- or multilateral character where an entity or fund from an industrialized country invests in a project in a developing country. However a third option has gained prominence – the unilateral option where the project development is planned and financed within the developing country.

In the bilateral CDM model, one or more developed country investors develop, finance and possibly implement the CDM project. Contract details are agreed directly between partners on a project-by-project basis.

Multilateral CDMs take the approach of a mutual fund in which invest-ments flow through a centrally managed fund to projects in host countries. Investors are not directly involved in project financing and development. The fund selects the projects on behalf of investors who are subsequently issued CERs generated by the projects. Fund management is often in the hands of development finance institutions such as the World Bank's Prototype Carbon Fund.

Each of these different structures has advantages and disadvantages. Unilateral CDMs have lower transaction costs and give more incentives to developing countries. However, the risks can be higher and the price for the credits is never fixed in advance. In addition, these projects do not contribute to the transfer of technology, which is one of the criteria for judging the additionality of projects. Bilateral structures offer limited geographical coverage to potential host countries. However, this approach is attractive to corporations in industrialized countries, which want maximum flexibility and minimum bureaucratic interference. The multi-lateral approach has the potential to include poorer host countries while shielding investors from individual project failure.

Additionality is the fundamental criterion for the recognition of a project. Under this criterion, the project developers must, from a business as usual scenario, show that their project will result in GHG emissions reductions that would not occur otherwise. The difference between the level of emissions in the BAU scenario and in the scenario with the CDM project determines rights to CERs. The additionality test is essentially composed of three elements: environmental additionality (does the project reduce emissions below the BAU scenario?), investment additionality (does access to CERs make the project viable?) and technological additionality (does the project lead to a transfer of technologies in the host country?).

The Marrakesh Accords implicitly recognize that investment additionality can be a means of proving the environmental additionality of the project, but is not necessarily the only way (other barriers to investment such as technological barriers or availability of capital may also prove the environmental additionality of a project). Finally, economic additionality is also considered. This requires that the capital provided by the developed countries is not used as a substitute for traditional aid to developing countries.

Correspondence of the project developers, for instance with banks or other investors, can be used to justify that carbon credits were considered as a source of revenue in the decision-making process before the investment was agreed. The project developer must be able to demonstrate that the project would not have been developed without the additional incomes generated by the carbon credits.

Most project design documents (PDD) include an analysis of the net present value (NPV) of a project. However, assumptions about the lifetime of a project and uncertainties about the price of fossil fuels or electricity in the context of renewable energy and energy-efficiency projects rarely allow unambiguous assessment of a project's profitability. The paradox of a PDD is that this is a business plan whose aim is to prove that the project is unprofitable or presents significant risks and that the investment decision is rational only when expected CERs are taken into account. Indeed, if the PDD indicated that the project were an excellent investment opportunity, this could challenge its additional character. The drafting of this document is therefore not an easy task for developers more accustomed to writing optimistic scenarios to raise the necessary capital from banks or their shareholders.

The Marrakesh Accords have also issued two restrictions on the use of CERs. First, they ban nuclear energy projects from the CDM. They then set a limitation on the use of carbon sinks: on an annual basis only 1 per cent of the 1990 level of GHG emissions from Annex I Parties can be offset between 2008 and 2012. The European Union defined other rules for the recognition of CERs in the EU ETS (see below).

Finally, buying CERs is not limited to states. We will see in the following sections that European companies involved in the EU ETS can use CERs. One consequence is that companies located in the EU but with facilities in non-Annex I countries are encouraged to invest in GHG emissions reductions on these sites.

The CDM project cycle

As a first step, a project developer makes an initial assessment as to whether the project is eligible under the CDM. If this initial assessment is positive then the project developer can develop and submit a project idea note (PIN) to one or more carbon credit buyers in the marketplace to gauge the level of interest in the project. The PIN will subsequently be screened by the recipient entities against the CDM rules and their investment criteria. The information requested in the PIN depends on the specific rules of the buyer. Even so there are great similarities between most of the PIN formats. Development of a PIN is not a requirement of the CDM process but represents an opportunity for the developer to receive feedback on whether or not the project is of interest. Moreover, most private buyers prefer to see PINs as their first form of contact with project developers.

The project design document (PDD) is the key documentation in the project cycle. The PDD is submitted to a designated operational entity for validation and, once validated, to the CDM EB for registration. Drafting a PDD is mandatory: no project can earn CERs without its validation by a DOE and registration by the Executive Board.

There is also a specific requirement to invite local stakeholders to comment. This local stakeholder consultation process is distinct from the invitation for comments from stakeholders by the designated operational entity, during the project validation phase. Stakeholders at the international level are invited to provide their comments regarding the specific CDM components of the activity. In contrast to local stakeholders the international stakeholders are not actively approached; they are made aware of new CDM projects through a website. The rationale is to empower the international and/or national community, especially NGOs, to monitor projects proposed for the CDM.

CDM projects have to be approved by the host country. Host country approval is one of the key components to ensure that governments retain sovereignty over their natural resources. Apart from approving the development of the proposed project under CDM, it is also the host country's responsibility to confirm whether the CDM project activity will help it meet its own sustainable development criteria. The Marrakesh Accords do not provide specific guidance on the form or content this approval should take, except to note that it should be a 'written' approval from its designated national authority. In practice, an official Letter of Approval from the designated national authority will serve as evidence of host country acceptance. The letter should state that the host country accepts the project and recognizes its contribution to sustainable development. Each country wishing to participate in the CDM – either as a host country or as an investor and buyer of CERs – has to establish an office responsible for CDM-related issues, the designated national authority. In general DNAs is linked to the ministry for the environment (but sometimes industry or energy ministries are involved).

The next stage is the validation. This is the process of evaluation by the designated operational entity (DOE) of all relevant documents for a CDM project activity against the requirements for CDM as set out in the Kyoto Protocol and the Marrakesh Accords. Validation occurs at the outset of a project and is distinct from verification, which occurs during the operation of the project. In effect, the validation process confirms that all the information conveyed and assumptions made within the PDD are accurate and/or reasonable. The DOE will confirm data on GHG emissions, as well as data and assumptions made regarding technical, social, political, regulatory and economic impacts of the project activity included in the PDD. It is the responsibility of the project developer to arrange for validation and to contract, and pay for, the services of a DOE. Proof of additionality is often the critical element in the validation process.

Based on the review and comments provided, the DOE will make a decision as to whether the project can be validated. The designated operational entity should make the validation report publicly available upon transmission to the Executive Board. The DOE solicits public comments on the validation report, which is then submitted to the Executive Board. The EB makes DOE validations available for public comment for 30 days on the UNFCCC website and collects comments from the general public on the report.

Registration of the project with the CDM EB is the act of formal acceptance of the validated project. The request for registration of a CDM project is the responsibility of the DOE. The DOE submits the validation report and host country's approval to the Executive Board for registration. The registration of the project with the EB will be final after a maximum of eight weeks after validation and the submission of the project to the Executive Board, unless a review is requested. Until the review is finalized by the EB, the decision for validation is not final and so the project cannot be registered.

Since CERs can accrue from the point of validation during this first stage of the CDM, certain projects may already be implemented prior to registration. From the point of implementation onwards, the project developer needs to monitor project performance, according to the procedures laid out in the validated monitoring plan of the PDD. The monitoring results have to be submitted to a designated operational entity for verification and certification. The business as usual scenario – or baseline – may or may not have to be monitored, depending on the requirements of the buyer, during the period for which the baseline has been fixed and validated by a DOE. Even if the buyer does require monitoring, the baseline is fixed for at least seven years, at which point it may have to be adjusted according to new data.

At the very minimum, technical project performance, including the project output and the related GHG emissions have to be monitored. In addition, environmental impacts and leakage effects of the project have to be monitored (an example of leakages is CH_4 emissions that come out of a reservoir dam in a hydroelectricity project). Where possible, the monitoring should be carried out in accordance with existing monitoring activities. For example, the monitoring of a power generation project should be linked with activities related to the sale of electricity. Although the monitoring plan should specify the frequency of monitoring activities, no specific frequency is required. However, CERs can only be issued after verification of the monitored data. The frequency of monitoring does not necessarily have to be equal to the frequency of verification. Based on the monitoring results, the GHG emissions reductions from the CDM project activity can be calculated and submitted for verification as CERs. CERs are based on reductions during the specific time period for which the monitoring results are provided.

The project developer is responsible for contracting a designated operational entity to carry out the verification process. Verification is the periodic review and *ex-post* determination of the monitored GHG emissions reductions that have occurred as a result of the CDM project. The DOE verifies the data collected by the developer according to the monitoring plan. As previously noted, the DOE contracted for verification should not be the same one that carried out the validation process, except in the case of small-scale projects or when specific approval has been granted by the CDM Executive Board.

The frequency of verification is mainly a choice of the project developer, assuming the DOE accepts the decision. Frequent verification (for example, every year instead of every three years) increases transaction costs, but also allows for more frequent transfer of CERs.

The DOE must make the monitoring report publicly available and submit a verification report to the Executive Board, which also must be made publicly available.

Finally, certification is the written assurance by a designated operational entity that during the specified time period a project activity achieved the reductions in GHG emissions as stated and verified, in compliance with all relevant criteria. This process of certification is required for CDM projects. The DOE also conducts validation and verification and is liable for possible mistakes, misrepresentations and fraud in this process. Certification is effectively a form of liability transfer; once the DOE has signed off, any underperformance of the CDM project with respect to the quantity or quality of the CERs is the responsibility of the DOE. Consequently a DOE must carry adequate liability insurance.

The certification report prepared by the DOE should consist of a request to the CDM EB to issue CERs for an amount corresponding with the emissions reductions that have been verified by the DOE. When the CDM EB approves the issuance of CERs, the CDM registry administrator, working under the authority of the Executive Board, will forward the CERs into the appropriate accounts.

In January 2009 the number of CERs that should be issued before 2012 by registered projects was 1463 million (or 290 million for each year from the commitment period; approximately the GHG emissions of the Netherlands and Denmark together). If we include expected credits from validated projects waiting for registration (228 million CERs expected by 2012) and projects in the validation stage (1221 million expected CERs), more than 2900 million should be added to the initial cap (AAUs). The final figure will probably be a bit lower for two reasons: first, a significant number of projects seeking validation will not receive it; second expected CERs are sometimes overestimated (because they do

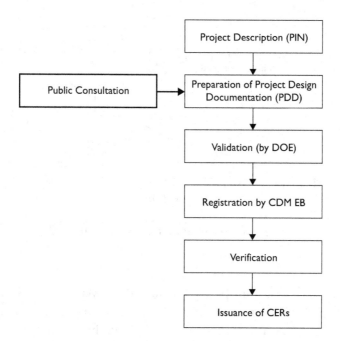

Figure 3.5 Stages for a CDM project

not take into account delays or technical difficulties that can arise in any large industrial project).

Investment fund and CERs prices

According to the *Caisse des Dépôts* in November 2007, the total volume of carbon credit funds (95 per cent of CERs, the rest being composed of ERUs) stood at about €7 billion. In total nearly 58 carbon funds existed in November 2007 (Cochran and Leguet, 2007).

The profile of market players changed significantly over time. Before 2004 public funds or multilateral agencies were the only players in the carbon market. The prototype carbon fund of the World Bank and the Dutch and Japanese investment programmes represented most of the investments in CDM/JI projects. Since 2005 and the launch of the EU Emissions Trading Scheme within the EU, we have witnessed an explosion of private investments, including banks in search of capital gains for their clients in a new and growing sector.

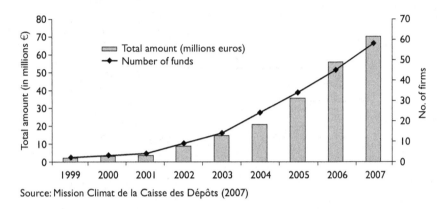

Source: Mission Climat de la Caisse des Dépôts (2007)

Figure 3.6 Investment fund volumes since 1999

We have seen that some projects include the buyer of credits from a very early stage (PDD or even PIN). The table opposite shows major companies or institutions that have guaranteed the purchase of credits in the preliminary phase. First there are two consulting and brokerage firms that specialize in the field of origination and trade of CERs – the British

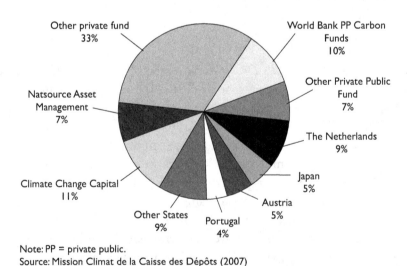

Note: PP = private public.
Source: Mission Climat de la Caisse des Dépôts (2007)

Figure 3.7 Investment funds in Kyoto credits

Table 3.4 *Major authorized buyers in CDM projects (February 2009)*

Companies/institutions	Number of Projects
Ecosecurities	306
Tricorona (Carbon Asset Management Sweden)	134
AgCert	97
EDF Trading	87
IBRD (World Bank)	82
RWE	82
Cargill International	82
Mitsubishi	82
Trading Emissions	72
Vitol	70
ENEL	69
Carbon Resource Management	63
CAMCO	62
MGM Carbon Portfolio	61
Marubeni	61

Source: UNEP RISOE, www.cdmpipeline.org

company Ecosecurities and the Swedish Tricorona. Then there is the World Bank, through its financial arm the International Bank for Reconstruction and Development (IBRD), one of the first players to invest in CDM. The major European energy utilities follow. Most often they invest in their subsidiaries in non-Annex-I countries and expect to get CERs to use in the EU ETS. The other companies are newer and/or smaller specialized firms.

Today most retail banks have their in-house carbon finance department and traders specializing in emissions trading. Between May 2007 and November 2008 prices for CERs were in the range €14–25. Following the economic downturn, prices collapsed down to €8 in February 2009, posing a threat to project developers and investors in carbon reductions projects.

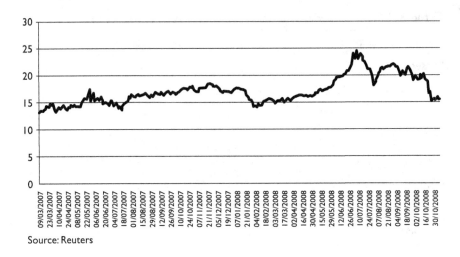

Source: Reuters

Figure 3.8 CERs prices on the secondary market

Critical analysis of the CDM

The Clean Development Mechanism is the subject of much criticism. The aim of the mechanism is to assist developing countries, via the transfer of technology and financial resources, to pursue their development in a low-carbon and sustainable manner. Many people doubt that the CDM can achieve such an ambitious goal. We summarize below five frequent criticisms of CDM projects.

Transaction costs

The validation, registration, monitoring, verification and certification procedures entail transaction costs that can prove insurmountable barriers for developers of projects, particularly those of small-scale projects. Moreover, this activity is normally undertaken by consultants based in developed countries. This criticism is not new; the original Marrakesh agreements provided a simplified procedure for small-scale projects. They are allowed to use simplified methodologies and a monitoring plan. In addition, the same operational entity (DOE) may proceed to the validation, verification and certification stages (which is not the case for ordinary CDM projects).

Three types of small-scale CDM projects were defined in the Marrakesh agreements:

- Renewable energy project activities with a maximum output capacity equivalent of up to 15MW;
- Energy-efficiency improvement project activities that reduce energy consumption on the supply and/or demand side, by up to the equivalent of 15GWh per year; and
- Other project activities that both reduce anthropogenic emissions by sources and directly emit less than 15,000 tonnes of CO_2e annually.

Despite these measures, transaction costs remain high, according to estimates ranging from €16,000 to €100,000 for a small-scale project (see Table 3.5). In some cases, the transaction costs can represent as much as €3 per issued CER (without taking the capital investment and the potential profit margin from the project developers into account).

It is likely that these costs will reduce over time with experience and harmonization of procedures. For example, in 2004/2005, the number of approved methodologies was still relatively low and the developer often had to write and ask for approval for its own methodology, which increased the number of days of consultancy. However, it is inevitable that the transaction costs of the current procedures will always prove burdensome for the small-scale projects that the CDM aims to encourage.

Geographical distribution of projects

Another frequent criticism concerns the geographical spread of the projects (and hence of capital transfer). More than 85 per cent of the issued credits come from five countries (China, India, Brazil, South Korea and Mexico). These five countries are among those that face the least difficulty in attracting foreign capital. Only 3 per cent of the credits come from Africa and among them most are from South Africa or the Maghreb countries. In practice the ambition of a mechanism that would contribute to the sustainable development of Africa and the poorest countries in the world using wind turbines and photovoltaic panels has not been realized. However, these statistics should not understate the fact that China, India and Brazil are highly disparate countries where access to electricity and new technology is very unevenly distributed. So there is little doubt that

Table 3.5 *Transaction costs of a small-scale CDM*

Transactions costs Small Scale CDM	Pilot Study	Pilot Study	Ecosecurities	Tractebel Engineering
	KEUR	EUR/tCO$_2$	KEUR	KEUR
	2005	2005	2004	2004
Pre-implementation costs	11–51	0.08–1.28	85	65
Pre-feasibility study	3–17	0.04–0.39	20	5
Drafting of PDD	3–15	0.01–0.30	35	35
Validation costs	3–14	0.03–0.51	15	15
Approbation by DNA	–	–	–	10
Registration	1–7	0.02–0.09	15	–
Implementation costs	4–25	8	15	5
CERs transfer	1–19	0.04–0.05	7	5
Other costs	1–5	0.01–0.07	–	10
Total	16–100	0.19–2.85	100	95

Source: Pype, 2006

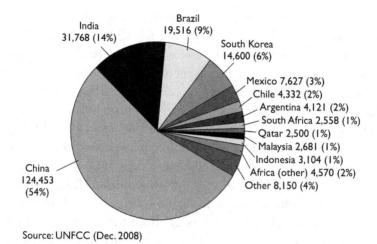

Source: UNFCC (Dec. 2008)

Figure 3.9 CERs projects registered by host country

many CDM projects have allowed additional investment in very poor regions where foreign investments do not reach in a BAU scenario. Overall many projects are beneficial to the environment and local populations; but these are not necessarily those projects that deliver the greatest amount of CERs.

Types of projects

The origin of credits is also the subject of criticism. In practice, larger projects are concentrated in the most profitable activities. Economically and environmentally this is desirable and the foundation for the establishment of an emissions market. However, the CDM was also intended to deliver on the third and least tangible pillar of sustainable development, i.e. improving the social conditions in local communities. Although the majority of projects developed in the energy (small hydropower, wind farms, etc.) or waste (waste recycling, recovery of CH_4, etc.) sectors improve social conditions around the project site, this is not true for big industrial projects involving the destruction of F-gases or large dams. Unfortunately these large projects represent the lion's share of the issued credits so far.

For example, the destruction of HFCs and PFCs, which accounts for just 1 per cent of registered projects, generates more than 30 per cent of the

CERs and is considered a highly profitable low-risk investment. The success of this type of project also comes from its obvious additionality. Indeed, in the absence of CDM there is no incentive to eliminate HFCs (because it does not result in a saving of energy or in the production of clean electricity or biofuel). These project activities are always additional since credits are the sole source of income for the investor. In a renewable energy project (such as a wind farm), the electricity generated is still the main source of income and it is often difficult for an investor to demonstrate that he would not have invested in the absence of the CDM.

The magnitude of the issue of the destruction of HFCs projects first came to light following an article in *Nature* (Wara, 2007). It is alleged that the destruction of HFC23 – a byproduct from the manufacture of refrigerants with one of the highest GWPs – creates distortions in the carbon market. In February 2007, with a CER market price of about €10, financial support to HFC23 destruction projects through CERs is expected to be €4.7 billion (for CERs expected until 2012). More ominously, the author found that developers of HFC23 projects can earn twice as much from the destruction of this gas as from the production of the refrigerants themselves (their core business). It is a major distortion of the market since these manufacturers have an interest in producing more refrigerants than are necessary for the market only because their production is subsidized by the CDM. Michael Wara believes it would cost only $100 million if capture and destruction of HFC facilities were fully and directly subsidized; whereas via the CDM it costs more than $6 billion. In addition, the CDM is also alleged to have encouraged some developing countries not to adopt strict regulations on HFCs in order not to hamper this transfer of capital. In fact, if China and India had legislated to make the destruction of HFCs mandatory, these destruction projects would no longer have been regarded as additional. The solution proposed by Wara is to limit CDM projects solely to CO_2.

Insufficient financial support for new technologies

Some critics point to the observation that the CDM seems to have failed to support new technology (Salter, 2004; Pearson, 2007). This criticism is particularly widespread in the case of renewable energy projects. Table 3.6, which dates from 2004 but is still cited in the academic literature in 2007, is used to argue this point.

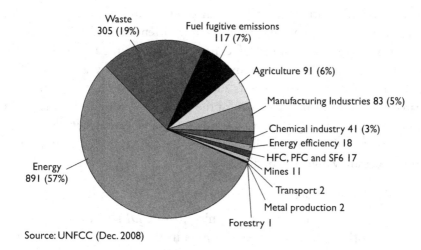

Source: UNFCC (Dec. 2008)

Figure 3.10 Number of registered projects by business

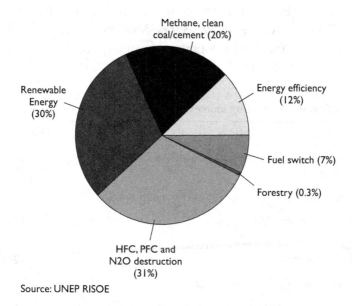

Source: UNEP RISOE

Figure 3.11 Expected CERs by activity

Although this critique was relevant in 2004, it can now be countered that recent developments have increased the role of renewables in the CDM. In February 2008 the number of expected CERs annually issued from renewable energy projects is approximately 65 million per year. With a 2008 CER price of €15, this represents support of $1.5 billion, half of the estimated annual investment in 2004 for the period 2005–2010. Thanks to the leverage effect, the capital flow towards renewable energies in developing countries is significantly higher, indicating that the CDM has an important impact, certainly higher than direct aid.

Overall climate impact

Since it is used as an offset mechanism, the CDM is, at best, climate neutral. To the extent that some projects in the CDM portfolio are not additional to business as usual, it has a negative impact on global emissions. If the CDM is likely to occupy a central role beyond 2012, some reforms will be needed to ensure the CDM's environmental integrity (Lutken, S. and Michaelowa, A., 2008). In particular, the EU Commission considers that the scheme should be phased out for advanced developing countries and highly competitive economic sectors and replaced by a crediting mechanism covering whole sectors. More positively, the CDM may also pave the way for the development of cap-and-trade systems in countries like China, India and Brazil.

Table 3.6 *Renewables funding sources in developing countries*

Funding source (forecast in 2004)	Amount US$/year
Renewables investment in developing countries, 2005–2010, annual average	3,000,000,000
Development aid in renewables, 1989–1999, annual average	986,000,000
GEF including leveraged investment	295,000,000
Renewables CDM including carbon credits and leveraged investment up to 2012	124,000,000
GEF renewable energy expenditure, 2002	59,000,000
Carbon credits from CDM for renewable energy up to 2012	15,000,000

Note: GEF = Global Environmental Facility.
Source: Salter, 2004

The Joint Implementation

Introduction: Differences from the CDM

The rules and practicalities of the Joint Implementation (JI) flexibility mechanism were also specified by the Marrakesh Accords in November 2001. Projects undertaken under the JI are carried out in an Annex I Party. To avoid double-counting, the issuance of emission reduction units (ERUs) must correspond to a cancellation of a corresponding amount of assigned amounts units (AAUs). By requiring JI credits to come from a host country's pool of AAUs, the Kyoto Protocol ensures that the total amount of emissions credits among Annex I Parties does not change for the duration of the Kyoto Protocol's first commitment period. To illustrate, suppose the UK finances a project for the reduction of 10,000 tonnes of CO_2e in Russia. The UK then receives 10,000 ERUs. Thanks to this project Russia needs fewer AAUs (its real emissions are reduced by 10,000 tonnes, so that's 10,000 AAUs not needed by Russia). In order to avoid double-counting of the reduction (i.e. the fact that two countries benefit from the same reduction project), ERUs issued by Russia must come from its reserve of AAUs. Given the link between ERUs and AAUs, ERUs can only be issued during the commitment period, i.e. between 2008 and 2012 inclusive.

As for the CDM, JI projects must satisfy additionality criteria. However, the risk associated with approving non-additional projects is limited as credits are taken from the pool of AAUs. The approval of a project that is not additional would be disadvantageous for the host country, but would not increase the cap.

The procedure for developing a JI project was supposed to be simple and fast, with an agreement between the parties at the centre of the procedure. However the use of this procedure is possible only if the host country meets all eligibility criteria set by the UN and if it has actually adopted guidelines for the recognition of JI projects. In practice most JI projects currently in the pipeline follow a second track (JI Track 2) inspired by the CDM.

The different steps of a JI Track 2 project

When the host country does not meet all the criteria and is therefore ineligible, the Marrakesh agreements allow a second way to develop JI projects, known as 'Track 2'. This procedure was inspired by the CDM. The development of a project within the framework of the JI Track 2 is overseen by the JI Supervisory Committee (JISC), an international body that is comparable to the CDM EB.

Note that even when a host country meets all eligibility criteria, the JI can be developed under the second track on a voluntary basis. If the project host does not meet the eligibility criteria, the project can only be developed within the Track 2 framework. The role of the DOE is performed by accredited independent entities (AIE). Before 2008, there were only Track 2 projects under way. There are also fears that Track 1, because of the important role given to the host country in the assessment of additionality and the determination of the amount of emissions reductions, could greenwash Russian or Ukrainian hot air (AAUs surplus due to economic collapse after 1990).

The project cycle of a JI Track 2 project is virtually identical to the CDM cycle; only the vocabulary is different. The DOE is called AIE and the validation stage is called determination. Accredited NGOs and the public can also make comments on the project.

Environmental integrity is guaranteed because the credits generated do not add to existing emissions but replace AAUs. With the JI, it is in the

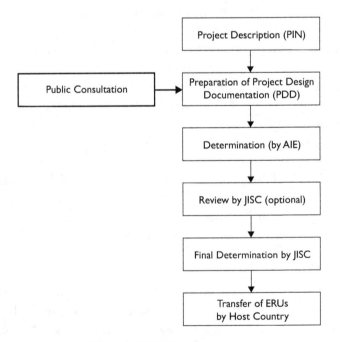

Figure 3.12 JI project cycle

interest of the host country to ensure that the projects generate effective and measurable emissions reductions. If this is not the case, the host country would transfer more ERUs than the actual emissions reductions, thereby weakening its ability to meet its reduction target. In other words, with this mechanism, the host country has no interest in choosing a high emissions baseline. This is not the case for CDM projects where both project developers and host countries want as much reduction as possible, making an impartial control by DOE and the Executive Board a prerequisite to ensure the credibility of the system under the CDM.

Distribution of JI projects

Russia and Ukraine will issue most of the ERUs (86 per cent). Germany is the only European Union country to have developed JI Track 2 projects. New Zealand and other developed countries have proposed some projects but it is likely that these projects will follow the Track 1 procedure. Potential reductions at low prices for foreign investors are increasingly rare in OECD countries. Indeed, the Annex I OECD countries have already an interest in achieving the reductions to save AAUs.

Of the 113 projects listed in March 2008, those related to recovery of CH_4 (or avoiding CH_4 losses in gas fields) and the cement/coal sectors accounted for more than 40 per cent. The projects related to energy (renewable, energy efficiency and fuel switching) accounted for more than half of the projects.

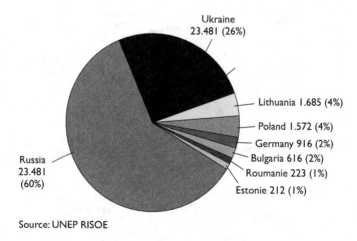

Source: UNEP RISOE

Figure 3.13 Expected ERUs by host country

If we analyse the share of expected ERUs by type of project, the proportion of energy projects is much lower, with a greater proportion in CH_4 recovery and coal/cement projects.

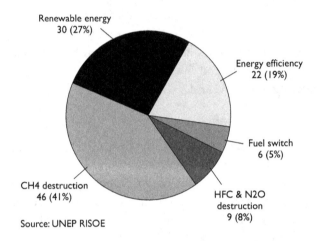

Renewable energy
30 (27%)

Energy efficiency
22 (19%)

Fuel switch
6 (5%)

CH4 destruction
46 (41%)

HFC & N2O
destruction
9 (8%)

Source: UNEP RISOE

Figure 3.14 Distribution by project activity

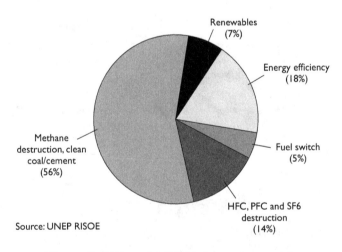

Renewables
(7%)

Energy efficiency
(18%)

Fuel switch
(5%)

Methane
destruction, clean
coal/cement
(56%)

HFC, PFC and SF6
destruction
(14%)

Source: UNEP RISOE

Figure 3.15 Expected ERUs by project activity

Emissions trading under Kyoto

Supply and demand for allowances

Supply and demand for allowances under Kyoto will be determined by the actual emissions of Annex B Parties during the commitment period 2008–2012. The following chart helps to explain the 'geopolitics of carbon'. This chart compares the difference between AAUs that the countries will receive in 2008 and the GHG emissions in 2005 (the latest year for which official emissions figures are available). The differences between countries could slightly reduce thanks to reduction efforts in the European Union and economic growth in Russia and Ukraine. But overall these changes are likely to remain minor and not significantly affect rankings. Regardless of policies and measures undertaken since 2006, Russia and Ukraine will have a surplus and the EU15, Japan and Canada will have a deficit of allowances (annual emissions higher than the number of annual AAUs). The deficit for the EU25 is considerably lower than for the EU15 because most new Member States (e.g. Romania, Bulgaria and Poland) have a surplus of AAUs.

Overall, the market will be long (in surplus). If the US had ratified, the market would have been short. In 2005, the US emitted 1448 million tonnes of CO_2e, more than the number of allowances that they would have received if they had ratified Kyoto. As already mentioned, the significant surplus of allowances in countries from the former Eastern bloc is a consequence of the collapse of heavy industries in these countries after the fall of their communist regimes. Logically, with a system based on historical emissions, a country or region facing industrial decline is likely to receive too many allowances. By 2012, over one billion CERs should be issued, i.e. over 200 million additional credits for each year of the compliance period.

Due to the dominant position of Russia and Ukraine on the supply side, some authors believe it is not impossible that these countries could form a cartel, similar to the one that exists between oil-exporting countries (OPEC) (Grubb, 2004). Although the comparison is justified, the context is very different and the financial amounts involved are much lower.

Over-allocation to countries in transition is often criticized by the detractors of the international carbon market. Many states are likely to meet their objectives through the purchase of Russian and Ukrainian AAUs. But in the absence of a generous allocation these two countries in transition would probably have remained outside the Kyoto Protocol. To address this problem, some buyers have sought assurance that their money will be used for environmental purposes before buying Russian and Ukrainian AAUs.

The country with the highest Kyoto bill (for credit purchase) will be Canada, where the annual cost of compliance could be as high as €60 per capita (0.2 per cent of the GDP).

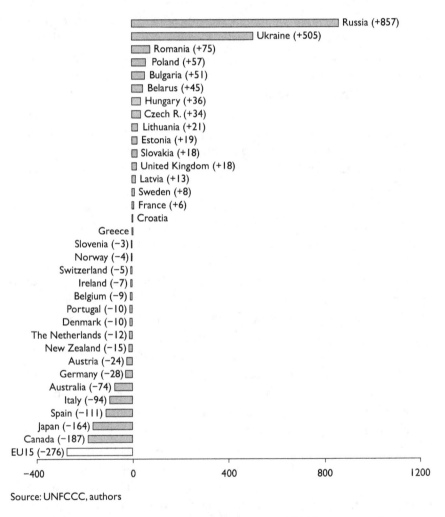

Source: UNFCCC, authors

Figure 3.16 Distance between baseline and 2005 emissions for
Annex B countries

Discrimination between Kyoto units

Although Kyoto makes no mention of restrictions on the fungibility of different units defined by the Protocol – AAUs, CERs, ERUs, RMUs can all be added to achieve the target – there is variation in the prices of the different units. This arises mainly from private sector purchases, which take into account the political and reputational risks in the purchase price of the units. Political risk comes from the uncertainty of the units that will eventually be accepted and used by governments (e.g. will the UK accept Russian AAUs without conditions?).

The environmental integrity of the market established by the Kyoto Protocol is also sometimes called into question because of the initial allocation that favoured economies of the former Eastern bloc. Russia, Ukraine, Bulgaria and Romania will have a number of Assigned Amount Units far above their actual emissions. These emissions rights that are available on the market and are not the result of emissions reduction efforts are often referred to as hot air. To ensure real environmental benefits, some buyers require that the money they give is reinvested in environmental protection measures (green investment schemes, GISs).[13] For the buyer, this guarantees that these funds will not be used to fund military or polluting activities, but rather to benefit renewable energy projects or environmental awareness programs.

Conclusion

This chapter has outlined the main features of the trading provisions of the Kyoto Protocol. The Protocol was initially adopted because of a unique set of circumstances – the warnings of the IPCC, the absence of mandatory limits on GHG emissions for individual nations and of enforcement provisions in the Convention, the success of the Montreal Protocol, the implementation of a cap-and-trade scheme in the US to combat acid rain and so on.

Although the trading provisions are likely to stay in, they were initially a controversial policy. The scope of the initial cap reflects a political negotiation rather than an optimization of environmental considerations. Often criticized for its lack of ambition, Kyoto should rather be seen as taking the first steps at a time when consensus on climate change was weaker than today, limiting potential action. Issues such as 'hot air', concerns about additionality for some CDM or JI projects, and the lack of transparency and liquidity of the carbon market itself will need to be considered carefully in any successor agreement. This must be a prerequisite for the next protocol to be more environmentally effective.

In the non-binding 'Washington Declaration' agreed on 16 February 2007, heads of government from Canada, France, Germany, Italy, Japan, Russia, United Kingdom, the United States, Brazil, China, India, Mexico and South Africa (G8 + 5) agreed in principle on the outline of a successor to the Kyoto Protocol and envisaged a global cap-and-trade system that would apply to both industrialized nations and developing countries. This suggests that there is strong support for carbon markets to remain a key feature of the global climate change regime.

Notes

1   NO_x is a generic term for mono-nitrogen oxides (NO and NO_2).
2   Short tons. One short ton is equivalent to 0.90718 metric tonne.
3   The difference between these two approaches is explained by industrial chemistry. While NO_x emissions depend on the technologies, because most NO_x is formed by a temperature-dependent reaction between nitrogen and oxygen in the air, SO_2 emissions come from complete oxidation of the sulfur content of fuels (this is similar with CO_2). The development of low-NO_x burners provides a partial technical solution that is relatively low cost. In contrast, high levels of SO_2 abatement require 'end of pipe' flue gas desulfurization technology – this has been used in Europe and elsewhere to deliver higher levels of abatement than in the US, but is more costly than the use of lower sulfur fuels.
4   For more details on the negotiations see Stone, 1992.
5   For more details on the negotiations see Breidenich et al, 1998.
6   The Montreal Protocol (September 1987) to the Vienna Convention for the Protection of the Ozone Layer (March 1985) was the first treaty to protect the atmosphere against the effects of human activities and imposes absolute and measurable targets. Its objective is to protect the ozone layer from the effects of certain industrial gases. It entered into force on 1 January 1989. All parties agreed to freeze the consumption of major chlorofluorocarbons (CFCs) at 1986 levels, and reduce consumption by 50 per cent within 10 years.
7   Council Decision of 25 April 2002 concerning the approval, on behalf of the European Community, of the Kyoto Protocol to the United Nations Framework Convention on Climate Change and the joint fulfilment of commitments thereunder (Official Journal L 130, 15/05/2002).
8   Annex B countries are the 40 countries listed in the Annex B of the Kyoto Protocol that have emissions reduction obligations. Although the terms 'Annex I' and 'Annex B' are often used interchangeably, countries invited to take part in the CDM are the Annex I countries. There are few differences between the two lists: Turkey is part of Annex I but is not listed in Annex B; Croatia, Liechtenstein, Monaco and Slovenia are part of Annex B but not listed in Annex I.

9   Report of the Conference of the Parties serving as the meeting of the Parties to the Kyoto
     Protocol on its first session, held at Montreal from 28 November to 10 December 2005,
     Part II, 16/CMP.1, Land use, land-use change and forestry.
10   Essentially aviation fuel must neither evaporate or freeze at the low pressures and
     temperatures encountered in the upper troposphere.
11   E.g. for the UK, the 2020 Energy Review found that more than 50 per cent of transport
     energy use and 25 per cent of total CO_2 emissions might result from aviation by 2050,
     www.cabinetoffice.gov.uk/~/media/assets/www.cabinetoffice.gov.uk/strategy/piuf per
     cent20pdf.ashx
12   Report of the Conference of the Parties serving as the meeting of the Parties to the Kyoto
     Protocol on its first session, held at Montreal from 28 November to 10 December 2005,
     Part I, 3/CMP.1, Modalities and procedures for a clean development mechanism as
     defined in Article 12 of the Kyoto Protocol.
13   To learn more on GIS, see e.g. World Bank, 2004. *Options for designing a Green Investment
     Scheme in Bulgaria*, Report No 29998.

References

Bonduelle, A. (2002) 'Les dix défauts du Protocole de Kyoto', in Y. Petit (dir.), *Le Protocole de
     Kyoto: Mise en œuvre et implications*, Presses Universitaires de Strasbourg, Strasbourg, p74
Breidenich, C., Magraw, D., Rowberg, A. and Rubin, J. W. (1998) 'The Kyoto Protocol to the
     United Nations Framework Convention on Climate Changes', *American Journal of
     International Law*, vol 92, no 2, pp315–331
Cochran, I. T. and Leguet, B. (2007) 'Fonds d'investissement CO_2: l'essor des capitaux privés',
     Note d'étude de la Mission climat de la Caisse des dépôts, no 12, 33pp
Den Elzen, M. G. J. and De Moor, A. P. G. (2002) 'Analyzing the Kyoto Protocol under the
     Marrakesh Accords: Economic effectiveness', *Ecological Economics*, vol 43, no 2–3, pp141–158
Den Elzen, M. G. J., Schaeffer, M. and Lucas, P. (2005) 'Differentiating future commitments on
     the basis of countries' relative historical responsibility for climate change: Uncertainties in the
     "Brazilian proposal" in the context of a policy implementation', *Climatic Change*, vol 71, no
     3, pp277–301
EU Council (1998) Document 97/02/98 du Conseil de l'UE du 19 juin 1998, reflétant les
     résultats des travaux du conseil 'environnement' des 16 et 17 juin 1998 annexe I
Grubb, M. (2004), 'The economics of the Kyoto Protocol', in A. D. Owen and N. Hanley (ed)
     The Economics of Climate Change, Routledge, London, pp72–114
Höhne, N. and Blok, K. (2005) 'Calculating historical contributions to climate change –
     discussing the "Brazilian proposal"', *Climatic Change*, vol 71, no 1–2, pp141–173
Joskow, P., Schmalensee, R. and Bailey, E. M. (1998) 'The market for sulfur dioxide emissions',
     American Economic Review, vol 88, no 4, pp669–685
Lutken, S. and Michaelowa, A. (2008) *Corporate Strategies and the Clean Development
     Mechanism*, Edward Edgar, London
Meyer, A. (2000) *Contraction & Convergence: The Global Solution to Climate Change*,
     Schumacher Briefings, vol 5, Green Books, Bristol, UK
Müller, B. (1999) 'Justice in global warming negotiations: How to obtain a procedurally fair
     compromise', *Journal of Energy Literature*, vol 5, no 2,
     www.oxfordclimatepolicy.org/publications/j2ed.pdf

Pearson, B. (2007) 'Market failure: Why the Clean Development Mechanism won't promote clean development', *Journal of Cleaner Production*, vol 15, no 2, pp247–252

Pype, J. (2006) 'Opzetten van projecten onder het mechanisme voor schone ontwikkeling. Vroege analyse sleutel tot succes', *Revue E tijdschrift*, vol 122, no 4, pp36–41

Salter, L. (2004) 'A clean energy future? The role of the CDM in promoting renewable energy in developing countries', WWF International, July, 11pp

Starkey, R. (2008) 'Allocating emissions rights: Are equal shares, fair shares?', Tyndall Working Paper 118, www.tyndall.ac.uk/publications/working_papers/twp118.pdf

Stone, C. (1992) 'Beyond Rio: Insuring against global warming', *American Journal of International Law*, vol 86, no 3, pp445–488

UNEP RISOE (2009) www.cdmpipeline.org, accessed 17 February 2009

UN General Assembly (1990) 'Protection of Global Climate for Present and Future Generations of Mankind', G.A. Res. 45/212

Wara, M. (2007) 'Is the global carbon market working?', *Nature*, vol 445, pp595–596

Chapter 4

The EU Emissions Trading Scheme

Introduction

The Kyoto Protocol established the principle of trading carbon emissions between countries to achieve cost advantages in the reduction of greenhouse gas emissions. However, the most significant emitters are not states themselves, but the businesses, households and transport systems within their boundaries. Effective carbon markets therefore need to engage these actors.

The European Union's Emissions Trading Scheme (EU ETS) is, to date, the largest carbon trading scheme established. This chapter sets out the political and economic context within which this market was established. It goes on to describe the principle elements of the market – the cap that establishes a value for carbon, how the emissions rights have been defined and distributed, and how emissions are reported and enforced.

This is followed by a short section that summarizes the (still developing) issues associated with accounting and taxation of the value of emissions permits. We then provide a short description of the way in which the carbon market has developed, including the price and traded volumes, and how this has affected the energy sector. Throughout we emphasize that the EU ETS is innovative – it is therefore a learning process for all involved. We then follow with a description of current and planned changes, including the addition of new countries, sectors and gases.

We conclude with a consideration of other instruments of carbon policy in the EU. We investigate the interaction of the carbon market with these policies, including national schemes for carbon trading and support for renewable energy and energy efficiency. We also look at the prospects for more radical change in carbon markets to include smaller emitters.

Political Context

The ratification of the Kyoto Protocol

By ratifying the Kyoto Protocol, the EU committed to reducing its emissions by 8 per cent during the period 2008–2012 compared to 1990. Despite significant reductions in the UK[1] and Germany[2] in the 1990s, many European countries were experiencing enormous difficulties in curbing their emissions. The EU then decided to set a ceiling on emissions from its main industrial sites and to implement an emissions market with the aim of reducing CO_2 emissions and achieving the Kyoto Protocol target.

Uncertainty on the entry into force of the Kyoto Protocol

Between 2000 and 2003, the uncertainty surrounding the entry into force of the Protocol was real. The United States had announced that it would not ratify and consequently Russia's participation became crucial to make up the quorum for the Protocol to come into force. Before ratifying, Russia took its time to thoroughly evaluate the benefits and it seems likely that Russia used its pivotal position to exercise pressure on parties that were most strongly in favour of the Protocol (Henry and Sundstrom, 2007).

Wishing to take the lead in the fight against global warming and faced with this uncertainty, the EU proposed the establishment of an emissions trading scheme for its industries, whose viability would not be linked to the future of the Kyoto Protocol. In doing so, the EU clearly indicated the direction it wanted to follow in the fight against climate change. Once the Protocol's coming into force was secured, the EU recognized (under certain conditions) credits issued via the CDM and JI flexibility mechanisms, providing a link between the EU market and the Kyoto mechanisms.

The failure of a carbon tax

During the 1990s, the European Commission studied and proposed the adoption of a fully harmonized energy/carbon tax for the EU (Commission of the European Communities, 1996). The idea of a hybrid carbon/energy tax was to provide both incentives for energy efficiency with all energy sources as well as a classical Pigovian tax, in particular as a compromise to address the very different carbon contents of electricity in different EU countries. However, the proposal failed for

a number of reasons, principally the concern of European energy industries about the competitiveness impacts of a tax in the absence of similar
measures in the US and Asia. The different traditions in tax policy in
different European countries, e.g. the balance between business and
personal taxation, led to difficulties in agreeing a common position. In
some countries concerns about relinquishing control over such a central
area of national policy as taxation added to the difficulties. Without
fiscal policy being subject to unanimity within the treaties of the EU,
agreement was not possible.

With rising concern about the seriousness of climate change and the
beginning of carbon trading schemes at the national level, the Commission
judged it easier to secure agreement within environmental policy to an
alternative system of emissions trading focusing on large industrial
polluters. This second attempt was more easily accepted by industries and
other stakeholders.

The development of disparate national initiatives

The development of carbon markets by Member States at the national
level is another reason why Europe decided to develop its own scheme.
Disparate national schemes might have led to a complex system and
undermined the EU will for more harmonization. As explained in a
Green Paper (Commission of the European Communities, 2000), the
European Commission wished to establish a common emissions market
in order to avoid distortions of competition. The following sections
describe the two most advanced national emissions trading systems: the
Danish and UK ETS.

The Danish CO_2 emissions trading system was restricted to the electricity sector, which accounted for almost 40 per cent of Danish emissions
in 2002. The European Commission considered this system to constitute
state aid because allowances were allocated free based on grandfathering
(Alexis, 2004). Despite this criticism, the Commission finally accepted
the Danish system, in particular because it had a limited lifetime and
could provide an interesting learning opportunity for the EU. The
Commission also pointed out that the grandfathering practice was a
problem for new entrants. The Commission nevertheless insisted on the
principle that in future a reserve for new entrants should be included
(CEPS, 2002).

The UK ETS was the world's first large-scale greenhouse gas (GHG) emissions trading scheme. The system included both incentives and allocations of allowances. Although development was supported financially by the UK Government, the initiative was largely designed and driven forward by a stakeholder group, the Emissions Trading Group, with the understanding that, initially at least, participation in the scheme would be on a voluntary basis. The primary aims of the scheme were to secure cost-effective GHG emissions reductions, to give UK companies early experience of emissions trading and to encourage the establishment of emissions trading centres in London. With the establishment of the EU ETS, there was no longer a case for a UK-based scheme to address industrial sector CO_2 emissions, but the mechanism is being revived to cover large emitters outside the scope of the EU scheme.

In the initial UK ETS, incentives were granted for absolute GHG emissions reductions. There were three types of participant in the scheme. First there were 31 direct participants (DPs). The government provided a £215 million financial incentive for organizations that agreed to make absolute reductions in emissions against their historic levels (a 1998–2000 average baseline). An auction held over the internet in March 2002 distributed the emissions reduction targets for each DP and the share of incentive money each would receive. The DPs covered a range of sizes and sectors, from global companies such as BP and Shell to banks and supermarkets, through to smaller players such as London's Natural History Museum. These DPs were committed to delivering just under 1.1MtC (~4MTCO$_2$) from the baseline by the end of the scheme in 2006. The second type of participants were climate change agreement participants (CCAPs). These were companies in energy-intensive sectors who were eligible for an 80 per cent discount to their Climate Change Levy (CCL, the UK business energy tax) subject to meeting a target for emissions reduction in a sectoral Climate Change Agreement (CCA). By participating in the UK ETS these companies were able to meet these commitments by engaging in emissions trading if they so chose. In addition to these two, the UK ETS also allowed other parties to participate in the Scheme as traders without compliance commitments, so that any individual or organization was free to enter the market and trade allowances on a speculative basis (trading participants). The DPs had a variety of different motivations for joining the Scheme. A common reason was that the Scheme was a valuable opportunity to gain familiarity with the implications of an ETS for their business. In all cases the financial incentive offered by government was essential, offsetting the costs and risks associated with participation. CCAPs on the other hand required and received no financial incentive in addition to the 80 per cent CCL discount – participation simply allowed a more cost-effective route to delivering the CCA. The system was designed to be broadly consistent with the CCAs, with emissions due to electricity generation accounted for at the point of electricity use. This provided a direct incentive to improve the efficiency of electricity use. It also avoided windfall profits (see below) to the electricity generators observed in the first phase of the EU ETS (Sijm et al, 2006). But the main political driver for this approach (and indeed for the CCL) in the UK was to avoid additional costs falling on household electricity use.

The European Commission also considered the UK ETS as state aid (as defined in Article 87 of the EC Treaty). Moreover, the system was considered to be very different from the one proposed by the Commission (because the UK's system was voluntary and downstream). Nevertheless, the Commission also approved the system for various reasons, mainly because of the limited duration of the programme and the excellent learning opportunity it represented. The UK Emissions Trading Scheme ended in December 2006, with final reconciliation completed in March 2007.

The UK ETS has been subject to significant criticism concerning the GHG emissions reduction achieved. Prices certainly fell to a very low level (£2/tCO$_2$) implying that, as in the first phase of the EU ETS, very little additional activity was required on the part of participants (NERA, 2004). This seems to have been particularly true for emitters of non-CO$_2$ GHGs such as hydrofluorocarbons, where very significant reductions in emissions were made in advance of the scheme commencing, but not factored into baselines. The incentive payments for reductions below historic baseline amounted to >£50/tCO$_2$, clearly far higher than market prices. Prices tended to fall at the end of CCA milestone periods, implying that the sale of excess allowances from the CCAPs may have been responsible. Yet it is also likely that the organizations that chose to participate as DPs were largely a self-selecting group that had a low-cost GHG abatement potential or a declining baseline. This would seem to be an inevitable consequence of a voluntary scheme and illustrates the same difficulties as seen in the CDM in establishing baselines for project-based systems that are both fair and transparent.

The characteristics of the EU emissions market

General principles

Directive 2003/87/EC established a scheme for GHG emissions allowance trading within the EU.[3] This scheme is known as the EU Emissions Trading Scheme (EU ETS). Written before the Kyoto Protocol came into force, the directive was not conditional on any international agreement. Even without the Kyoto Protocol, the EU would have developed its carbon market, although the provisions for trading in the Protocol certainly influenced the scheme.

The EU ETS was the first international emissions trading system and currently covers more than 10,000 installations in the energy and industrial sectors. The ETS is a cap-and-trade scheme, i.e. the overall level of emissions is capped, but up to this limit participants are allowed to buy and sell emissions rights (allowances) according to their needs. The scheme covers nearly half of the EU's CO_2 emissions and 40 per cent of the EU's total GHG emissions. In December 2006 the Commission issued a legislative proposal, suggesting the inclusion of the aviation sector in the EU ETS in 2011 or 2012, backed up further by a legislative resolution of the European Parliament on 8 July 2008.

The ETS set a price for carbon and demonstrated how GHG emissions trading could work for businesses (Soleille, 2006). The first phrase put in place the policy infrastructure. However, the environmental benefits were limited because of over-allocation of permits by most Member States. This was mainly due to baseline industrial emissions projections that were far too high (Ellerman and Buchner, 2007). Once official data on 2005 emissions verified this over-allocation, the market responded as one might expect when supply is much greater than demand: the price crashed (see below). Despite these problems, phase 1 of the ETS was a successful first step and precedent for subsequent phases and other ETS schemes around the world.

In addition to the need for reliable and verified emissions data, the first phase showed that it is important to consider distortions of competition between Member States and to harmonize the monitoring, verification and reporting rules as well as the limits set on the import of CERs and ERUs as part of scheme design.

Cap and period

Period

The ETS was launched on 1 January 2005. The first phase lasted three years until the end of 2007. This period was presented by the Commission as a 'learning by doing' phase designed to prepare for the second trading period. Beginning on 1 January 2008, the second phase is scheduled for five years until the end of 2012. An essential characteristic of phase 2 is that it coincides with the first commitment period of the Kyoto Protocol, during which the EU and other industrialized countries must meet the GHG emissions targets. For the second trading period, the Commission tightened the cap by reducing emission allocations on average by 6.5 per cent compared with the 2005 verified emissions. The aim is to ensure that Member States meet their commitments under the Kyoto Protocol and promote a carbon price that encourages abatement.

The cap

The ceiling for emissions is set individually for each installation as part of each country's national allocation plan (NAP). The total volume of the cap is therefore the sum of allowances allocated on a case-by-case basis at each installation. Each Member State of the EU is responsible for ensuring allocations under each NAP meet the national emission target set by the commission.

The installations included in the scope of the ETS are:

- combustion installations with a rated thermal input exceeding 20 MW;
- mineral oil refineries;
- coke ovens;
- iron production and processing;
- mining;
- installations for the manufacture of glass;
- installations for the manufacture of ceramic products;
- industrial plants for the production of pulp and paper.

The 20MW threshold is relatively low and thus has included many quite small combustion installations. Some individual large buildings (e.g. the European Parliament in Brussels) are included in the system because of the power of their boiler. Many companies in industries not separately named in the directive (e.g. textiles, food, construction and engineering) are also covered by the ETS because of this. The 740 biggest emitters (7 per cent) covered by the scheme account for 80 per cent of the emissions, while the 7400 smallest emitters account for less than 5 per cent of the emissions (EEA, 2007b). The 1100 smallest emitters were responsible for the emissions of a mere 93,000 tonnes of CO_2, a statistically insignificant amount (less than 0.01 per cent of total emissions covered).

Defining emission rights

The rights granted under the EU ETS are called EU allowances (EUA). An EUA is equal to one metric tonne of CO_2 equivalent (CO_2e). Directive 2004/101/EC (commonly referred to as the *linking directive*) creates a link between the EU ETS and the flexibility mechanisms of the Kyoto Protocol (CDM and JI projects).[4] The directive establishes a triple equality between an EU allowance, a Certified Emissions Reduction and a Emissions Reduction Unit. This Directive also specifies certain conditions for the use of ERUs and CERs in the ETS. For example, the credits issued through land use, land use change and forestry (LULUCF) projects are not allowed in the EU ETS. The credits issued through the production of hydroelectricity with a production capacity greater than 20MW must comply with the specific sustainability criteria, including those mentioned in the final report of the World Commission on Dams.

Since the EU is the biggest player in the international carbon market, these additional criteria have an impact on the fungibility of allowances internationally. A credit issued from a large hydroelectric project that does not comply with the World Commission on Dams guidelines or forestry credits may be devalued because of the weaker demand for these credits. In addition, EU ETS criteria require a rigorous tracing of the origin of the Kyoto credits and which must be integrated into the registries.

Each national allocation plan has a set ceiling on the number of credits that may be imported. For the second phase this limit, expressed as a percentage of the ceiling set on installations in the national allocation plans, varies from 0 per cent in Estonia to 20 per cent in Spain, Germany and Lithuania. In Belgium the figure is different in each region and is on average 8.4 per cent.

Allocation

For each ETS phase, Member States prepare their national allocation plans (NAP), to achieve their total level of allowed emissions and allowances to each installation located on their territory.

At the end of each year, installations must surrender a number of allowances equal to their emissions. Companies that keep their emissions below the level of their allowances can sell their surplus. For those who emit more, they can either take emissions reductions measures (for instance by investing in more efficient technologies or using low-carbon energy sources), or buy extra allowances on the market.

The emissions targets of each participant at each site is determined at the national level (at the regional level in Belgium). National allocation plans describe, among other things, how a country distributes emissions rights between different sectors and companies within each sector.

If not carefully managed, this regional approach can lead to protectionism, environmental dumping and distortions of competition (Grubb et al, 2005). For example, three technically similar power stations will not receive the same number of allowances in Germany, in the Walloon Region or in Luxembourg. Consequently, the generosity of Member States in the allocation of allowances has become one of the main criteria for choosing the location of a new industrial site (Grubb and Neuhoff, 2006). Apart from the evident risk of favouritism, this approach has also been criticized because of its extreme complexity. The Belgian case is a good example. Due to the regionalization of environmental policy and an exception for nuclear installations that fall within the jurisdiction of the federal authority, the Belgian NAP is composed of four separate parts, making Belgium the only Member State to define different rules for the allocation of allowances to its installations according to their regional location (Luypaert and Brohé, 2006).

Auctioning is often suggested as a solution in order to reduce the influence that Member States have in the free allocation of allowances to their industry (Hepburn et al, 2006). Auctioning was already an option in the first two phases but one that few states have used. In the first phase Hungary auctioned 2.4 million allowances during two sales held in late 2006 and early 2007, Ireland auctioned 1.2 million allowances in two sales and Lithuania sold half a million EUAs in September 2007 (when the price was below 10 cents) (Vertis Environmental Finance, 2008). However, in total just 0.12 per cent of the EUAs available in the first phase were auctioned.

The EU ETS auction procedure aims to set a uniform price for all successful bidders – the clearing price. To do this, bids are sought for allowances, then the bids received are listed in descending order by price (if there are bids at the same price, earlier bids are ranked higher). The bids are then accepted in turn from the top of the ranked list downwards. The successful bid volumes are added up until the total reaches the total number of allowances to be sold. The last successful bid's price is deemed to be the clearing price, and all successful bids receive allowances at this price. If the total volume of bids is less than the total number of allowances to be sold, the lowest valid bid price is the clearing price. The submitted bids may not be withdrawn or changed after the end of the bidding phase and the auction is 'blind', i.e. bids are not visible to competing bidders.

Besides allocating allowances to existing enterprises, NAPs also provide a reserve for new entrants, i.e. companies created after the implementation of the scheme.

Monitoring and reporting of emissions

Each year, no later than 30 April, each company must surrender a number of allowances corresponding to its actual emissions in the previous year. The monitoring and reporting of emissions is governed by decision 2007/589/EC (which amends Decision 2004/156/EC).[5,6]

For monitoring of emissions, installations can choose between a method based on calculations and a method based on continuous measurement.[7] In the case of the latter, the operator must demonstrate the reliability of the method and have it approved by a competent authority. The uncertainties in the calculation of emissions in the ETS are fewer than those within the framework of the Kyoto Protocol because of its more limited scope. It is easier to monitor energy flows and gas concentrations at an installation level than at a country level.

Recent amendments to the guidelines make reporting easier for installations through the adoption of emissions factors for commercial fuels and by relaxing supervision rules for small companies (less than 25,000 tonnes of CO_2 per year), thereby reducing costs of compliance.

Registries

In order to track exchanges of EUAs and meet the requirements of the Kyoto Protocol, it is mandatory for each Member State to have a national registry. This is governed by Decision 280/2004/EC of the European Parliament. As a signatory to the Kyoto Protocol, the Community is also obliged to keep a separate registry. These registries ensure the accurate accounting for all units under the Kyoto Protocol plus the accurate accounting for allowances under the EU ETS. Not only companies but also people may open an account anywhere in an EC registry.

The Community Independent Transaction Log (CITL) records the issuance, transfer, cancellation and banking of allowances that take place in the registries (Community registry and national registries). When the national allocation plans are accepted by the Commission, this information is encoded in the CITL (Halleux et al, 2006).

The CITL currently manages the transfer of EU allowances, and since 2008 is complemented by the ITL, which tracks the exchange of AAUs and other Kyoto units. For instance, from 2008, when a French company sells EUAs to a German company, an equivalent amount of AAUs is transferred from the French registry to the German one. The purchase of CERs or ERUs by an installation covered by the EU ETS increases the amount of allowances available for the country in which the installation is located.

Penalties

Participating companies must surrender allowances to cover their emissions by 30 April of the following calendar year. If a company does not surrender a sufficient number of allowances, a fine of €40 per tonne of CO_2 (tCO_2) for each tonne was charged during the period 2005–2007. As from 2008, the penalty is €100/tCO_2. This fine is a penalty for lateness of surrender; it should not be considered as a price ceiling as it does not exempt the company from acquiring the missing allowances, i.e. a company in default must still redeem the missing allowances the following year.

Legal and accounting issues related to the EU ETS

The legal status of EUAs

The EU ETS has also raised legal issues that were not considered before implementation (Peeters, 2003). The European Directive 2003/87/EC did not define the legal nature of the allowances. A key issue is whether allowances should be considered as a commodity or good, or as an equity or financial instrument. This is ambiguous under the directive and thus the legal status of allowances could vary across the EU Member States, with allowances being classed as a commodity in one country and a financial instrument in another. Similar questions also arise over whether allowances should be regarded as property rights or licences. These are issues where consistency would be useful but, in practice, it has been difficult to harmonize the legal definition. Trades in derivatives of allowances such as futures and options are clearly financial instruments and are treated as such for tax and accounting purposes. The legal nature is an important feature, as it determines the accounting treatment of EUAs. The European Commission did not provide details on the accounting rules to use. This lack of clarity is the subject of much discussion within companies and these uncertainties certainly increased implementation costs. In practice, at a European level, we see that the accounting treatment is rarely specified in the annual accounts and jurisprudence is not yet clear on the nature of the allowances. A definition from the Commission at the outset or at the very least a consultation with the stakeholders before implementation could have reduced the risk of different interpretations in different countries.

IFRIC 3

The International Accounting Standards Board (IASB) on 2 December 2004 issued IFRIC 3, dealing with the accounting treatment of emissions rights. According to this interpretation:

- Emissions rights (allowances) are intangible assets that should be recognized in financial statements in accordance with IAS 38 on Intangible Assets. This means that when allowances are acquired on the market they are valued at their acquisition cost. When they are obtained for less than their fair value (for instance for free) they are valued at their fair value. Note that the fair value of an asset is the amount for which that asset could be exchanged between well-informed and consenting parties operating in competitive conditions.

- When allowances are issued to a participant by government for less than their fair value, the difference between the amount paid (if any) and their fair value is a government grant that is accounted for in accordance with IAS 20 Accounting for Government Grants and Disclosure of Government Assistance.

- As a participant produces emissions, it recognizes a provision for its obligation to deliver allowances in accordance with IAS 37 Provisions, Contingent Liabilities and Contingent Assets. This provision is normally measured at the market value of the allowances needed to settle it.

If an active market as defined in IAS 38 is in place, companies may opt for the revaluation model, which, as opposed to the cost model, encourages recording the difference between book value and fair value directly in equity.

Various criticisms have been made of this interpretation. For example, the European Financial Reporting Advisory Group (EFRAG), in its opinion of 6 May 2005 to the European Commission (in which it advised not to adopt IFRIC 3), noted that the simultaneous application of different standards has the effect of creating mismatches. According to EFRAG, applying IFRIC 3 will not always result in economic reality being reflected 'because the accounting required by IFRIC in IFRIC 3 is constrained by the interpretation of the interplay of the existing standards IAS 38 Intangible Assets, IAS 20 Accounting for Government Grants and Disclosure of Government Assistance and IAS 37 Provisions, Contingent Liabilities and Contingent Assets'. This creates a mismatch where some items are measured at cost (IAS 38 and IAS 20) and others at fair value (IAS 37) and whereby some gains and losses are reported in profit or loss (IAS 37 and IAS 20) and others in equity (IAS 38). These accounting mismatches are all the more critical because there is economic interdependency between the assets and liability involved in the scheme: emissions rights are granted to allow entities to settle their liability for emissions made up to a specified level; emissions rights are the only assets eligible for settlement of the liability for emissions made.

For instance, under the cost model described in IFRIC 3, the allowances are valued at cost and the corresponding liability at fair value. When changes in the market price for the allowances appear, the income statement may be affected by a mismatch that is created by the mixed measurement model. Under IFRIC 3's revaluation model there is a mismatch in relation to the income statement both during the interim periods and at year-end, because revaluation gains are recognized directly in equity while expenses relating to the liability are recognized in profit or loss. As a result of these criticisms, the IASB voted on 25 June 2005 to withdraw IFRIC 3.

Treatment of VAT

Regarding the treatment of value-added tax (VAT), the EU has stated that the transfer of GHG emissions allowances as described in Article 12 of Directive 2003/87/EC, when made for consideration by a taxable person, is a taxable supply of services falling within the scope of Article 9(2)(e) of Directive 77/388/EEC. None of the exemptions provided for in Article 13 of Directive 77/388/EEC can be applied to these allowance transfers.

Evolution of demand and price

During the first year of phase 1, the demand for allowances did not follow the actual level of emissions. Between January 2005 (launch of the scheme) and April 2006 when consolidated results of the first audit reports were released, the allowance price had been rising in a quasi-continuous manner, essentially due to risk-adverse behaviours from installations likely to have excess allowances and speculative behaviours by brokerage firms or banks. A sharp increase in prices in June 2005 was mainly due to the inactivity of hydropower in Spain and fears of a cold winter that had significantly increased the forward price of natural gas. The only significant decrease in prices in 2005 (30 per cent) was recorded in July when natural gas prices fell back to their May level, making gas more competitive than coal. This fall was amplified by the first rumours of over-allocation in the new Member States. The dramatic fall in prices, down to 3 cents at the end of 2007, was mainly due to the problem of over-allocation. Many Member States were too generous with the allocation of permits, leading to an excess of supply over demand.

In practice this first experience has demonstrated the difficulty of ensuring uniform rules and limiting over-allocation when the allocation is made by Member States. This problem was addressed in the second phase with the Commission more severe in their review of national allocation plans. During the first phase lack of reference data and fears of harming the competitiveness of businesses led some Member States to place too much faith in expected growth figures from industry. Today the audited figures for each installation are known and installations that received a substantial surplus generally receive much less during the second phase.

Figures 4.2 and 4.3 indicate the extent of over-allocations in the Member States. First in five countries – UK, Ireland, Italy, Spain and Austria – companies emitted more than the allowances they received. It is interesting to note that even in these countries many firms received too many allowances, so that we can speak of sectoral over-allocation. For example, in Spain companies with excess allowances received on average 13 per cent more emissions rights than their emissions. Gross shortage for companies is quite important and exceeded 20 per cent in the United Kingdom, Ireland and Spain. The three Baltic States were the most generous, allocating between 29 and 46 per cent more than the actual emissions. These large over-allocations in Lithuania, Latvia and Estonia, however, have little impact in absolute terms given the relative small size of these countries. The EU over-allocation average amounted to 2.5 per cent of the total cap. In absolute terms the top three over-allocations occurred in Poland (31 million EUAs in surplus), France (22 million) and Germany (17 million), although in the case of Germany there were large differences between industrial sites.

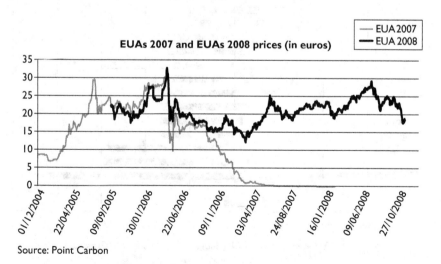

Source: Point Carbon

Figure 4.1 Evolution of EUAs prices

British-based companies suffered the heaviest deficit with a lack of allowances exceeding 40 million.

In the United Kingdom it is useful to note that the allowance shortage was almost exclusively borne by power plants. They bore a deficit of 46 million EUAs in 2006 (ENDS Report, 2008). The internationally competitive sectors of British industry were not pressured by the British NAP. For example the chemical industry and refineries each enjoyed an over-allocation of 2 million allowances. Metallurgy received 3 million EUAs in excess of its actual emissions and offshore sites (oil and gas) over 2 million. In practice the apparent severity of the British allocation simply avoided the windfall profits recorded by most electricity generators in continental Europe.

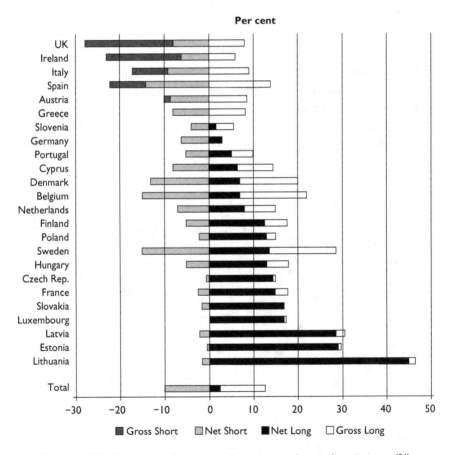

Figure 4.2 Differences between allocation and actual emissions (%)

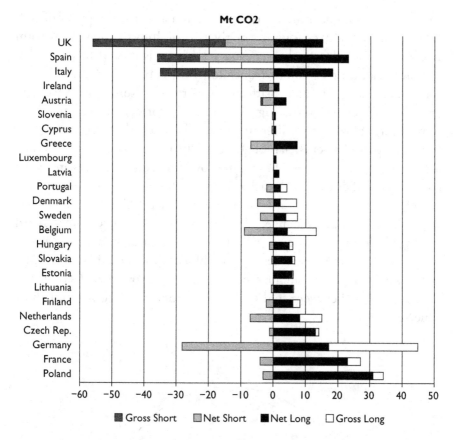

Mt CO2

Figure 4.3 Differences between allocation and actual emissions (million EUAs)

Trading platforms

Trading platforms play a fundamental role in giving price signals and ensuring market liquidity (Frémont, 2005). The primary function of these centralized electronic marketplaces is to contribute to the fluidity of the market and offer their customers the following benefits:

- reduced transaction costs;
- reduction of risks;
- guarantee of anonymity;
- timeliness of transactions;
- price transparency.

ECX, the largest operator, is based in London and is a subsidiary of ICE (InterContinentalExchange, formerly IPE or International Petroleum Exchange), a platform whose primary business is related to petroleum products transactions. Another operator, EEX is based in Berlin. EEX is the leading energy trading platform in Germany. Nordpool, Powernext and EXAA are energy trading platforms in Norway, France and Italy respectively. However, while competition between these different platforms has played a beneficial role for participants in the ETS, most transactions are still agreed over the counter (over-the-counter trades are where companies deal directly with each other).

Reflecting the growing interest in the market for CO_2 allowances, the largest global stock exchange, NYSE Euronext, launched a specialized trading platform dedicated to environmental products in January 2008 in association with the Caisse des Dépôts, Bluenext. It should be noted that NYSE Euronext is a shareholder in Powernext and, Powernext Carbon and Powernext Weather were sold to NYSE Euronext before the launch of BlueNext.

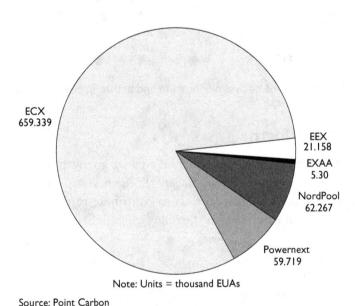

Note: Units = thousand EUAs

Source: Point Carbon

Figure 4.4 Trade volumes by platform

Impact of EUAs prices on the energy sector

The energy sector (electricity and heat) accounts for about half of the emissions covered by the ETS. It is therefore interesting to assess how this system impacts on the choice of technologies, on the price of electricity and on the profitability of the sector.

Influence on the merit order

Electricity companies rarely use their installations at full capacity. Overall capacity needs to exceed average output by a large margin, because demand is variable, electricity is expensive to store, and security of supply requires surplus capacity to meet unexpected demand spikes. Indeed, production capacity is higher than even the expected peak load, in order to maintain supply under exceptional conditions (e.g. disruption of hydroelectric installations due to drought, rapid surges in demand due to exceptional occurrences such as a major sporting event, and unplanned 'outages'). This means that most of the time, power generating companies choose to run their installations with the lowest marginal cost of production, in 'merit order'.

In practice nuclear power plants are 'must run' installations because of the high cost of safely stopping and restarting a reactor. Wind turbines and other renewable energy sources are always used to full available capacity because running costs are very low. The merit order can thus generally be reduced to a competition between coal and natural gas (for economic reasons oil power plants are used very little in most European countries). However, the recent increase in the use of biomass (pellets, olive kernels, sewage sludge, etc.) can complicate this. In the jargon of the electricity sector, a proxy of the profitability of a coal power station is given by the 'dark spread'. The dark spread is the theoretical gross income of a coal-fired power plant from selling a unit of electricity, having bought the fuel required to produce this unit of electricity as well as factoring in other costs such as operation and maintenance, capital and other financial costs. In practice the dark spread is the price of electricity (in €/kWh for example) minus the price of coal (in the same units) divided by the efficiency of the plant. The equivalent of dark spread for gas-fired power plant is named the 'spark spread'. Following the entry into force of the ETS, electricity generators have added the price of allowances into these decision parameters – comparing 'clean spark spread' and 'clean dark spread' to determine their merit order. Generating the same amount of electricity from coal emits approximately twice as much CO_2 as using gas, giving gas a comparative advantage compared to the pre-ETS position. When the price of allowances is high this increases this competitive advantage.

The following figure shows clearly that in the UK gas was more competitive than coal in 2005 when the price of allowances was above €25. From 2008, given high gas prices, it is estimated that the price of the EUAs would need to reach €40 for the clean spark spread to exceed the clean dark spread. This explains the proliferation in the construction of coal power plants in Europe (while natural gas was the reference fuel for new power plants in the late 1980s and the 1990s), including in Germany, France and the Netherlands.

Windfall profits

The influence of the ETS on the price of electricity depends on two factors – the cost of the allowances associated with each unit of electricity generated, and the extent to which this is passed on to electricity consumers.

Generating electricity emits approximately one tonne of CO_2 per MWh using coal or one tonne of CO_2 per 2–2.5MWh using gas.[8] With electricity wholesale prices typically €30/MWh, this implies that impacts were therefore limited in 2007 when the price of allowances remained below €5.

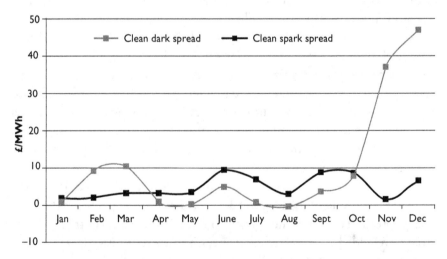

Figure 4.5 Clean dark spread and clean spark spread in the UK in 2005

The biggest potential impact of the ETS on emissions from the electricity sector is therefore on the choice of fuel, through differential prices, rather than on demand through increased costs.

With permits grandfathered to electricity generators, aggregate costs to power generating companies do not rise as a result of the allocation process. It might therefore be expected that costs to consumers would not be affected. However, this is not the way that the market works. The allowances given to generating companies represent an asset that is not affected by decisions about generation mix or pricing. The costs of additional allowances, on the other hand, are affected by these decisions and therefore form part of the variable costs of generation. In a competitive market, it is expected that prices will be determined by these variable costs, and therefore that carbon allowance prices are passed on to consumers whether the permits are grandfathered or auctioned. The extent to which this happens depends on actual market conditions. Experience from the first phase of the EU ETS showed that there was a significant pass-through of the CO_2 costs from the producer to the end-user, particularly in the residential sector even though energy companies did not pay for grandfathered permits. It is feared that the lack of auctioning in phase 2 will see a repeat of this problem (Sijm et al, 2006).

Developments of the EU ETS

Introduction to recent developments[9]

Since its launch in January 2005, the ETS has been amended and more changes will be introduced from 2013 in order to respond to some of the failings of the scheme (over-allocation, windfall profits, etc.). One recent change is from 2008 the system goes beyond the borders of the EU to cover other members of the European Economic Area (EEA).

On 23 January 2008, the Commission revealed its climate change package, setting the targets for reducing emissions to 2020 as well as targets for renewable energy development by Member States.[11,12] This package also included a proposal to revise the EU Emissions Trading Scheme and a proposal for the geological disposal of CO_2 (carbon capture and sequestration (CCS) for CO_2 Capture and Storage).[13,14] On 11–12 December, the EU Council agreed a final version of the energy and climate change package. On 17 December, the European Parliament voted in favour of the energy and climate change 'package', with 610 votes for and 60 against amid 29 abstentions.

The total effort for greenhouse gas reduction is divided between the EU ETS and non-ETS sectors:

- a 21 per cent reduction in EU ETS sector emissions compared to 2005 by 2020;
- a reduction of around 10 per cent compared to 2005 for the sectors that are not covered by the EU ETS.

Taken together, this results in an overall reduction of –14 per cent in EU emissions compared with 2005, or a reduction of –20 per cent compared with 1990. Since a single, EU-wide cap under the EU ETS will be introduced from 2013 (see below), an effort sharing arrangement between Member States has been determined solely for the reduction in emissions from sectors not covered by the EU ETS.

These targets call for a reduction in emissions of at least 20 per cent by 2020 compared with 1990 levels, and by 30 per cent provided that other industrialized countries commit to comparable efforts in the framework of a global agreement, which it is planned to conclude in discussions at the Copenhagen Conference of the Parties to the Kyoto Protocol in late 2009.

The proposed amendments to the ETS fall under the co-decision procedure, which means that they must be approved by both the Council of ministers of the EU and the European Parliament to become law. Now that both the Council and the EU Parliament have agreed on an identical text, the proposal can become law in time to be implemented for the next phase of the ETS and to inform post-Kyoto negotiations.

Enlargement to other countries

The ETS applies not only to the 27 Member States of the EU, but since 2008 also to three other Member States of the European Economic Area (Norway, Iceland and Liechtenstein). The aim of the Commission is to make the ETS simpler and more transparent to encourage other countries and regions to join.

The Commission sees the EU ETS as an important building block in the development of a global network of emissions trading systems. Linking the

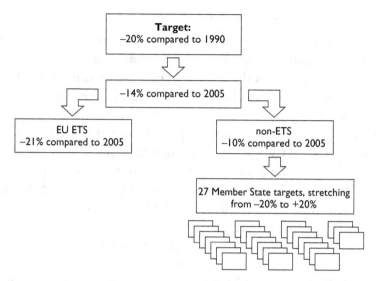

Figure 4.6 Sharing of EU GHG emissions reduction target in 2020

ETS with other national or regional cap-and-trade schemes would create a larger market, which could lower the overall cost of reducing GHG emissions. Theoretically, it would increase market liquidity and could reduce price volatility, both effects being beneficial to the functioning of the emissions market. This could help support a global network of exchange systems in which participants would be able to buy allowances in order to meet their respective reduction targets.

While the current Directive 2003/87/EC allows for linking the EU ETS with other industrialized countries that have ratified the Kyoto Protocol, the Commission would like to extend this to include any country or administrative entity (such as a state or group of states under a federal system) that has established a cap-and-trade system whose design elements would not undermine the environmental integrity of the EU ETS. This is a clear signal towards US initiatives in California and the Northeastern States.

This system of linked national schemes may prove to be an alternative to the current international system under the Kyoto Protocol. It also provides a way around the lack of ambition in setting targets and troubles with building consensus that have plagued international negotiations.

Inclusion of the aviation sector

In December 2006 the European Commission unveiled a proposal for a directive to include aviation in the ETS from 2012. A directive to this purpose was published in the Official Journal on 13 January 2009.[10] This would be a major change as the present scheme does not include emissions from transport.

Air transport has seen dramatic growth over the last two decades. According to the IPCC, the sector contributes 2 per cent of global emissions and is the fastest-growing source of GHGs contributing to climate change. While the EU's total emissions covered by the Kyoto Protocol fell by 4 per cent from 1990 to 2006, its GHG emissions from international aviation increased by 96 per cent (EEA, 2007a). Even though there has been significant improvement in aircraft technology (i.e. noise reduced by 75 per cent and fuel efficiency improved by 70 per cent over the last 40 years) and in operational efficiency, this has not been enough to neutralize the effect of increased traffic.

If the aviation sector continues to grow and remains excluded from climate change mitigation policies, reductions in other sectors would be seriously undermined. Figure 4.7 shows the business as usual scenario for aviation alongside the EU's long-term target (60 per cent decrease in GHG emissions by 2050) for other sources. This clearly highlights the need for inclusion of the aviation sector in carbon regulation.

Another important aspect of GHG emissions from international air transport is their exclusion from the Kyoto Protocol (see Chapter 1, p11). The directive provides for aviation to be introduced in two steps.[15] From the start of 2011 emissions from all domestic and international flights between EU airports will be covered. One year later, at the start of 2012, the scope will be expanded to cover emissions from all international flights – to or from anywhere in the world – that arrive at or depart from EU airports.

Expansion to other sectors and gases

The ETS covers installations performing specific activities. From the beginning it has covered (above certain capacity thresholds) power plants and other combustion plants, oil refineries, coke ovens, iron and steel plants and factories producing cement, glass, lime, bricks, ceramics, pulp,

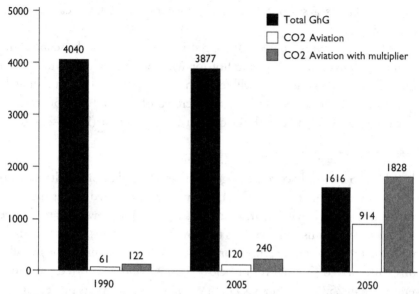

(in MtCO2e / source: Annual European Community greenhouse gas inventory 1990–2005 and inventory report 2007)

Figure 4.7 Emissions in the aviation sector compared with total emissions in the EU15

paper and paperboard. Until now the scheme only covers CO_2 emissions. From 2013 revised EU ETS will include additional sectors and GHGs. CO_2 emissions from the manufacture of petrochemicals, ammonia and aluminium, as well as emissions of nitrous oxide (NO_x) from the production of nitric acid, adipic acid and glyoxylic acid and emissions of perfluorocarbons (PFCs) from the aluminium sector will be included. The capture and geological storage of GHG emissions will also be covered within the scope of the scheme as a source for generating emission credits. The EU is very hopeful about the development of this new technology, although to date it has not been applied on an industrial scale. Despite the infancy of this technology, the Commission considered in January 2007 that 'by 2030, electricity and heat will increasingly need to be produced from low-carbon sources and extensive near-zero emission fossil fuel power plants with CO_2 capture and storage'.[16] The ETS would then have a role to play as a support scheme for operators of CO_2 capture and storage sites.

The Commission estimates that the proposed extension to the scope of the scheme, coupled with the possibility for Member States to exclude small installations (see next section), will result in a net expansion of approximately 6 per cent, which corresponds to an increase of up to 120–130 million tonnes of CO_2e compared with the current EU ETS phase (2008–2012).

Exclusion for small installations

The EU ETS currently covers a large number of installations emitting relatively small amounts of CO_2. Doubts have been expressed about the cost-effectiveness of their participation in the system. In its new climate change package, the Commission proposes to allow Member States to exclude these smaller installations with certain conditions. As a consequence, the installations with a rated thermal input below 35MW, whose reported emissions were less than 25,000 tonnes CO_2e for each of the three years preceding the year of application, could be excluded from the system as long as they are subject to certain measures to reduce emissions. In the original proposal from the Commission, the thresholds were respectively 25MW and 10,000 tonnes CO_2e. This opt out would cover some 4200 installations, accounting collectively for around 0.7 per cent of the total ETS emissions. Under the new arrangements, it is expected more than half of the covered installations may choose the opt out.

Setting an EU-wide cap

Faced with criticism of the distortions in competition created by the 27 national allocation plans in phase 3, the caps will be replaced by an EU-wide cap. This cap would then be lowered in a linear manner from 2013. National allocation plans will not be needed and the Commission will allocate allowances on the basis of harmonized rules.

It is intended that a significantly higher share of allowances would be auctioned instead of allocated free of charge. The Member States will still have the responsibility for organizing the auctions. The distribution of the auctioning rights to Member States are to be based primarily on historical emissions. However, some of the rights would be redistributed from Member States with high per capita income to Member States with lower per capita income.

The starting point for the planned decrease in emissions allowances from 2013 is the average total amount of allowances to be issued by Member States for the 2008–2012 period, adjusted to reflect the extension of the system from 2013. The linear reduction factor is set at 1.74 per cent per annum and was calculated to achieve overall reduction target of 20 per cent of GHG emissions compared to 1990 levels (equivalent to a 14 per cent reduction compared to 2005). The Commission put forward that a larger reduction should be required in the EU ETS because it is cheaper and easier than in the transport or domestic sectors, which remain outside the scheme's scope. According to the Commission, a reduction of 21 per cent (compared to 2005) in EU ETS sector by 2020 and a reduction of about 10 per cent for those areas that are not covered by the EU ETS is a way of sharing the burden that minimizes overall reduction costs. The Commission has also suggested this linear factor of 1.74 per cent should continue to apply beyond the end of the trading period in 2020 and should determine the cap for the fourth trading period (2021–2028) and beyond.

Some allowances are likely to be still allocated for free, but only in certain cases. Auctioning will become the basic principle for allocation from 2013 onwards. According to the Commission auctioning offers greater simplicity, efficiency and transparency. It also reduces the risk of windfall profits discussed earlier. The plan is for around 20 per cent of the total quantity of allowances will be auctioned in 2013, and this proportion to increase in each year with a view to reaching 70 per cent in 2020 and 100 per cent in 2027 (compared to only 0.12 per cent auctioning of the allowances auctioned during phase 1). The auctioning rate will be higher for electricity generators, with a rate of at least 30 per cent in 2013, increasing progressively to 100 per cent no later than 2020. In the original proposal the auctioning rate in 2013 was set at 100 per cent for the power sector and 60 per cent for the other sectors.

Allowances allocated free of charge will be distributed according to EU-wide rules so that all companies in the EU whose activities are similar would receive consistent treatment. For example a benchmark could be used where a number of allowances is given according to historical output as opposed to estimates of future pollution. Such rules would reward operators who have taken early action.

Note that an exception is made for sectors where the risk of 'carbon leakage' is high, i.e. sectors where international competitive pressures could lead to relocation outside the EU. According to the new climate package, 5 per cent of the total quantity of allowances are to be put in a reserve for new installations or airlines that integrate with the system after 2013 (new entrants). Any allowance remaining should be distributed to Member States for auctioning. Allowances issued from 1 January 2013 are also to be held in the community registry instead of in national registries.

A common threshold for the use of CDM/JI credits

The ETS recognizes (under certain conditions and with certain limits) credits issued by CDM and JI projects. In addition, the rules concerning the use of those credits vary from one Member State to another. With the revised directive the EU harmonizes the rules.

The new rules limit the use of those credits to 50 per cent of the EU-wide reductions over the period 2008–2020. In practice, this means that participants will be able to use credits up to a maximum of 11 per cent of their allocation during the period 2008–2012. A top up may be allowed for participants with the lowest proportion of free allocation for the 2008–2012 period. New sectors and new entrants in the third trading period will have a guaranteed minimum access to CDM/JI type credits of 4.5 per cent of their verified emissions during the period 2013–2020. For the aviation sector, the minimum access will be 1.5 per cent.

Based on stricter emissions reduction in the context of a satisfactory international agreement, the Commission has signalled additional access to credits could be allowed, as well as the use of additional types of project credits or other mechanisms created under such an agreement.

New mechanism projects

With the revised EU ETS, projects in EU Member States that reduce emissions of GHGs in sectors that are not covered by the scheme could issue credits. These domestic baseline and credits projects would be managed according to common EU rules in order to be tradable throughout the system.

The role of a new international agreement and permit allocation

When an international agreement is reached, the Commission will revise or repeal the EU-wide rules for free allocation of allowances due to competitiveness concerns. Moreover, if other countries take significant action, then the EU cap may be reduced by up to 30 per cent compared with 1990 levels.

2020 effort-sharing

The 2020 targets for EU Member States (expressed in comparison with 2005 levels) for sources not covered by the EU ETS were passed by the EU Parliament on 17 December 2008.[17] These limitations on non-EU ETS sectors mainly come from road transport, heating and agriculture.

According to the Commission the use of the year 2005 has two advantages compared to the common reference to 1990. First these goals are more understandable, since they refer to the current situation. Second 2005 figures are more accurate than those for 1990 given the progress in the measurement of emissions. The reformed phase 3 ETS also recognizes the right to use CERs to achieve these goals, up to a maximum of 3 per cent of emissions of 2005 (almost one third of the 10 per cent discount required in the non-ETS sector). Member States that have to reduce their non-ETS emissions, or are only allowed to increase them by up to 5 per cent, can also use an additional 1 per cent of CER credits (Austria, Finland, Denmark, Italy, Spain, Belgium, Luxembourg, Portugal, Ireland, Slovenia, Cyprus

Table 4.1 *Limitations of GHG emissions in non-ETS sectors by 2020 in comparison with 2005 levels*

Percentage of emissions from reference year (2005)					
Austria	84	Germany	86	Netherlands	84
Belgium	85	Greece	96	Poland	114
Bulgaria	120	Hungary	110	Portugal	101
Cyprus	95	Ireland	80	Romania	119
Czech Republic	109	Italy	87	Slovakia	113
Denmark	80	Latvia	117	Slovenia	104
Estonia	111	Lithuania	115	Spain	90
Finland	84	Luxembourg	80	Sweden	83
France	86	Malta	105	United Kingdom	84

and Sweden). These credits can come only from CDM projects in least developed countries and small island developing states, and have to be non-bankable and non-transferable.

Developments to complement the EU ETS

National trading schemes

National trading schemes for sectors covered by the EU ETS are now seen to be unnecessarily complex and unhelpful in delivering climate objectives. However, there is potential for using trading schemes to address sectors outside the EU ETS. The UK is the only EU Member State currently actively pursuing this approach, using the same legislative basis as for the (now ended) UK ETS.

The scheme will be called the Carbon Reduction Commitment (CRC).[18] It covers companies and other organizations that do not fall into sectors covered by the EU ETS, but who are sufficiently large to be significant energy users. Like the EU ETS it will be a mandatory cap-and-trade scheme, but of course restricted within the UK. The objective is to reduce emissions by 4.4MtCO$_2$ by 2020, below a baseline that is projected to grow significantly. Eligibility will be defined by electricity use in excess of 6GWh/year, and the scheme will cover all energy use, including electricity. It is therefore a downstream cap-and-trade system like the earlier UK ETS, with the primary objective of improving energy end-use efficiency, where the lowest cost emissions reductions are often to be found.

The 6GWh cut-off for eligibility means that only large organizations will be involved. There are expected to be 4–5000 participants. These are will be large commercial organizations (e.g. banks, hotel and restaurant chains, supermarkets), government offices, hospitals and universities. To prevent tactical restructuring to avoid the CRC, a private sector 'organization' will be defined as a company group. The exclusion of smaller organizations is intended to reduce administrative costs and political opposition. While the scheme will require EU State Aid approval, implications are limited because of the low-energy intensity of covered businesses. The scheme will be administered by the UK Environment Agency, which also acts as an administrator for the EU ETS. Any emissions already covered by the EU ETS of the UK Climate Change Agreements (CCA) will be excluded, except of course emissions from generation of electricity used by participants. To this extent there will be 'double coverage' of the two schemes, but with different responsibilities within the two schemes – upstream in the EU ETS, downstream in the CRC.

To make the scheme environmentally effective and to avoid the windfall profit problems of the EU ETS, it is proposed that all CRC emissions allocations will all be auctioned. To avoid the competitiveness concerns that this raises, it is proposed that auction revenues will be recycled to participants in proportion to the total emissions since the beginning of the scheme. This approach gives the smallest possible redistributive effect while retaining the carbon price incentive. Alternative recycling options, e.g. through reduced labour taxes or based on sectoral benchmarks, could have bigger environmental and economic benefits, but raise the risk of bigger objections from losers. In addition, it is proposed to implement a 'safety valve' on the carbon price within the scheme through a 'buy only link' to the EU ETS. In other words, even if the performance of the scheme participants is poor, the price will only be allowed to rise to level of the permits in EU ETS. Given the non-energy intensive nature of the participants (energy costs typically <3 per cent of total costs) the competitiveness impacts are likely to be very small. However this safety valve can also be considered to reduce the effectiveness of the mechanism. The 'buy only' nature of the link also preserves the integrity of the EU ETS. All businesses (except the very smallest) will continue to pay the CCL.

The scheme will begin with a initial 3-year phase, 2010–2012, in which allocations will be sold at a fixed price, with the full auctioning system in place from 2013, i.e. the post-Kyoto period.

Support for renewable energy and carbon markets

Throughout Europe there are national support mechanisms for the production and/or use of renewable energy, particularly electricity from new renewable sources such as solar, wind and biomass. It has been argued by some free-market economists that these support measures are now unnecessary because the EU ETS internalizes the cost of carbon in the most efficient manner. These arguments neglect two important considerations.

First, they assume that the existing price of carbon in current carbon markets is sufficient. In practice, most assessments of the costs of climate change indicate that a higher value would be required to internalize it fully and even then that the uncertainty inherent in climate change makes the identification of any unique 'correct price' difficult. Current carbon markets alone may therefore be inadequate to secure the changes in competitiveness of low-carbon fuels and technologies that are required for the transition to a low-carbon economy.

Second, there are additional reasons to support innovation and new technologies. It is well established that the costs of technology fall both with research and development and as markets for the technology grow. It is therefore quite possible, indeed likely, that the set of technologies that will prove optimum for delivering our energy needs in a low-carbon world do not yet exist or are only currently available at costs that are not competitive. Private inventors, developers and investors have some incentive from the prospect of future sales, but because intellectual property diffuses quite broadly over a long period, the initial developer does not secure all the economic benefits of the innovation. Free markets therefore tend to under-invest in innovation. This is the classic case for government to support the early stages of all types of potentially beneficial innovation. The case is much stronger for low-carbon technologies where it is clear that innovation is needed to develop the technologies for a sustainable energy system (see Chapter 2, Figure 2.7).

Renewable energy technologies form a group that can clearly benefit from cost reduction through market expansion, or 'learning by doing'. Particularly in the electricity market, they compete to produce a transportable commodity against well-established technologies using fossil and nuclear fuels. The argument that targeted support for renewable energy is 'unfair' is clearly invalid when the extent of historical public support for the development of competitor technologies is considered. Fossil fuel power generation benefited from the R&D undertaken in monopoly power systems throughout most of the last century, as well as from direct government support for other individual technologies in other sectors, notably for gas turbines in aviation. Nuclear power, although more recent, has now had more than 60 years of very substantial government support, particularly in the countries that have sought to develop nuclear technology for military purposes. Arguably therefore, a substantial period of support focused on renewable energy is a correction towards a 'level playing field' rather than unfair competition.

While there has been significant support for renewable technology within the EU's research, technology and demonstration (RTD) programmes, the largest support measures for early stage deployment have been national. This partly reflects the industrial policy drivers that are inherent in the case for national support of renewable energy. While all national support mechanisms need to comply with European law, given the drivers of innovation policy, it is inevitable that they are designed to maximize the chances of economic benefits accruing within the country of origin.

Moreover, it is clear that there are industrial success stories arising from national support. Denmark, despite being a relatively small economy, is a key player in the global wind industry, thanks in part to the 'first mover advantage' secured by small Danish wind manufacturing companies within Danish programmes in the 1970s. More recently, German leadership in the European photovoltaic (PV) sector probably owes something to the large German market for building integrated PV, established as a result of a relatively generous support mechanism.

For early stage deployment, there are two broad approaches to renewable electricity support: price premiums (often referred to as 'feed in tariffs' (FITs)) and volume obligations (usually through requirements for Renewable Energy Certificates (RECs), sometimes called Tradable Green Certificates (TGCs).[19] In essence, these mirror the two approaches to pricing carbon. The price can be fixed by regulation and the quantity allowed to vary (carbon tax and FIT). Or the total quantity fixed (carbon cap-and-trade or RECs) and the resulting commodity traded, allowing the price to vary. All the same arguments about equivalence under conditions of perfect certainty apply; as do all the same discussions about the relative merits of different approaches under uncertainty (see Chapter 2).

As with the choice between carbon taxation and carbon trading, in practice the choice has usually been made on grounds of political feasibility or expediency. Despite the theoretical equivalence of the approaches, the 'price fixing' approach of FITs has seemed unattractive to governments committed to less intervention in markets, e.g. US, UK and Australia, but more attractive in the European continental tradition of managed markets. In Europe, at least, there seems to be a growing analytical consensus on the merits of the FIT approach (Mitchell and Connor, 2004). This is based on two considerations. The first is purely empirical – renewable electricity production, particularly wind energy, has expanded significantly more quickly in markets using FITs (notably Germany and Spain) than in those using RECs (notably the UK). Of course this could be due to a number of different factors including well-documented problems in securing permission for land-use change. The second argument is more theoretical, but supported by market players. It is that support from financial institutions is more difficult to obtain when the project cash flow is dependent on a variable priced certificate rather than on a fixed price tariff.

There are voluntary markets for renewable electricity, just as for carbon. These have been useful in establishing the validity of 'green energy' as a concept in the market for a physically undifferentiated commodity such as electricity. Many of the monitoring and certification systems required to establish either FIT or REC systems have their roots in early attempts by entrepreneurs and supportive institutions to establish premium green energy products. In some cases, market share of a few percentage points was established. Such voluntary product schemes will probably continue to exist. Nevertheless, problems of establishing 'additionality' in markets where there is a significant product arising from a regulatory intervention make voluntary green products unlikely to reach mainstream consumers, at least in Europe.

Perhaps inevitably in the EU context, there are ongoing debates about the extent to which a unified or harmonized European wide scheme would be preferable to a patchwork of national schemes based on different approaches, definitions and rules. In the context of a European market in electricity, a European wide scheme would seem a logical outcome. However, the objectives of renewable energy policies, as well as the availability and costs of resources, and the existing support schemes are so different that a fully unified system seems unlikely to meet the needs of all Member States.

In this context, some progress has been made. There is already a functioning harmonized system of defining renewable electricity – the Renewable Energy Guarantee of Origin (REGO) system. This system requires Member States, on request from a renewable generator, to identify and certificate renewable electricity produced within their boundaries. However, there is no requirement to accept REGOs from the certification systems of other Member States within their own renewable electricity support schemes. So REGOs provide some confidence in the veracity of claims that imported electricity is renewable,[20] but they do not themselves provide the basis for financial incentives driven by national support programmes.

Some attempts have been made by the European Commission during 2008 to use REGOs as the basis for establishing a more harmonized support system. A system of tradable REGOs linked to requirements for delivery of specified amounts of renewable electricity would be a move in this direction. However, it would be a step towards a European REC system. It would require detailed but important changes in support mechanisms to align definitions and adjust targets. It could also tend to undermine FIT systems, which would be unpopular, as these are widely seen as more effective than RECs systems, especially in those Member States with FITs. So no agreement on this is likely. In the short term at least, emphasis is likely to be on the strengthening and improvement of national schemes.

In the context of this chapter, it is important not only to consider the reason for policy instruments to support renewable energy to supplement the EU ETS, but also the interaction of such support schemes with the EU ETS. Before the advent of the EU ETS, renewable energy support schemes were widely considered as part of attempts to internalize climate change. In the narrow sense of the tariffs or certificate values including the value of carbon abatement, that is now difficult to justify in the context of an electricity system that is subject to a carbon cap, with a separate market in carbon.

It should also not be forgotten that there are other potential objectives for renewable energy. Renewables offer reduction in most forms of pollution and other environmental stresses as well. Indeed some policy objectives are not environmental in character. The early Danish support for wind energy, now seen as a climate policy exemplar, began as an intervention to diversify energy supplies away from oil. Energy security remains an important goal for renewables policy in many countries. Through this diversification renewables also offer social and economic advantages in terms of job creation and the development of indigenous industries.

Renewable energy support schemes should still be seen primarily as part of the overall strategy for carbon emissions reduction in Europe, as elsewhere. As explained above, the interaction between two externalities (carbon and underinvestment in innovation) justifies a more dynamic approach to carbon policy than can be delivered by a single carbon price. Long-term carbon policy requires not just least cost emissions reduction now, but the creation of options that provide the potential for cheaper, non-marginal reductions in future.

Support for energy efficiency and carbon markets

European countries and the EU have developed separate support mechanisms for energy efficiency. As with renewable energy, these have been questioned in the context of the EU ETS by those who assume that carbon pricing will internalize the cost of carbon in the most efficient manner.

Carbon pricing policy is designed largely on the assumption that 'correct' pricing across the economy will deliver emissions reduction at least cost. In the context of energy-efficiency market interventions, there are two important points to make. First that the EU ETS does not price carbon into all energy-efficiency decisions. Second, there is abundant evidence that the theory of a perfect market is not very good for many energy-using decisions, i.e. there are market failures other than the failure to price carbon adequately. We will treat these separately.

The scope of the EU ETS is set out above. About 60 per cent of EU carbon emissions remain entirely outside its scope: these include fuel use in transport, homes, agriculture and much non-energy-intensive industry, commerce and the public sector. It is well established that there is a significant potential to improve energy use, and thereby reduce carbon emissions, in these sectors. Indeed, for the reasons set out below, it is very likely that the energy-efficiency potential as a percentage is larger in these sectors than in the energy sector itself and the energy-intensive industries included in the EU ETS. Proposed changes to the EU ETS will alter this to some extent through the inclusion of aviation in 2011/2012, but the broad issue is unchanged – much of EU energy use is outside the scope of the EU ETS. Intervention to improve energy efficiency in these sectors is justified because of this limited scope.

Energy-efficiency intervention is also justified across the economy because of a number of market failures that restrict investment in cost-effective technology. These market failures, and policy interventions to address them, are unrelated to and predate concern about climate change. There are many taxonomies of these barriers to energy efficiency (Sorrell et al, 2004). Most include imperfect information, myopia in investment, lack of alignment of responsibility for energy efficiency and its benefits (e.g. between landlords and tenants) and failure of capital markets to lend to cost-effective products. Among energy-efficiency analysts there is broad agreement that these are widely and deeply ingrained features of energy markets, not a short-lived concern. In particular, the 'rational economic actor' assumption of economic theory does not provide a very thorough explanation of observed human behaviour, and there seems no reason to expect that it ever will.

The result of these market failures is that there are numerous opportunities for improved energy efficiency that are cost-effective even without a positive price for carbon. In other words, the marginal cost abatement curve for carbon emissions reduction has a significant negative cost section. This idea has been popularized by McKinsey (Endquist et al, 2007). The details of this analysis have been rightly criticized, but the basic analysis is well-established, although not referenced by McKinsey, with detailed analysis for many countries and sectors stretching back to the 1970s. These have been thoroughly peer-reviewed and are broadly accepted by the IPCC (Levine et al, 2007).

The reasons there is such a well-established literature are important. Policy support for energy efficiency predates concerns about climate change and carbon emissions. Indeed, improved energy efficiency is widely accepted as supporting all key goals of energy policy, economic, social and security-related, as well as environmental policy. Policies and measures to support energy efficiency are therefore well understood, although concerns about carbon emissions clearly add weight to their importance.

The existence of market failures implies that market-based solutions are not necessarily the most efficient means of intervention within the market. This theoretical observation is supported by evidence from actual interventions within markets for energy-using goods. Some of the most cost-effective are relatively straightforward 'command and control' regulation. Most notable are standards for buildings and for energy-using appliances (e.g. boilers, refrigerators, automobiles). Building energy standards were introduced in most developed countries in the aftermath of the 1970s oil shocks and are now very widely used, with climate change concerns driving higher standards in most countries. Similarly, standards for electrical appliances are now very widely used. A straightforward regulatory approach not only reduces regulatory (transaction) costs; provided that sufficient notice of future standards is given, the approach also provides industry with a clear framework in which to develop new products and to mass-manufacture them, with consequent cost reductions. Nowhere is there a serious suggestion to policy makers that a market-based approach with no minimum standard would be preferable.

Despite its 'non-market' approach, energy-efficiency regulation has important implications for carbon markets. Improved end-use efficiency, particularly for electricity, tends to reduce carbon emissions within the cap of any emissions trading scheme. To the extent that this is driven by policy intervention in the form of standards (or related policies such as negotiated agreements), policy makers need to ensure that carbon caps are set with an awareness of future changes in market structure. The effect can be significant – for example the proposed phase-out of traditional incandescent lighting in Europe and some other countries will improve energy efficiency, and therefore reduce associated carbon emissions, by a factor of four in those lighting markets where incandescent lamps are currently dominant. However, these changes can be modelled and allowed for in carbon market policy.

The implications for project-based carbon markets are more complex. The logic of instruments such us the Joint Implementation and the Clean Development Mechanism is that project credits should be based on 'additional' energy and/or GHG savings. The quantification of additionality is therefore critical in these instruments and the commonly used approach is to define the extent of additionality from a baseline of the legal minimum standard or the current market average. This potentially raises the prospect of perverse incentives for energy efficiency within the CDM in particular.[21] If additionality is measured over and above the minimum standard in the host country, then that country will reduce its eligibility for CDM credits for any given energy-efficiency project by tightening its energy-efficiency standards. It will have an incentive under the CDM to set lax standards in order to maximize its receipt of carbon credits. This problem can obviously be addressed by basing credits on a more objective and international standard. However, it is not a trivial problem – using a baseline of 'best available technology' clearly eliminates all projects and even a baseline of 'currently cost-effective' technology sets a standard well above what might actually occur in markets without intervention.

There is one area of energy efficiency policy where trading is beginning to be used – energy-efficiency obligations for energy companies. There is a long history of using energy retailers as the mechanism for delivering energy efficiency improvements. The origin was in regulated monopoly electricity markets in the US, particularly in the 1980s before market liberalization became fashionable. The intervention was generally referred to as 'least cost planning' or 'integrated resource planning (IRP)' with the implication that monopoly utilities should invest in energy efficiency as opposed to new supply if this provided a lower cost option than new supply (which because of barriers to energy efficiency it invariably did). The form of intervention has gradually been modified, starting in the UK and spreading particularly to other European countries, to deal with the competitive structure of energy supply markets in many countries. Rather than a least cost resource plan, the policy works through energy-efficiency obligations for energy retailers or distributors, specified in energy or carbon saved. The trend is for these obligations to be tradable through an 'energy efficiency certificate' approach. The certificates are usually referred to as Tradable White Certificates (TWC) to distinguish them from carbon trading (black certificates) and renewable energy trading (green certificates (TGCs)).

The initial UK approach of suppliers' obligations has been adopted and made more obviously tradable in other European countries, notably France and Italy, and now beginning elsewhere within the OECD.[22] Initial experience is broadly positive, although in many countries the policy is too new to have been fully evaluated (Lees, 2006).

To the extent that TWC schemes apply to electricity use in Europe, the same relationship applies to the EU ETS as for renewable electricity trading, i.e. value of carbon is not fully captured in the TWC. However, given that the intervention largely promotes the use of cost-effective technology, it is beneficial for other reasons. However, in practice TWC schemes almost certainly do reduce carbon emissions. UK carbon caps for power generators in the EU ETS have explicitly assumed full delivery of energy efficiency obligations and European policy for the EU ETS post-2013 can be expected to follow the same approach. Importantly, TWCs are generally being applied to all fuels used in the sectors covered by the obligations, which are largely outside the scope of the EU ETS, and therefore for these fuels the TWC can be understood to include the carbon value of the energy saved.

To date this approach to delivering energy efficiency has been limited solely to a project mechanism approach with TWCs granted for defined energy-efficiency projects. In most cases the credits for energy-efficiency projects are set *ex ante*, i.e. the number of certificates for investing in a specific technology (e.g. an A-rated refrigerator) are defined in advance by the scheme regulator, from a knowledge of the efficiency of the technology and its baseline competitor. For well-understood technologies the likely error is small and far outweighed by the benefits of reduced transaction costs. Where this type of approach is not followed, notably in the CDM where expensive *ex post* monitoring has been required, energy-efficiency projects have not been developed despite being the most cost-effective carbon reduction opportunities. This aspect of TWC schemes has important lessons for programmatic CDM.

To date there have been no attempts to implement 'cap-and-trade' obligations on energy suppliers with respect to the energy use of their customers. However, ideas for such an approach have been put forward, most notably for consultation by UK Government. However, there is evidence that energy suppliers are unlikely to be able to influence their customers' energy use on the scale and with the certainty required for this to be a feasible approach (Eyre, 2008).

Proposals for radical extension of the scope of trading

As set out above, current schemes and plans for emissions trading focus on large industrial sources, including power generation, with plans for extension to aviation. However, a large and growing fraction of carbon emissions are from smaller sources in buildings, land vehicles and light industry. Although there are no examples of carbon trading being extended to these emitters, proposals to do this have been made. There are several variants on the same broad concept, but basically two models:

- The original proposal was called Tradable Energy Quotas (TEQs) in which the whole economy is carbon capped, with allowances distributed free to individuals and auctioned to businesses (Fleming, 1997). The same broad approach, but with a variety of distribution mechanisms is used in other proposed schemes, such as 'Cap and Share' and 'Sky Trust' (Barnes, 2003; Matthews, 2007).
- Variants are restricted to energy use under the direct control of individuals, i.e. household energy and personal transport, generally now known under the broad heading of personal carbon trading (PCT) (Hillman and Fawcett, 2004; Fawcett et al, 2007).

TEQs have the property of only requiring enforcement at the top of the energy chain, i.e. the point of extraction or import of fossil fuels. This makes administration in principle fairly straightforward (Fleming, 2008). The objective is to set a price for carbon across the economy, with an equitable initial distribution of permits. The assumption is that supply of permits could then be used to control emissions in a manner that would be both fair and effective – the schemes are seen as a 'silver bullet' for climate mitigation policy. However, the proposed scope overlaps with the EU ETS, which most analysts now take as a policy 'given'. While it is possible to describe a gradual transition of the EU ETS towards the TEQs proposal, it is not a straightforward change (Anderson and Starkey, 2005). In general, these variants have been designed by eco-innovators working in isolation from the policy process. Although scheme designs have been mapped out, the practical challenges of administration, enforcement and political acceptability have not been addressed in detail.

In contrast, PCT has been designed to be complementary to the EU ETS.[23] It would require downstream measurement and enforcement with the aim of engaging energy users more actively in carbon emissions reduction. Indeed, the proponents of PCT do not generally regard the scheme as a pure economic instrument. On the contrary, PCT is seen as qualitatively different from carbon taxation and upstream trading and, through the personalization of carbon allocation, as a means of changing attitudes to and engagement with energy and carbon issues.

Either variant would have the attraction of addressing personal carbon emissions directly and transparently, and the pitfalls of upstream windfalls by granting property rights to final consumers. In principle, any allocation system could be used, although the only option considered in any detail has been equal per capita allowances, because of its apparent equity. The usual proposed scope is wider than a household energy supplier obligation, covering personal transport.

This combination of broad scope and conceptual simplicity has attracted political attention in the UK, leading to a number of detailed studies (Accenture, 2008; CSE, 2008; Defra, 2008; Enviros, 2008). The broad conclusions from these are that a PCT system is technically feasible, but expensive to set up and maintain. Public acceptability is unknown and difficult to judge in the absence of a worked-up and operational scheme. The UK Government has concluded that the costs are unlikely to be justified by benefits over and above other approaches to reducing emissions. This conclusion seems valid if it is assumed that PCT operates purely as an economic instrument, as upstream alternatives would be equally effective, while being simpler and cheaper to implement (e.g. the approach to transport emissions in the Australian emissions trading scheme, the Carbon Pollution Reduction Scheme). However, PCT proponents claim its effectiveness may be largely through psychological and social factors rather than price elasticity. In the absence of evidence this difference of opinion cannot be resolved. Ultimately a decision to implement PCT in any jurisdiction is likely to depend on political conditions. Allocation of emissions rights to citizens and placing them under an obligation to share responsibility for emissions reduction would mark a major shift in the political economy of the environment.

Conclusion

This chapter has outlined the role of carbon trading in the climate policy of the EU. The policy was initially adopted because of a unique set of circumstances – the trading provisions of the Kyoto Protocol, the desire for European leadership to address climate change, the difficulties with carbon tax proposals and the need to avoid competing national initiatives.

Although the existence of the EU ETS is now broadly accepted, it was initially a controversial policy. Its design reflected the need to gain support, or at least acceptance, from a wide variety of stakeholders, including national governments and industrial sectors with diverging priorities. The scope of the initial cap reflects a political negotiation rather than an optimization of economic or environmental outputs. This explains some outcomes that are now widely criticized. These include the decision to allow Member States to set caps, over allocation resulting in the collapse of the carbon price, and the windfall gains for electricity generators that result from free allocation of permits.

Despite this chequered history, the EU ETS is a landmark in climate policy. The scale of the market is unrivalled in comparison to any other existing carbon market; and the link to the CDM, although doubtless reducing the carbon price, has resulted in significant carbon finance for the developing world. Although EU ETS permit prices have varied, this has led to changes that now mean it does affect some investment and operational decisions. Furthermore, flexibility inherent in the market-based approach has allowed prices to adjust in response to the current economic crisis. The experience of free allocation has led to increased auctioning. In short, recognition of the desirability of it has been a learning process as the scheme expands to include the new Member States of the EU, aviation emissions and other GHGs.

Emissions trading, or any form of carbon pricing, can never be expected to be a complete carbon policy. The EU and its Member States continue with other complementary initiatives, most notably to promote innovation in low-carbon technologies that are currently too expensive to benefit from carbon markets (especially renewable energy) and to promote energy efficiency, as this is constrained by other market failures.

Notes

1   Partly because of a fuel switch from coal to natural gas.
2   Mainly because of the collapse of heavy industries in former German Democratic Republic.
3   Directive 2003/87/EC of the European Parliament and of the Council of 13 October 2003 establishing a scheme for greenhouse gas emission allowance trading within the Community and amending Council Directive 96/61/EC.
4   Directive 2004/101/EC of the European Parliament and of the Council of 27 October 2004 amending Directive 2003/87/EC establishing a scheme for greenhouse gas emission allowance trading within the Community, in respect of the Kyoto Protocol's project mechanisms.
5   Commission Decision of 18 July 2007 establishing guidelines for the monitoring and reporting of greenhouse gas emissions pursuant to Directive 2003/87/EC of the European Parliament and of the Council.
6   Commission Decision of 29/01/2004 establishing guidelines for the monitoring and reporting of greenhouse gas emissions pursuant to Directive 2003/87/EC of the European Parliament and of the Council.
7   With this method, CO_2 emissions are calculated using the following equation:
$$CO_2 = \text{activity data} * \text{emission factor} * \text{oxidation factor}.$$
Activity data includes information on the flow of materials, fuel consumption, input material or production. Emission factors are based on the carbon content of fuels or inbound materials and are expressed in tCO_2/TJ (combustion emissions), tCO_2/t or tCO_2/Nm^3 (process emissions). The oxidation factor is the proportion of carbon that is oxidized to CO_2 during the process.
8   Exact numbers depend on fuel quality and power station efficiency.
9   European Commission, Q&A on the Commission's proposal to revise the EU ETS, MEMO/08/35, Brussels, 23 January 2008.
10 Directive 2008/101/EC of the European Parliament and of the Council of 19 November 2008 amending Directive 2003/87/EC so as to include aviation activities in the scheme for greenhouse gas emission allowance trading within the Community (Text with EEA relevance).

11 Proposal for a Decision of the European Parliament and of the Council on the effort of Member States to reduce their greenhouse gas emissions to meet the Community's greenhouse gas emission reduction commitments up to 2020, Brussels, 23 January 2008, COM(2008) 30 final.

12 Proposal for a Directive of the European Parliament and of the Council on the promotion of the use of energy from renewable sources, Brussels, 23 January 2008, COM(2008) 19 final.

13 Proposal for a Directive amending Directive 2003/87/EC so as to improve and extend the greenhouse gas emission allowance trading system of the Community, Brussels, 23 January 2008, COM(2008) 16 final.

14 Proposal for a Directive of the European Parliament and of the Council on the geological storage of carbon dioxide and amending Council Directives 85/337/EEC, 96/61/EC, Directives 2000/60/EC, 2001/80/EC, 2004/35/EC, 2006/12/EC and Regulation (EC) No 1013/200, Brussels, 23 January 2008, COM(2008) 18 final.

15 Proposal for a Directive of the European Parliament and of the Council amending Directive 2003/87/EC so as to include aviation activities in the scheme for greenhouse gas emission allowance trading within the Community, Brussels, 20 December 2006, COM(2006) 818 final.

16 Communication from the Commission to the European Council and the European Parliament, 'An Energy Policy for Europe', Brussels, 10 January 2007, COM(2007) 1 final.

17 Position of the European Parliament adopted at first reading on 17 December 2008 with a view to the adoption of Decision No .../2009/EC of the European Parliament and of the Council on the effort of Member States to reduce their greenhouse gas emissions to meet the Community's greenhouse gas emission reduction commitments up to 2020.

18 The CRC was initially known as the Energy Performance Commitment (EPC) but the name was changed to avoid confusion with Energy Performance Certificates that form the UK certification system for building required by the Energy Performance of Buildings Directive.

19 Or in the US, where regulated monopoly markets remain more common, Renewable Portfolio Standards, RPS.

20 For more information refer to: www.ofgem.gov.uk/Sustainability/Environmnt/REGOs/Pages/REGOs.aspx

21 In practice the existing rules of the CDM have largely precluded use of energy efficiency to date, but this has been recognized as problematic.

22 See for example Vine and Hamrin, 2008; Bertoldi and Rezessy, 2008; Pavan, 2008.

23 PCT proposals include electricity use that is within the EU ETS, but the carbon reduction measures that the two approaches would incentivize are different – EU ETS upstream and PCT downstream.

References

Accenture (2008) 'An analysis of the technical feasibility and potential cost of a personal carbon trading scheme', Report to Defra, UK

Alexis, A. (2004) 'Protection de l'environnement et aides d'État: La mise en application du principe du pollueur-payeur', R.A.E.-L.A.E, pp629–640

Anderson, K. and Starkey, R. (2005) 'Domestic Tradable Quotas: A policy instrument for reducing greenhouse gas emissions from energy use', Tyndall Centre Technical Report No. 39

Barnes, P. (2003) Who Owns the Sky? *Our Common Assets and the Future of Capitalism*, Island Press, Washington DC

Bertoldi, P. and Rezessy, S. (2008) 'Assessment of White Certificate Schemes in Europe', Proceedings of ACEEE Summer Study on Energy Efficiency in Buildings

CEPS (2002) 'Greenhouse gas emissions trading in Europe: Conditions for environmental credibility and economic efficiency', CEPS Task Force Report No 43

Commission of the European Communities (1996) 'Energy: Consequences of the proposed carbon/energy tax', SEC (92)

Commission of the European Communities (2000) 'Green Paper on greenhouse gas emissions trading within the European Union', COM (2000) 87 final, pp8–20

CSE (2008) 'Centre for Sustainable Energy. Personal carbon trading: Equity and distributional impacts', A report to Defra, UK

Defra (2008) 'Personal carbon trading: An assessment of the potential effectiveness and strategic fit', Defra, UK

EEA (2007a) 'Annual European Community greenhouse gas inventory 1990–2005 and inventory report 2007', Technical Report no 7, EEA

EEA (2007b) 'Application of the Emissions Trading Directive by EU Member States, reporting year 2006', EEA Technical Report No 4/2007

Ellerman, A. D. and Buchner, B. K. (2007) 'The European Union Emissions Trading Scheme: Origins, allocation and early results', *Review of Environmental Economics and Policy*, vol 1, no 1, pp66–87

Endquist, P.-A., Nauclér, T. and Rosander, J. (2007) 'A cost curve for greenhouse reduction', *The McKinsey Quarterly*, vol 1, pp36–45

ENDS Report (2008) 'Two thirds of UK EU ETS installations in surplus', *ENDS Report*, vol 397, p9

Enviros (2008) 'Enviros and opinion leader research: Personal carbon trading – public acceptability', A report to Defra, UK

Eyre, N. (2008) 'Regulation of energy suppliers to save energy: Lessons from the UK debate', Proceedings of the British Institute of Energy Economists, Oxford

Fawcett, T., Bottrill, C., Boardman, B. and Lye, G. (2007) 'Trialling personal carbon allowance', UKERC Research Report DR/2007/02

Fleming, D. (1997) 'Tradable quotas: Setting limits to carbon emissions', Discussion Paper 11, *The Lean Economy Initiative*, London

Fleming, D. (2008) 'DEFRA's pre-feasibility study into personal carbon trading: A missed opportunity', The Lean Economy Connection, London

Frémont, R. (2005) 'Les plates-formes de marché et le fonctionnement du système de quotas CO_2', *Note d'étude de la Mission climat de la Caisse des dépôts*, no 3, www.caissedesdepots.fr/IMG/pdf/note3_plateformes_210605.pdf

Grubb, M. and Neuhoff, K. (2006) 'Allocation and competitiveness in the EU Emissions Trading Scheme: Policy overview', *Climate Policy*, vol 6, pp7–30

Grubb, M., Azar, C. and Persson, U. (2005) 'Allowance allocation in the European Emission Trading System: A commentary', *Climate Policy*, vol 5, pp127–136

Halleux, J. F., Velghe, R. and Pype, J. (2006) 'The development of the Kyoto Protocol and European Union Emissions Trading Scheme Registry Systems', *Revue E tijdschrift*, vol 122, no 4, pp29–34

Henry, L. A. and Sundstrom, L. M. (2007) 'Russia and the Kyoto Protocol: Seeking an alignment of interests and image', *Global Environmental Politics*, vol 7, no 4, pp47–69

Hepburn, C., Grubb, M., Neuhoff, K., Matthes, F. and Tse, M. (2006) 'Auctioning of EU ETS phase II allowances: How and why?', *Climate Policy*, vol 6, no 1, pp137–160

Hillman, M. and Fawcett, T. (2004) *How We Can Save the Planet*, Penguin Books, London

IPCC (1999) *Aviation and the Global Atmosphere*, Cambridge University Press, Cambridge

Lees, E. (2006) 'Evaluation of the Energy Efficiency Commitment 2002–2005', Report to Defra, Eoin Lees Energy

Levine, M. D., Ürge-Vorsatz, D., Blok, K., Geng, L., Harvey, D. and 8 others (2007) 'Residential and commercial buildings', in *Climate Change 2007: Mitigation*, Contribution of Working Group III to the Fourth Assessment Report of the Intergovernmental Panel on Climate Change, Cambridge University Press, Cambridge

Luypaert, N. and Brohé, A. (2006) 'Les plans d'allocations de quotas en Belgique: Entre objectif environnemental et réalisme économique', *Revue E tijdschrift*, vol 122, no 4, pp22–28

Matthews, L. (2007) 'Memorandum of evidence to the UK House of Commons Environmental Audit Committee', www.capandshare.org/download_files/C&S_EAC_submission.pdf, accessed 1 March 2009

Mitchell, C. and Connor, P. (2004) 'Renewable energy policy in the UK 1990–2003', Centre for Management under Regulation, Warwick Business School, University of Warwick

NERA (2004) 'Review of the first and second years of the UK Emissions Trading Scheme', Defra, UK

Pavan, M. (2008) 'Not Just Energy Savings: Emerging Regulatory Challenges from the Implementation of Tradable White Certificates', Proceedings of ACEEE Summer Study on Energy Efficiency in Buildings

Peeters, M. (2003) 'Emissions trading as a new dimension to European environmental law: The political agreement of the European Council on greenhouse gas allowance trading', *European Environmental Law Review*, vol 12, no 3, pp82–92

Sijm, J., Neuhoff, K. and Chen, Y. (2006) 'CO_2 cost pass-through and windfall profits in the power sector', *Climate Policy*, vol 6, no 1, pp49–72

Soleille, S. (2006) 'Greenhouse gas emission trading schemes: A new tool for the environmental regulator's kit', *Energy Policy*, vol 34, no 13, pp1473–1477

Sorrell, S., O'Malley, E., Shleich, J. and Scott, S. (2004) *The Economics of Energy Efficiency: Barriers to Cost-Effective Investment*, Edward Elgar, Cheltenham

Vertis Environmental Finance (2008) www.vertisfinance.com, accessed 20 October 2008

Vine, E. and Hamrin, J. (2008) 'Energy savings certificates: A market-based tool for reducing greenhouse gas emissions', *Energy Policy*, vol 36, pp467–476

Chapter 5

US Carbon Markets

Introduction

The election of President Barack Obama to the White House in Washington DC represents a structural shift in climate policy in the United States strongly favouring the development of emissions trading in America. This is especially significant as America is one of the largest emitters of GHGs in the world and the system developed there will exert a powerful influence in other markets in Europe and elsewhere.

While America pioneered emissions trading in its regulation of sulfur dioxide from around 1990 (Feldman and Raufer, 1987), the development of a national carbon market has been slow to emerge. However, recent federal inaction has not meant the complete stalling of America's engagement with CO_2 emissions trading. Over the last decade, lack of progress at a national level with emissions trading has often masked to the international community action being taken at a state level. In addition to establishing three regional emission trading schemes, also including some provinces in Canada, at least 17 states have established state-wide emissions targets, often in vigorous competition with one another. For example, the state of New York has instituted a 5 per cent cut in emissions by 2010 (relative to 1990) and many of the New England states have targets to reduce emissions by 10 per cent by 2020 (again, relative to 1990). A number of states (such as California, Florida, New Mexico, Oregon, Massachusetts and Vermont) have also adopted 2050 targets ranging from cuts of 75 per cent to 85 per cent (relative to 1990). Moreover, in recent years, a number of carbon trading bills have been debated in Congress and several regional cap-and-trade schemes have emerged. These include the Regional Greenhouse Gas Initiative (RGGI), the Western Climate Initiative and the Midwestern Greenhouse Gas Accord and will encompass most of America's emissions when fully implemented.

These initiatives are likely to be brought into focus around a new economy-wide national emissions trading system with the long-term aim of reducing national emissions by 80 per cent by 2050 (White House, 2009). This is likely to take either two broad forms – one that coordinates the existing nascent regional trading schemes from the bottom up, or alternatively implements a new scheme top-down from the federal level to the states. A tension here may be emerging between the ability of states to take stronger action based on regional consensus, reflecting more local contingencies and the benefits from coordinated action, such as avoiding carbon leakage between states.

Some have argued that the new President's energy policy aspires to represent a 'Green New Deal' reminiscent of Franklin D. Roosevelt's plan to reform the economy and banking sector after the Great Depression in 1933. Roosevelt's New Deal was characterized by transformative reforms such as the institution of the first social security system, radical new banking regulations and massive public spending (and government debt) on infrastructure through the Tennessee Valley Authority.

Emissions trading is only one part of the Obama–Biden New Energy plan. In this initial plan the new administration also aims to spend $150 billion over 10 years and create 5 million jobs in clean energy, put 1 million plug-in hybrid cars on the road by 2015 and have 10 per cent of electricity coming from renewable energy by 2012. These reforms are closely related to America's energy security goals to reduce reliance on imported oil (especially from Russia, the Middle East and Venezuela). Indeed, energy security should be considered alongside climate policy to have a full appreciation for how emissions trading may develop.

America has now adopted a new vision for the future. History will judge the extent to which it fulfils its ambitions. In this chapter, we trace the contribution of emissions trading in America's first steps along this path to a clean and secure energy future.

Political context

The pre-Kyoto period

For many years, the US was the largest GHG emitter in the world only recently surpassed by China. While the US is home to 5 per cent of the

Earth's population, it produces approximately 20 per cent of the world's anthropogenic GHGs[1] (Bang et al, 2007). In 2006, the most recent year of data, America's emissions were $7054MtCO_2e$ and had increased 14.7 per cent since 1990. As such, the world has looked to the US to assume a leadership position on climate change, just as it has typically done in other areas of international relations.

In the early 1990s, President George H. W. Bush supported global action on GHGs, signing the UNFCCC treaty in October 1992, five months after the Earth Summit in Rio with a two thirds approval in the Senate. This treaty committed signatory governments to a 'non-binding aim' to reduce atmospheric concentrations of GHGs. More fundamental for the subsequent negotiations, it enshrined the principle of 'common but differentiated responsibilities' between developed and developing nations in the effort to reduce global GHG emissions. The first Bush administration was also an active supporter of cap-and-trade policies to solve environmental problems, supporting the 1990 amendments to the Clean Air Act, which were the first legal actions establishing a mandatory emissions trading scheme.

The Clinton–Gore administration started its mandate in 1992 with ambitious plans for domestic GHG emissions reductions, in particular with a proposal for a British thermal unit (BTU)-based tax on energy fuels. This tax would have internalized the cost to society arising from the use of fossil fuels, raising revenue that could then be funnelled to encouraging resource conservation. The administration's proposal was met with strong opposition as numerous interest groups fought hard to weaken the legislation's chances of success, and was eventually defeated in the Senate Finance Committee (Lisowski, 2002, p167). As a result, the administration's subsequent effort, the 1993 Climate Change Action Plan (CCAP), was based largely on voluntary programmes seeking to provide technical assistance to companies wishing to improve energy efficiency. The CCAP aimed to return US GHG emissions to 1990 levels by the year 2000 with domestic actions alone; however, it also recognized the enormous potential for cost-effective emissions reductions in other countries (Clinton and Gore, 1993). This action plan set the ground rules for a US initiative on Joint Implementation, a pilot programme that directly inspired the Kyoto Protocol flexibility mechanisms (both CDM and JI project-based mechanisms). The purpose of this programme was to:

- encourage the rapid development and implementation of cooperative, mutually voluntary projects between US and foreign partners aimed at reducing net emissions of GHGs, particularly those promoting technology cooperation with and sustainable development in developing countries and transitional economies;
- promote a broad range of cooperative, mutually voluntary projects to test and evaluate methodologies for measuring, tracking and verifying the costs and benefits of emissions reduction;
- establish an empirical basis to contribute to the formulation of international criteria for Joint Implementation;
- encourage private sector investment and innovation in the development and dissemination of technologies for reducing net emissions of GHGs; and
- encourage participating countries to adopt more complete climate protection programmes, including national inventories, baselines, policies and measures, and appropriate specific commitments.

Following the coming into force of the UNFCCC in 1994, the Clinton–Gore administration insisted on an international comprehensive approach to emissions abatement, involving sources, sinks and a basket of greenhouse gases. At the first COP (COP1) in Berlin in 1995, the parties agreed to the 'Berlin mandate', which exempted non-Annex I countries from assuming binding emissions obligations. At COP2 in Geneva in 1996, American negotiators agreed to assume 'legally binding mid-term [emissions] targets' along with the other Annex I parties.

On 25 July 1997, before the Kyoto Protocol was finalized (although it had been fully negotiated, and a penultimate draft was finished), the US Senate unanimously passed by a 95–0 vote the Byrd-Hagel Resolution (S. Res. 98, 105th US Congress), which stated that the US Senate would not ratify any protocol that did not include binding targets and timetables for developing as well as industrialized nations or that would result in serious harm to the US economy (Bang et al, 2007).

The idea of using an international system of tradable emissions permits to regulate carbon was first promulgated by American negotiators in the lead-up to Kyoto in 1997 who argued vigorously (against early resistance from the European Union) in favour of emissions trading. They supported their case, citing the successful experience of shifting away from traditional command-and-control methods for the regulation of sulfur dioxide emissions from coal plants and lead in gasoline.

The US and the Kyoto Protocol

The Byrd-Hagel Resolution, passed just five months before the Kyoto conference, effectively limited the American negotiating position there. In Kyoto, US negotiators were not able to secure quantitative commitments for developing countries inserted in the treaty. This prevented the administration from putting the Kyoto Protocol to a vote in the Senate. However, despite this failure from the US negotiators, the final version of the Protocol was shaped significantly by the US. In particular, the Kyoto Protocol came to include all the flexibility mechanisms originally proposed by the US. On 12 November 1998, Vice President Al Gore symbolically signed the Protocol. However, both Gore and Senator Joseph Lieberman indicated that the Protocol would not be submitted to the Senate for ratification until there was participation by the developing nations. In 2001, President George W. Bush made clear that he would not send the 'fatally flawed' Kyoto Protocol to the Senate for ratification and that the US would not implement the Kyoto targets during his presidency (Christiansen, 2003).

The G.W. Bush years

As a presidential candidate, George W. Bush favoured a new multi-pollutant regime that would include mandatory caps on CO_2 emissions from utilities in order to curb carbon emissions. However, once elected, President Bush changed his approach, favouring voluntary initiatives. The reason for not capping GHG emissions was the fear of higher electricity prices caused by a shift from relatively cheap coal power plants to cleaner but more expensive alternatives. The Bush administration considered that 'the current uncertainty surrounding climate change implies that a realistic policy should involve a gradual, measured response, not a risky, precipitous one' (Council of Economic Advisors, 2002, quoted in Christiansen, 2003). Compared to 'an arbitrary short-term emission limit (i.e. absolute cap)', such an approach would offer 'insurance consistent with existing climate science without putting the economy at risk' (Council of Economic Advisors, 2002, quoted in Christiansen, 2003).

In February 2002, the Bush administration launched its Global Climate Change Initiative. The key policy goal of this plan was to reduce the GHG intensity of the US economy, measured as GHG emissions per unit of total gross domestic product, by 18 per cent over the period 2002–2012. According to President Bush, meeting this goal would be 'comparable to the average progress that nations participating in the Kyoto protocol are required to achieve'. However, many analysts considered this strategy to be equivalent to a business as usual scenario. For instance, van Vuuren et al (2002) demonstrated that the goal of an 18 per cent decline in GHG emissions intensity was largely consistent with historical trends in technology improvements and would have occurred without any initiative. Moreover, the initiative relied solely on voluntary cooperation and technology subsidies. The administration suggested that monitoring and reporting emissions should be voluntary even though establishing such procedures to ensure effective operation of emissions trading schemes and project-based mechanisms would have been essential to facilitate future linkages between American and international climate strategies (Christiansen, 2003).

On the international stage, the Bush administration entered into bilateral agreements on climate change with several industrialized and developing countries, including China, India, Japan, Australia, Canada, Italy and the European Union (EU); however, these agreements were limited to science and technology research partnerships and did not set quantitative emissions goals.

An observed shift in public opinion in the US did not lead to a change in the Bush administration's climate change policies during its second term. Although American scepticism about climate change was in the mainstream in 2000, a 2007 poll found that 84 per cent of Americans saw human activity as at least contributing to warming and that 90 per cent of Democrats, 80 per cent of independents and 60 per cent of Republicans thought immediate action was required (Broder and Connelly, 2007). The impact of the American documentary film *An Inconvenient Truth* certainly played a crucial role in this opinion shift toward recognition of global warming as a major issue with serious implications for human life. In 2007, the Nobel Peace Prize was awarded to the IPCC and Al Gore for their wide-reaching efforts to draw attention to the dangers of global warming.

At the end of 2007, President Bush signed the Energy Independence and Security Act of 2007. The law called for a number of energy improvements in the American economy, including new efficiency and environmental standards for cars (the first increase in fuel economy standards since the 1970s),[2] appliances and fuel sources. The legislation will increase fuel efficiency standards for cars and trucks by 40 per cent, from 25 to 35 miles per gallon (or from 9.4l/100km to 6.7l/100km) by 2020. However, these measures alone are insufficient to reverse the US emission trends. In December 2007 Gore was very critical of the Bush years and noted it was 'unfortunate' that the US 'has been the principal obstacle to progress in solving the climate crisis' (Gore, quoted in Jordan, 2007).

Though the Bush administration has consistently opposed any kind of mandated limitation on US GHG emissions, systematically and erroneously confusing a cap on emissions with a limit on economic growth, there have been a number of legislative cap-and-trade proposals designed specifically to address GHG emissions in Congress. In the following section we introduce the most recent bills, which have catalysed the legislative debate on the issue. These are the bills that set the scene for the development of emissions trading under the 111th Congress and Obama Presidency. Further, this lack of decisive Congressional action and presidential leadership has driven cities, states, regions and even individual businesses[3] to call openly and directly for binding federal limits.

Unlike the international system embraced in the UNFCCC, the US has generally taken a 'voluntary' approach to regulating emissions. Although this 'voluntary' theme originated in the Congress in the early 1990s (as President George H. W. Bush supported stronger action), it has since switched to the executive, where President George W. Bush pushed for voluntary measures and Congress increasingly suggested government intervention. Similarly, Congress has shifted from being the obstacle to US participation in international climate agreements in the 1990s (when it refused to ratify the Kyoto Protocol) to being the impetus, seeing the introduction of numerous bills and proposals establishing national cap-and-trade systems since the early 2000s (see below).

Federal cap and trade bills since 2007

Introduction

All proposed climate change legislation has shared common features. First, each requires the US Environmental Protection Agency (EPA) to promulgate an annual national cap on the emissions of the GHGs listed in the Kyoto Protocol (note that these Acts do not refer to the Protocol but enumerate the same six gases or family of gases) and use the GWP set out by the UNFCCC to convert them into a CO_2 equivalent. Second, all call for the national cap to decline over a period of years according to a defined schedule designed to keep the atmospheric emissions levels below those predicted to cause abrupt or runaway climate change. During the 110th Congress (3 January 2007 – 3 January 2009), ten economy-wide cap-and-trade bills were proposed (Pew Center, 2008a). Here we present the five most recent proposals from the Senate and the five most recent from the House of Representatives, in chronological order.

Box 5.1 US federal legislative process

The two chambers of the US Congress work in parallel to develop, debate and pass new laws, introducing hundreds of proposals in the Senate and House of Representatives each year – but with only a few becoming federal law. A proposal must overcome several procedural stages before it can be sent to the President's desk for signature into law. After a proposal is submitted in a chamber, it is referred to one or more committees with jurisdiction over the bill's subject. The main committees with jurisdiction over climate policy are the Environment and Public Works Committee in the Senate and the Energy and Commerce Committee in the House (Hight and Silva-Chávez, 2008, p28).

The chairs of the relevant committees, who are members of the majority party, decide whether the committee will consider the proposal. If a committee chooses not to consider a proposal, it 'dies' in committee and proceeds no further in the legislative process. If the committee chooses to consider a proposal, it gathers information enabling it to decide whether to approve or reject the proposal.[4] If a committee approves a legislative proposal, it is sent to the full Senate or House membership for consideration and is debated according to each chamber's rules.[5] Once a bill is approved by one house, it is sent to the other, which may pass, reject or amend it. In order for the bill to become law, both houses must agree to identical versions of the bill, which is arranged in conference committee (including members of both chambers) if different versions are passed out of the House and Senate. After passage by both houses, the final version of the bill is submitted to the President, who may choose to sign the bill, thereby making it law, or veto the bill, returning it to Congress with his objections. In the latter case, the bill only becomes law if each House of Congress votes to override the veto with a two-thirds majority. Finally, the President may choose to take no action, neither signing nor vetoing the bill. In such a case, the Constitution states that the bill automatically becomes law after 10 days unless Congress adjourns (ends a legislative session) during the 10-day period, after which the bill dies. Thus, the President may veto legislation passed at the end of a congressional session simply by ignoring it – a manoeuvre known as the 'pocket veto'.

The McCain-Lieberman Climate Stewardship and Innovation Act (US Senate, 2007a)

Introduction to the proposal

In 2003, Senators Joseph Lieberman (Democrat) and John McCain (Republican) introduced the Climate Stewardship Act, the first legislative proposal to implement a national cap-and-trade programme to regulate GHG emissions.[6] The Climate Stewardship Act skipped the normal committee-based process and was instead introduced directly to the full Senate membership for a vote in October 2003, where it was rejected by a vote of 43–55. However, the number of Senators who voted in favour of the proposal demonstrated openness in the Senate toward setting a mandatory emissions cap (Hight and Silva-Chávez, 2008, p18). Many of its key provisions – including cap-and-trade, banking and the use of offsets to lower compliance costs – became foundations for subsequent proposals to tackle US GHG emissions. The original Climate Stewardship Act sought to reduce emissions to 2000 levels by 2010 by capping emissions from the electricity, transportation, industrial and commercial sectors and by allowing trading of emission rights.

Under a slightly modified title, but with similar provisions, the Climate Stewardship and Innovation Act (S. 1151) was reintroduced to a new Congress in 2005. This Act essentially included the same aspects as the 2003 version, and in addition called for the federal government to play a stronger role in researching and commercializing new energy technologies, including nuclear power plants. Further, it would have capped the 2010 aggregate emissions level for the covered sectors at 2000 levels. It eventually failed in the summer of 2005 as Republicans opposed it by a 49–6 margin and Democrats supported it 37–10.

Yet another version of the Climate Stewardship and Innovation Act (S. 280) was presented in 2007 and involved the provision for the emissions cap, immobile in previous incarnations, to be gradually reduced. Here we will analyse this version, of which both presidential candidates John McCain and Barack Obama were co-sponsors.

Scope

The programme in the 2007 version involves all six Kyoto gases. It requires specific, named entities that own or control an emissions source in the electric power, industrial and commercial sectors of the US economy to submit to the EPA, beginning in 2012, one tradable allowance for every metric tonne of GHGs emitted. The proposal suggests the inclusion of the transportation sector and controlled upstream (i.e. at the refineries), while the electric utilities and other large sources would be controlled down-stream (i.e. closer to the point of emissions).

Cap and allocation

In this proposal, all major sectors of the American economy would be required to reduce GHG emissions to 2004 levels by 2012. After this the cap would be lowered gradually to reach one third of 2004 levels by 2050. This effectively mandates emission reductions to 2004 levels by 2012, 1990 levels by 2020, 20 per cent below 1990 by 2030 and 60 per cent below 1990 by 2050.

Allowance allocation would be split between free allocation and auctioning as determined by the EPA administrator, taking into consideration such issues as consumer impact and competitiveness, however, no detailed plan has yet been articulated.

Penalties, offsets and other volatility control mechanisms

Any covered entity that fails to comply for a year would be liable to a civil penalty equalling three times the market value (determined on the last day of the year at issue) of the tradable allowances necessary for the entity to meet its requirements on the date of the emission that resulted in the violation. Under this proposal, tradable allowances may be sold, exchanged, purchased, retired, borrowed (with a 5-year forward limit and interest payable) or offset.

The proposal sets a 30 per cent limit on the use of offsets. The different types of offsets that would be recognized under the scheme include:

- allowances from another nation's market if specific criteria are met (completeness, accuracy and transparency of the other nation's system; enforceable limit in the other nation; withdrawing of the allowance in the other nation's market);
- registered net increase in sequestration;
- registered reduction by a person that is not a covered entity;
- international credits.

International credits are tradable allowances earned from developing countries' activities that result in 'certified emissions reductions'. Note that even if the name of the credits is exactly the same as the Clean Development Mechanism, this proposal does not mention the Kyoto Protocol. This means that its CERs are not automatically fungible with CERs issued by the CDM Executive Board. Note that the proposal allows for a future linking with the CDM as it states that the tradability with reductions earned under other similar international programmes should be ensured.

Other aspects

The bill also includes provisions intended to encourage the development and deployment of low-carbon energy technologies before the cap would take effect in 2010. These provisions include support for cleaner vehicles and fuels, as well as power generation options including coal gasification and nuclear generation.

The Sanders-Boxer Global Warming Pollution Reduction Act (US Senate, 2007b)

Introduction to the proposal

The Global Warming Pollution Reduction Act was also introduced in January 2007, and amends the Clean Air Act by including provisions regulating GHG emissions. According to the authors, it works with caps but does not necessarily use trade – allowing the exchange of allowances but not relying upon it – and primarily encourages technological development and improvements.

Scope

This programme targets all six Kyoto gases. Notably, the car industry will be required to meet emissions standards, including every car manufactured from 2016. In the electricity sector, it is also proposed that all generation units would have to meet an emission standard similar to a new combined-cycle natural gas generating unit.

Cap and allocation

This bill proposes to cap emissions at 2010 levels, gradually tightening it back to 1990 levels by 2020. Thereafter, the proposal becomes more ambitious than the McCain-Lieberman Bill, requiring reductions by 27 per cent below 1990 levels by 2030. In 2040, emissions should then decrease by an additional 27 per cent below 1990 levels, and in 2050 emissions should finally reach 80 per cent below the reference year. As with the 2007 Climate Stewardship and Innovation Act, the EPA will split allowance allocation between free allocation and auctioning.

Penalties, offsets and other volatility controls mechanisms

There are specific penalties for utilities that fail to meet their target. Again, because trading is not a major feature of this proposal, little information on the compliance aspects that usually form the cornerstone of an efficient carbon market exist in the legislation, although the proposal does provide for offsets generated from biological sequestration. A safety valve called the 'technology-indexed stop price' in the proposal exists within this legislation. If the price of an allowance rises above the technology-indexed stop price, the cap remains stagnant and does not decline until either the price drops below the stop level or three years passes, whichever occurs first.

Other aspects

The programme may recognize early reductions if they are made under state or local laws.

The Kerry-Snowe Global Warming Reduction Act (US Senate, 2007c)

Introduction to the proposal

The bipartisan Kerry-Snowe Act of 2007 is another demonstration of the strong support in the US Senate for a cap-and-trade system designed to tackle rising US emissions.

Scope

As with the previously mentioned proposals, this legislation accounts for all six Kyoto gases; however, special attention is paid to the electricity sector, for which it outlines requirements regarding energy efficiency and peak load reduction. Further, the bill directly mandates that the US generate 20 per cent of its electricity from renewable sources by 2020.

Cap and allocation

If passed, the bill would require that the US cap emissions at 2010 levels and then reduce them gradually. The first target would be to reduce emissions to the 1990 level in 2020. After that, an annual reduction of 2.5 per cent would be implemented until 2029, followed by a 3.5 per cent reduction per year between 2030 and 2050. Overall, the ambition is to emit 62 per cent fewer GHGs than the 1990s level in 2050. The split between auctioning and free allocation is not specified in the proposal, with the (as-yet) unspecified amount of auctioned allowances to be determined by the President.

Penalties, offsets and other volatility control mechanisms

The civil penalty amount for each quantity of uncovered emissions would equal twice the market price for an allowance as of 31 December of the calendar year in which allowances were missing. The Kerry-Snowe programme would support sequestration in the forest and agricultural sectors. However, the proposal does not define the overall role of offsetting in helping to reduce the cost of compliance, nor does it include rules to limit price volatility.

Other aspects

A fund for technology, research and development would be set up to encourage environmentally friendly innovation. Standards for vehicles, energy efficiency and renewable energy would play a pre-eminent role. The Kerry-Snowe bill would also require issuers of securities to disclose to investors certain climate change-related risks to the issuer.

The Bingaman-Specter Low Carbon Economy Act (US Senate, 2007d)

Introduction to the proposal

The Bingaman-Specter Act is a bipartisan cap-and-trade. It aims to achieve a significant emissions reduction level while benefiting and protecting both employment and consumers. Although this proposal gained media attention in the summer of 2007, it is no longer at the centre of the Senate climate debate following the release of the Lieberman-Warner proposal (see below). However, as chairman of the energy committee, Senator Bingaman is expected to play a key role in any future climate change policy in the US (Rosenzweig et al, 2008).

Scope

The act takes into account all six Kyoto gases, and regulates oil and natural gas producers, coal consumers and non-CO_2 GHG producers by targeting natural gas and petroleum emissions upstream and coal emissions downstream.

Cap and allocation

The cap-and-trade proposal does not impose emissions controls until 2012, by 2020 it requires that emissions return to 2006 levels and by 2030 emissions must drop to 1990 levels.

The bill initially provides for a free allocation of roughly three quarters (76 per cent) of available allowances, requiring that the remaining 24 per cent be sold via an auction. The proceeds of the auction are proposed to be earmarked for for technology research, development and deployment, and climate change adaptation. Under the proposed bill, auctioning would rise from 24 per cent during the 2012–2017 period to 53 per cent in 2030.

Penalties, offsets and other volatility control mechanisms

As in the McCain-Lieberman Bill, any covered entity that fails to submit allowances (or credits or a 'Technology Accelerator Payment' (TAP) in lieu of an allowance) would be liable for a civil penalty, equal to three times the TAP price for that calendar year. The Technology Accelerator Payment's goal is to limit economic uncertainty and price volatility. In practice, the government would allow firms to make a payment at a fixed price in lieu of submitting allowances. This fee – the 'Technology Accelerator

Payment' – starts at $12 per metric tonne of CO_2e in the first year of the programme and rises steadily each year thereafter at 5 per cent above the rate of inflation. If technology improves rapidly and if additional GHG reduction policies are adopted, the TAP option will never be engaged. Conversely, if technology improves less rapidly than expected and programme costs exceed predictions, companies could make a payment into an 'Energy Technology Deployment Fund' at the TAP price, to cover some or all of their allowance submission requirements. This safety-valve provision is unique among the proposed cap-and-trade bills and might inspire future initiatives.

Domestic offsets would include biosequestration and industrial offsets. Some international systems would also be authorized to offset internal emissions but with a 10 per cent limit.

Other aspects

Under this proposal, major incentives would be given to plants equipped with CCS. For every ton of CO_2 sequestered, one credit would be automatically allocated. This system would also be applied to facilities built or retrofitted by 2030, but only during the first 10 years of their operation. Overall, $25 billion a year technology fund would be established for R&D into improved technologies and adaptation measures. 20 per cent of this fund would support the 'dual goals' of export promotion and emissions reduction in rapidly developing countries. In order to encourage prompt action, 1 per cent of allowances would be given free of charge to those registering GHG reductions before enactment.

The Boxer-Lieberman-Warner Climate Security Act of 2008 (US Senate, 2008)

Introduction to the proposal

The Lieberman-Warner Climate Security Act was the first cap-and-trade legislation to be approved by the Senate Committee on Environment and Public Works (US Senate, 2007e). The proposal is an amalgamation of several cap-and-trade bills developed in the Senate in 2006/2007. On 6 June 2008, the bill fell a dozen votes short of the 60-vote threshold it needed to overcome a Republican filibuster despite strong bipartisan support.[7] The 48–36 vote for the climate bill came after fierce debate in which opponents charged that it would damage the US economy and drive up gasoline and other energy prices. Democratic supporters of the measure accused Republicans of spreading misinformation about it. The legislation collapsed for a variety of reasons, including the poor timing of debate about the bill, which occurred while much of the country was focused on record-high $4-a-gallon gasoline. On 2 June the White House issued a statement pledging to veto the bill. According to President Bush, 'S. 3036 and the Boxer Amendment would, in effect, constitute one of the largest tax and spend bills in our Nation's history, costing Americans dramatically more than the BTU energy tax proposals rejected by the Congress in 1993' (White House Office of Management and Budget, 2008). The White House predicted that the bill would jeopardize US competitiveness and drive jobs abroad, often simply creating carbon leakages to other countries. Although the proposal was blocked, it will probably serve as a foundation for future legislative proposals, along with the draft proposal introduced by Representatives Dingell and Boucher in the House of Representatives (Hight and Silva-Chávez, 2008, p4). It also highlights how powerful the argument of carbon leakage plays out on the political stage and foreshadows proposals that look to address this issue through border-tariff proposals.

Scope

This proposal regulates GHG emissions released by large coal consumers, natural gas and petroleum processors, producers and importers, and producers of hydrochlorofluorocarbon refrigerants. The proposal's authors estimate that emissions from these sectors represent approximately 80 per cent of US GHG emissions. Emissions for transport fuels and natural gas would be controlled upstream (i.e. at the point of bulk sale of the fuels such as the refineries), while large emitters would be included downstream (i.e. closer to the point of emissions). There would be a separate HFC cap.

Cap and allocation

The proposal would cap GHG emissions from covered sources starting from 2012. The proposal aims to reduce emissions from covered facilities to 19 per cent below 2005 levels by 2020, and to 71 per cent below 2005 levels by 2050. It would set the first cap at 5775MtCO$_2$e in 2012 (4 per cent below the business as usual emissions projections).

Like the Lieberman-Warner bill, it initially provides a free allocation of roughly three quarters of available allowances for affected industries and special purposes, while auctioning the remaining quarter. The percentage of auctioned allowances would start at 21.5 per cent in 2012 and increase gradually to 69.5 per cent by 2031 onwards. Proceeds are to be earmarked for energy technology development, assistance for low- and middle-income energy consumers, climate change adaptation efforts in the US, and programmes to support energy independence and national security. The proposal would also establish a minimum reserve price for allowances to be sold each year in the auction. In 2012 the minimum reserve price would be $10 and would increase each year by 5 per cent above the annual inflation rate.

From 2012 to 2030, 19 per cent of the allowance account would be allocated free to electric power generators, 10 per cent to manufacturers, 2 per cent to fuel producers or importers, 1 per cent to rural electric cooperatives and 4 per cent to carbon capture and sequestration (CCS) activities. From 2012 to 2017, 5 per cent of allowances would be allocated to early actors. Roughly 30.5 per cent of allowances would be set aside from 2012 to 2050 for other entities, including states, load-serving entities and others.

Penalties, offsets and other volatility control mechanisms

Under this proposal, any covered facility that fails for any year to submit to one or more of the emission allowances is liable to pay an excess emissions penalty. The amount per missing allowance would be 'the greater of $200 or a dollar figure representing 3 times the mean market value of an emissions allowance during the calendar year for which the emissions allowances were due'. Offsets represent a central element of this proposal, since covered entities would be able to use different categories of offsets to meet up to 30 per cent of their annual emissions obligations.

The proposal would establish a programme to encourage farmers and foresters to generate income through the creation of certified domestic offset credits (for activities such as planting trees or engaging in farming practices that increase soil carbon). Installations could use these (domestic) credits to meet up to 15 per cent of their annual commitment. If the quantity of domestic offsets available is less than 15 per cent, the EPA administrator may allow installations to make up the difference with international emission allowances from countries with mandatory programmes and from international forest carbon credits. If the 15 per cent limit is not reached, an entity could carry over its unused domestic allowance quota into the next calendar year. In addition to the domestic offset provision, the proposal allows covered facilities to use international offset credits and international emissions allowances. The quantity of international offset credits (i.e. those generated through the Clean Development Mechanism and Joint Implementation provisions of the Kyoto Protocol) that an installation could use for compliance each year would be limited to 5 per cent of the installation's emissions cap for that year. If the quantity of international offset credits available were less than 5 per cent, the EPA administrator may permit allowances from countries with mandatory GHG programmes. If the 5 per cent limit were not reached, an installation may carry over its unused international allowance quota into the next calendar year.

The proposal also contains a programme to create offset credits for reductions in international deforestation. To be eligible a country must adopt a national commitment to reduce deforestation, and emissions accounting must be done at the national level. Installations would be able to use international forest carbon credits generated by these types of national programmes to meet 10 per cent of their annual commitments.

Trading and banking allowances would be unrestricted. Allowance borrowing would be limited to 15 per cent of an installation's compliance obligation for each calendar year, and allowances could be borrowed from compliance years no further than 5 years in the future. In addition, a 10 per cent annual interest rate would be applied to the repayment of borrowed allowances.

The proposal would also set up an annual 'cost containment auction' in which firms could buy a limited number of emissions allowances borrowed from the programme's later years if allowance prices rise above expected levels. Allowances borrowed from the emissions caps of 2030–2050 would be available for purchase at this auction at a predetermined 'cost containment auction price'. In 2012, this price would be between $22 and $30 and from this point on rise at 5 per cent above the annual inflation rate. If allowances were sold through the cost containment auction, 70 per cent of proceeds would be used to achieve make-up emissions reductions outside the cap and the remaining 30 per cent would be used for low-income assistance.

While this flexibility with forward borrowing and banking allows polluters to smooth the impact of the emissions trading scheme over time, if not carefully managed it could undermine the scheme's environmental integrity. For instance, firms may borrow from future years only to subsequently lobby for additional permits when their reduced allowances come through at a future date.

To control these risks to environmental integrity, the proposal would also limit the total number of allowances that could be sold in any given year under the cost containment auction. This limit would start at 8 per cent of the total allowance pool in 2012, and decrease by 1 per cent from each previous year's limit. Beginning in 2022, unused allowances in the cost containment auction pool would be returned to the general allowance account for sale.

The Boxer-Lieberman-Warner Climate Security Act is quite original as it is the only cap-and-trade proposal that would set a floor price. The minimum price would start at $10 per ton, rising by a 5 per cent each year above the inflation rate. If allowance costs fall below this floor price, the EPA is instructed to tighten the cap by reducing the number of allowances issued each year (so that the provision remains revenue neutral for the government).

Other aspects

The proposal also addresses the issue of carbon leakages through an 'international reserve allowance'. Beginning in 2014, importers of primary goods from countries that do not have comparable GHG controls to the US would be required to purchase special international reserve allowances to compensate for the GHG emissions associated with the production of their exports to the US. These allowances would be separate from and additional to the annual allowance cap. International allowances from acceptable carbon markets in other countries or approved international offset credits could also be accepted in lieu of international reserve allowances.

Box 5.2 Emissions trading and border tariff adjustments

These 'international reserve allowances' follow the logic of border tariff adjustments according to the degree to which carbon prices exist in exporting countries. Such provisions are designed to prevent 'carbon leakage' – when the production of goods allegedly leave a nation with a carbon constraint for another without such a constraint. They do this by taxing imports from the exporting country at a level similar to the price of carbon in the importer's domestic economy. Implementing such a system is likely to be highly controversial in the context of world trade law and runs the danger of triggering retaliatory action. For example, for Chinese exporters to America, it is likely that they would have to buy such permits (as the cost of carbon is greater in the US than in China) thus benefiting American producers of the same products (albeit at the cost of higher inflation and consumer prices). However, relative to Europe, America has lower carbon prices. If Europeans instituted a similar scheme, American exporters would find they had to face this extra trade barrier and would likely have to buy the European equivalent of 'international reserve allowances' themselves. Such border tariff adjustments also run the risk of being used for political purposes, rather than environmental, to lock certain countries out of international trade.

This demonstrates why caution should be exercised when considering the use of border tariff adjustments. In theory, using what economists call partial equilibrium analysis, it makes good sense to impose the full (environmental) costs of imports on foreign producers' exports. In practice, however there is already a wide range of implicit carbon prices across countries that can confound the powerful argument of this simple analysis. More concerning still is that such 'adjustments' would become a servant of trade protectionism rather than the environment – damaging the welfare of the average citizen for the privilege of a few highly organized industry groups.

The Boxer-Lieberman-Warner proposal also draws from the voluntary Carbon Disclosure Project (CDP, 2008) as it would require the Securities and Exchange Commission (SEC) to direct securities issuers to inform investors of material risks related to climate change. A final additional feature of the proposal is that it would provide bonus allocations for carbon capture and storage and for renewable projects.

The Olver-Gilchrest Climate Stewardship Act of 2007 (US House of Representatives, 2007a)

Introduction

The bipartisan Climate Stewardship Act was introduced in March 2004 by Representatives Wayne Gilchrest (Republican) and John W. Olver (Democrat), and is the House companion of the bill introduced in the Senate by Senators Lieberman and McCain in 2003. In addition, the 2007 version is a companion bill of S. 280 Climate Stewardship and Innovation Act but with reduced aid for new technologies.

Scope

The Olver-Gilchrest bill covers all six Kyoto gases. The transport sector would be regulated upstream (for example, at the point of sale of fuel by refineries) while electric utilities and large sources would be controlled downstream (closer to the point of emissions). All entities would be allowed to register their GHG emissions reductions and benefit from sequestrations achievements made since 1990 and before 2012. This caveat also applies to non-covered entities.

Cap and allocation

The medium targets of this proposal are similar to those in the McCain-Lieberman proposal (i.e. 2004 emission levels by 2012 and 1990 levels by 2020). The 2030 and 2050 targets are a bit more ambitious than the companion bill in the Senate, at 22 per cent and 70 per cent below 1990 levels respectively (compared with the 20 per cent and 60 per cent targets in the Senate bill). As in the McCain-Lieberman proposal, the EPA administrator would determine the split between auctioning and free allocation.

Penalties, offsets and other volatility control mechanisms

The penalty system is also similar to that developed in the McCain-Lieberman proposal, with it equalling three times the market value of the tradable allowances, as determined on the last day of the year at issue. The various types of offsets credits are also similar, but this bill is more stringent as it would limit the use of offsets to 15 per cent (only half of the limit in the Senate companion bill). Borrowing would be allowed for a period of 5 years at an as yet undetermined interest rate. Banking of allowances would also be allowed.

Table 5.1 *Comparative table of the Bills in Senate*

	McCain–Lieberman S. 280	Sanders–Boxer S. 309	Kerry–Snowe S. 485	Bingaman–Specter S. 1766	Lieberman–Warner S. 2191
Scope	Upstream for transportation; downstream for large sources (incl. electric utilities)	Point of regulation not specified	Point of regulation not specified	Upstream for natural gas and petroleum; downstream for coal	Upstream for transport fuels and natural gas; downstream for large coal users and GHG manufacturers; separate HFC cap
Cap	2004 level in 2012; 1990 level in 2020; 20% below 1990 in 2030; 60% below 1990 in 2050	2010 level in 2010; 1990 level in 2020; 27% below 1990 in 2030; 53% below 1990 in 2040; 80% below 1990 in 2050	2010 level in 2010; 1990 level in 2020; 2.5%/year reduction from 2020–2029; 3.5%/year reduction from 2030–2050; 62% below 1990 in 2050	2012 level in 2012; 2006 level in 2020; 1990 level in 2030; President may set long-term target ≥60% below 2006 level by 2050	4% below 2005 in 2012; 19% below 2005 in 2020; 71% below 2005 in 2050

Allocation	Split between free allocation and auctioning determined by Administrator	Cap and trade permitted but not required	Split between free allocation and auctioning determined by President	Some sector allocations are specified including: 9% to states, 53% to industry; Increasing auction: 24% 2012–2017, rising to 53% in 2030; 5% of allowance set aside for agriculture	Sector allowances total 75.5% in 2012; Increasing auction: 24.5% in 2012 rising to 58.75% 2032–2050; 4.25% set-aside for domestic agriculture and forestry
Offsets and other volatility control mechanisms	30% limit on use of offsets. 3 types of offsets (international, domestic and sequestration); Borrowing allowed	Provision for offsets generated from biological sequestration; 'Technology-indexed stop price' freezes cap if prices high relative to technology options	Provision for offsets generated from biosequestration	Biosequestration and industrial offsets; International offsets subject to 10% limit; $12/ton CO_2e price cap starting in 2012 and increasing 5%/year above inflation	30% limit on domestic and international offsets; Creates cost-containment auction using future year allowances; Borrowing up to 15% per company

Source: Pew Center on Global Climate Change, 2008a

Other aspects

Under this proposal every entity subject to regulation under the Act would have to submit a report regarding their GHG activities and also of the products imported from outside the country that might emit GHGs. Funds and incentives for technology research and development would be available, and the proposal specifically supports appropriate climate change mitigation strategies and programmes for developing countries and poor populations. Mitigating effects on low-income citizens of the US has also been marked as an important consideration under this proposal.

The Waxman Safe Climate Act of 2007 (US House of Representatives, 2007b)

Introduction

The 2006 version of the Safe Climate Act, sponsored by Representative Henry Waxman (Democrat) of California, was the House companion bill to Boxer-Sanders. The 2007 version diverges further from the Senate bill.

Scope

While all six Kyoto gases are explicitly covered in this Climate Act, the point at which they are regulated (upstream and/or downstream) is not yet specified. On the other hand, the proposal does state that emissions from motor vehicles need to be rapidly adjusted to an acceptable standard. This hits on a tender political issue involving the 'Big Three' automakers in the US: General Motors, Chrysler and Ford. Here the tension between the priorities of securing American automotive jobs and climate policies becomes pronounced. American-made cars have traditionally been larger and less fuel efficient than cars made in Europe and Asia – driven supposedly by consumer demands for larger, safer and more powerful vehicles. However, in the aftermath of the high petrol prices of 2006 to 2008 and the 2009 economic recession – cost conscious environmentalism is emerging as more important to consumers and policy makers. This is manifesting in a range of new fuel efficiency initiatives stemming from the White House as a quid pro quo of Federal bailout funds.

Box 5.3 Hybrid cars and the US automotive industry

Shortly after his inauguration President Obama announced a national target of 1 million plug in hybrids capable of 150 miles per gallon (64km/l or 1.57 l/100km) to be on the road by 2015 along with a $7000 tax concession for purchasing an 'advanced' vehicle. At the centrepiece of a Federal bailout of carmaker General Motors was the production of the $30,000 Chevrolet Volt, which is set for release in 2010. A key competitor to the General Motors Volt is a similar plug-in hybrid made in China by BYD, reported to be available for $21,000.

Cap and allocation

The bill sets targets for a 2 per cent reduction in GHG emissions each year from 2010 to 2050. The scope of the trading scheme under the bill is as yet undefined and the bill is almost completely silent on the detailed practicalities of the carbon market it would create.

As a target the bill specifies that emissions in 2010 should not exceed 2009 levels, decreasing by 2 per cent each year so emissions reach 1990 levels by 2020. Between 2020 and 2050 the cap would be tightened by 5 per cent each year with the goal that by 2050 emissions levels are 80 per cent below 1990 emissions. The President would determine the split (as yet unspecified) between free allocation and auctioning.

Penalties, offsets and other cost control

No provisions have been articulated dealing with penalties, offsets, or cost control instruments.

Other aspects

Early reductions would be recognized and rewarded. There would be standards for vehicles, efficiency and renewables. Beginning in 2010, the bill would require an annual increase in the percentage of electricity generated from renewable sources that is sold at the retail level in the US and would require this percentage to be at least 20 per cent of the total electricity sold by 2020. It would allow suppliers to achieve the targets through a market-based trading system (like the Tradable Green Certificates scheme in several

European countries). This 20 per cent target for renewables is similar to the EU target.

The Markey Investing in Climate Action and Protection Act (US House of Representatives, 2008a)

Introduction

Representative Edward Markey's (Democrat) bill has received support from many environmental NGOs, including powerful groups like Environmental Defense (ED), the Natural Resources Defense Council (NRDC) and Union of Concerned Scientists (UCS). Another key feature of this bill is that it also strives to redistribute revenue to low- and middle-income Americans. By tightening the cap, auctioning all permits and distributing some of the revenue as a dividend to those with incomes less than $70,000, Markey's plan is more progressive than the widely discussed Lieberman-Warner bill.

Scope

This Act would control all six Kyoto gases plus nitrogen trifluoride (NF_3). The following covered entities would be regulated under the cap: power plants and large industrial facilities; producers or importers of petroleum and coal-based liquid or gaseous fuels; producers or importers of hydrofluorocarbons, perfluorocarbons, sulfur hexafluoride and nitrogen trifluoride; local natural gas distribution companies; and geological carbon sequestration sites. Transport fuels would be regulated at the upstream level while electric utilities and large sources would be controlled downstream.

Cap and allocation

The first target is to stabilize emissions at 2005 levels by 2012. Markey's bill then calls for reductions of 20 per cent below 2005 levels by 2020, which is 7 per cent below the 1990 level. By 2050 it should achieve reductions of 85 per cent below 2005 levels.

Agriculture, forestry and small businesses would not be included in the cap regulations; nevertheless, incentives would be provided for them to reduce their emissions. The act's main priority is to establish an allocation system based solely on auctions. Over the period 2012–2019, auctioning would account for 94 per cent of total allocations, increasing to 100 per cent after 2020. Half the proposed auction revenue would be allocated to ease the increase in energy costs on households

Penalties, offsets and other cost control

The provisions for a non-compliant entity are similar to the Lieberman-Warner proposal: any covered facility/entity that fails for any year to submit one or more of the emission allowances for which it is liable must pay an amount per missing allowance equal to 'the greater of $200 or three times the fair market value of an emission allowance during the calendar year for which the emission allowances were due'. Offsetting would be allowed within a 15 per cent limit on the use of domestic offsets and a 15 per cent limit on the use of international emissions allowances.

Further, Markey's proposal would set up an Office of Carbon Market Oversight (OCMO) within the Federal Energy Regulatory Commission (FERC) to monitor the market for allowances, derivatives and offset credits. Borrowing would be allowed for a period of five years with a 10 per cent interest rate, while notably underground sequestration of CO_2 by geological injections would be regulated under an amendment of the Safe Drinking Act.

Other aspects

The proposal also seeks to encourage individual states to undertake early actions through a new energy-efficiency fund. Any goods manufactured in a country lacking an emissions cap would not be allowed importation without purchasing allowances to cover their carbon footprint (see Box 5.2 above on border tariff adjustments). Another major tenet of the bill is the funding it would provide to clean energy technology, energy efficiency, adaptation, job training and related measures, sourced in large part from auction revenues.

The Doggett Climate MATTERS Act of 2008 (US House of Representatives, 2008b)

Introduction

The Market, Auction, Trust and Trade Emissions Reduction System Act of 2008 – also called the Climate MATTERS Act – is a proposed federal programme aiming to reduce US emissions significantly by 2050. Its originality lies in the creation of an international reserve GHG emissions allowance programme, where proceeds from allowance sales would be used to mitigate the climate change's negative impacts on disadvantaged communities in World Trade Organization (WTO) participating countries. It would also establish the International Climate Change Commission within the US to determine annually whether a WTO participant country has taken appropriate actions to limit its GHG emissions.

Scope

The six Kyoto gases would be controlled under this proposal. While transport fuels and natural gas would be controlled upstream (from the point of emission), other large emissions sources – including large coal users – would be regulated downstream (nearer the point of emission).

Cap and allocation

Under the Climate MATTERS Act, emissions are not to be regulated below business as usual until 2012. Then, however, it argues to return emissions to 1990 levels by 2020 and 80 per cent below 1990 levels by 2050.

Doggett specifies allocations by sector: in 2012 5 per cent of allowances would be distributed free of charge to power plants and 10 per cent to energy-intensive manufacturers (which would gradually decrease to zero by 2020), with the remaining part auctioned. Of the revenues generated from these auctions 85 per cent would support a Citizen Protection Trust Fund (CPTF) for consumer assistance, adaptation measures, and technology research, development and implementation. This bill excludes agriculture, forestry and small businesses from the emissions cap but would provide incentives for these sectors to reduce their emissions.

Penalties, offsets and other cost controls

The provisions for non-compliant entities are similar to those under the Lieberman-Warner and Markey bills, meaning those failing to meet their reduction liabilities must pay the greater amount between $200 and three times the market value of the missing allowance.

Offsets would be authorized to a certain degree, with an overall limit set at 25 per cent. Additional limits are proposed for the different categories of offsets: 10 per cent on domestically sourced credits, 15 per cent on international emissions allowances and 15 per cent on international forest allowances. In addition, a 'Carbon Market Efficiency Board' would be established in order to 'monitor the market and implement cost relief including increased borrowing and offsets'.

Other aspects

A Citizen Protection Trust Fund (CPTF) would provide 1 per cent of its funding in 2012 to entities taking early action on climate change, decreasing to zero by 2015. Interestingly, the cap-and-trade programme performances and targets would be subject to a triannual National Academy of Sciences review.

Dingell-Boucher Discussion Draft (US House of Representatives, 2008c)

Introduction

Even while Congress was formally in recess for the 2008 elections, energy and climate change issues continued to receive high-level attention from the House Energy and Commerce Committee. A draft was released for the consideration of the new Congress meeting in January 2009 after bringing together four separate white papers on different aspects of climate policy, and numerous hearings (Alliance to Save Energy, 2008).

Scope

As in the Markey proposal, this discussion draft would control the six Kyoto gases plus nitrogen trifluoride (NF_3). Power plants, natural gas distribution companies, producers and importers of petroleum-based and coal-based liquid fuels and other sources of GHGs such as large industrial facilities, and geological sequestration sites that emit more than 25,000 tons of CO_2 or equivalent would be included under the cap. Transport fuels would be regulated upstream (at a point where the GHG emissions of the fuel can be easily accounted for), while electric utilities and large sources would be controlled downstream (closer to the source of emissions). All together, this scheme would cover around 88 per cent of US GHG emissions.

Cap and allocation

Caps would cover emissions starting in 2012 and mandate reductions to 6 per cent below 2005 levels by 2020, 44 per cent below 2005 levels by 2030, and 80 per cent below 2005 levels by 2050. A separate cap would be established for hydrofluorocarbons.

The allocation method provides for the free allocation of permits to begin with, gradually increasing to 100 per cent auctioning by 2026. While there are several options canvassed for allocating allowances, they are generally to be given to polluters according to historical emissions. Revenue from the sale of permits is earmarked to support energy efficiency and clean technology programmes for low-income households in sectors not directly exposed to the cap (such as small business and households).

Penalties, offsets and other cost controls

Trading and banking would be allowed with no restriction, however, borrowing allowances would be limited to up to five years into the future and only up to 15 per cent of the entities total obligation. Interest would also be payable (in the form of extra allowances) on borrowing from future periods at the rate of 8 per cent.

A strategic reserve of allowances would be set aside for auction to regulated entities with a set (and rising) minimum price. Firms covered by the scheme would also be allowed to buy international allowances from countries with similarly rigorous programmes. Verified domestic offsets (GHG reductions outside the scope of the cap) or international offsets could also be used for a portion of needed allowances. The proportion of offsets allowed to be accessed from these sources start at 5 per cent of the firm's cap at the start of the programme increasing to 30 per cent by 2024. From 2025 onwards, domestic offset credits could be used to satisfy up to 20 per cent of an installation's compliance obligation and international offset credits could be used without limitation.

Similar to the Lieberman-Warner proposal in the Senate, the House draft proposal also contains a provision that would standardize the types of international forestry offsets that installations may use for compliance.

The draft proposes the creation of an International Climate Change Commission that would assess which US trading partners have 'taken comparable action to limit [their] greenhouse gas emissions'. Countries that have not taken comparable action would be required to submit 'international reserve allowances' to compensate for the carbon footprint of the products they export to the US.

Just how such proposals (see Box 5.2) will work under the rules of the World Trade Organization will be a key issue in the future of American (and other) emission trading schemes. This will hinge on the extent to which low-

(or non-existant) carbon prices constitute domestic industry protection in exporting countries. If it can be shown that lack of environmental standards constitutes trade protection this would allow importing nations to legally impose tariffs.

Box 5.4 The Shrimp Turtle Case and environmental trade restrictions

In 1998, India, Malaysia, Pakistan and Thailand brought a case against the United States in the WTO appealing against a shrimp import ban that had been placed on their exports in America. At issue was whether the exporting countries were doing enough (or at least something comparable to American shrimpers) to protect threatened turtles from being killed in their shrimping operations. The WTO appellate panel held, 'We have *not* [emphasis added] decided that the sovereign nations that are Members of the WTO cannot adopt effective measures to protect endangered species, such as sea turtles. Clearly, they can and should.' The decision means that there is a legal precedent suggesting that nations may impose trade restrictions against other countries that do not comply with global environmental norms.

(See WTO Case Numbers 58 and 61, ruling adopted on 6 November 1998.)

Other aspects

On commencement of the scheme, 3 per cent of the allowances will be made free of charge to firms that have taken early action to reduce their emissions. This is in order to dissuade firms from increasing emissions before commencement of the scheme so to maximize their initial allocations. By 2026 no such allowances will be available.

Regional initiatives

Introduction

The stalling of American action on emissions trading at the national level in the late 1990s did not mean emissions trading schemes stopped being developed entirely. In 2001, Massachusetts established a cap-and-trade programme between state utilities followed by New Hampshire in 2002.

Table 5.2 *Comparative table of the Bills in the House of Representatives*

	Olver-Gilchrest *H.R. 620*	*Waxman* *H.R. 1590*	*Markey* *H.R. 6186*	*Doggett* *H.R. 6316*	*Dingell-Boucher* *Discussion Draft*
Scope	Upstream for transportation; downstream for large sources (incl. electric utilities)	Point of regulation not specified	Upstream for transportation; downstream for large sources (incl. electric utilities)	Upstream for natural gas and petroleum; downstream for coal and large sources	Upstream for transport fuels and natural gas; downstream for electric utilities and large sources
Cap	2004 level in 2012; 1990 level in 2020; 22% below 1990 in 2030; 70% below 1990 in 2050	2009 level in 2010; 1990 level in 2020; 5%/year reduction 2020–2050; 80% below 1990 in 2050	2005 level in 2012; 20% below 2005 in 2020; 85% below 2005 in 2050	2012 level in 2012; 1990 level in 2020; 80% below 1990 in 2050	6% below 2005 in 2020; 44% below 2005 in 2030; 80% below 2005 in 2050

Allocation	Split between free allocation and auctioning determined by Administrator	Split between free allocation and auctioning determined by President	Increasing auction: 94% 2012–2019, rising to 100% 2020–2050; Over 50% of auction proceeds used for tax credits/rebates to households for increases in energy costs	5% of allowances to power plants and 10% to energy-intensive manufacturers in 2012 (transitions to zero in 2020); 85% of auction revenues directed to fund for consumer assistance, adaptation, technology, early action, etc.	Four options: 1) most value to covered entities; 2) less value to covered entities and more value to complementary GHG reduction initiatives; 3) some value to adaptation; and 4) most value to consumer rebates. All options include 100% auction by 2026
Offsets and other volatility control mechanisms	15% limit on use of offsets; 3 types of offsets (international, domestic and sequestration); Borrowing allowed with interest	Not specified	15% limit on use of domestic offsets; 15% limit on use of international offsets; Borrowing allowed with interest	Overall limit of 25% on use of offsets with further limit on types; Borrowing foreseen	Increasing use of offsets: 5% initially reaching 35% by 2024; Cost-containment auction using future year reserve allowances; Borrowing up to 15% per company with interest.

Source: Pew Center on Global Climate Change, 2008a

These early experiments prompted other states to consider doing the same using their powers to regulate air emissions and environmental performance of electricity generating utilities (Rabe, 2004). This process eventually culminated in the Governor of New York, George Pataki, initiating the steps to form America's first regional cap-and-trade scheme – The Regional Greenhouse Gas Initiative.

In early 2009, three regional cap-and-trade programmes were in operation or development within the US. A total of 23 states (accounting for 36 per cent of total emissions) were full participants in these programmes, and an additional nine states were participating as observers.

Regional Greenhouse Gas Initiative

Introduction

The Regional Greenhouse Gas Initiative (RGGI) was the first mandatory US cap-and-trade programme for CO_2. The ten northeastern and mid-Atlantic states that are participating include: Connecticut, Delaware, Maine, Maryland, Massachusetts, New Hampshire, New Jersey, New York, Rhode Island and Vermont. An interesting feature of the development of

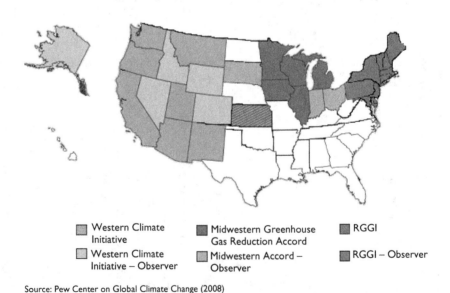

◩ Western Climate Initiative	◩ Midwestern Greenhouse Gas Reduction Accord	◩ RGGI
◻ Western Climate Initiative – Observer	◩ Midwestern Accord – Observer	◩ RGGI – Observer

Source: Pew Center on Global Climate Change (2008)

Figure 5.1 US regional initiatives

RGGI, is that it has been undertaken with relatively little consultation or support from the Federal Government (Rabe, 2008). That such a complex multijurisdictional agreement could be put in place without a powerful central bureaucracy (for example, contrast this with the EU ETS) is an important example of bottom-up climate politics at work.

On 20 December 2005, the governors of seven northeastern states (Connecticut, Delaware, Maine, New Hampshire, New Jersey, New York and Vermont) announced RGGI's creation, signing a memorandum of understanding (MOU) agreeing to implement the system over the coming years. At this stage Pennsylvania and the District of Columbia signed up as observers to the process. RGGI sets a cap on CO_2 emissions, allocates allowances via an auction and allows sources to trade emissions allowances.

In January 2007 governors of Massachusetts and Rhode Island signed the MOU, committing their states to joining the RGGI, making them the eighth and ninth states to participate. Maryland became the tenth official partici-pating state in April 2007. The first permit auction occurred in September 2008, the second in December 2008 and the third in March 2009.

These participating states negotiated state-wide caps largely based on historical emissions. Aggregated, these state caps form the regional RGGI cap in a process similar to the National Allocation Plans of the EU ETS.

Scope

RGGI sets a cap on emissions of CO_2 from fossil fuel-fired power plants of at least 25MW, covering about 225 facilities (RGGI, 2008).

Cap and allocation

The programme begins by capping emissions at 188 million short tons of CO_2 (current levels) in 2009 and after six years at this level it declines to 169 million short tons by 2018 (approx a 10 per cent reduction on current levels). The goal is to stabilize emissions between 2009 and 2014, at which point the cap will be reduced by 2.5 per cent each year between 2015 and 2018.

At least 25 per cent of each of emissions allowances must be set aside for consumer benefit programmes. This could include promoting renewable energy and energy efficiency or mitigating possible increases in energy prices to consumers. Significantly, most states are auctioning 100 per cent of emission allowances to industry. Some states (Connecticut, Maine,

Rhode Island and Vermont) have legislated that 100 per cent of auction revenue must be spent on consumer benefit programmes.

In September 2008 all 12.6 million allowances available for sale at the first auction of the US's first mandatory cap-and-trade scheme were sold. Six of the ten member states (Connecticut, Maine, Maryland, Massachusetts, Rhode Island and Vermont) participated, while the other four members did not participate, as they had not yet finalized their regulations for participation in the trading scheme. Regardless of this, all allowances purchased at the first auction may be used for compliance in any of the ten RGGI member states. Demand was almost four times higher than available supply with 59 participants from the energy, financial and environmental sectors submitting bids for nearly 52 million allowances (Trading Carbon, 2008). Bidding took place in a single-round, uniform price, sealed-bid, internet-based format. The September 2008 auction set a reserve price of $1.86 per ton of CO_2. While some had previously expressed concern that permits had been over-allocated, all 12.6 million allowances were sold at a clearing price of $3.07/short ton allowance (about €2.40/metric tonne). This low clearing price was widely anticipated, due to the general impression that the RGGI market will be 'long' (i.e. the supply of allowances is greater than the demand) in its first several years of operation (Hight and Silva-Chávez, 2008, p15). The first auction, bringing in a total of almost $39 million, was the largest carbon auction ever. This record was broken at the second auction where 31,505,898 allowances were sold for $3.38 per allowance.

Penalties, offsets and other cost controls

Covered entities are required to continuously monitor and report their emissions. Penalties for non-compliance will be enforced according to each state's rules. RGGI also allows the use of offset projects for compliance. Covered entities may use domestic carbon offsets to meet 3.3 per cent of their emissions obligations during each three-year trading phase. Offsets may be generated from five types of projects: (1) landfill methane capture and destruction; (2) reductions in emissions of sulfur hexafluoride; (3) sequestration of carbon through afforestation; (4) reduction or avoidance of CO_2 emissions from natural gas, oil or propane combustion through energy efficiency; and (5) avoided methane emissions from agricultural manure management operations. Offset projects may be located in any RGGI state or in any other state that has agreed to enforce RGGI project standards. To provide a safety valve on the upward pressure of prices, the limit on domestic offset use by RGGI participants rises to 5 per cent in the event that allowance prices exceed an average of $7/short ton (about €5/metric tonne) for 12 months. If prices exceed an average of $10/short ton (about €7/metric tonne) in a 12-month period, generators may use offsets to satisfy 10 per cent of their obligations and may purchase international offset credits (namely ERUs or CERs) to meet their responsibilities. This last provision may offer the first opportunity to link existing carbon markets with a US carbon market.

Carbon leakages are one problem that the designers of RGGI have had to grapple with (Arrandale, 2008). The problem is that while participating states can regulate electricity generated within their borders, nothing stops the importation of (potentially cheaper) electricity from non-participating states that are still linked to the grid that RGGI states draw on. Constitutionally, states are limited from restricting the flow of commerce (including electrons) across borders (Rabe, 2008). This issue is one that increased federal level involvement may help to solve.

The Western Climate Initiative (Western Climate Initiative, 2008)

Introduction

The Western Climate Initiative (WCI) plans to lay the foundation for an international cap-and-trade programme that would involve both the US and Canada. It involves the states of Arizona, California, Montana, New Mexico, Oregon, Utah and Washington, and the Canadian provinces of British Columbia, Manitoba, Ontario and Quebec. The seven US states represent about 20 per cent of the US economy, while the four Canadian provinces make up 70 per cent of the Canadian economy. Observer states include Alaska, Colorado, Idaho, Kansas, Nevada and Wyoming, Saskatchewan in Canada, and the Mexican states of Baja California, Chihuahua, Coahuila, Nuevo Leon, Sonora and Tamaulipas. Some of the participants independently have already developed a climate strategy. For instance, the largest participant, California, passed Assembly Bill 32 (signed into law in 2006) in order to reduce GHG emissions to 1990 levels by 2020 and to achieve a cut of 80 per cent of 1990 levels by 2050 (California Air Resources Board, 2008).

This law set the US's first economy-wide, binding plan to reduce emissions. Regardless of such state-wide initiatives, every participant will have to comply with the regional rules they have agreed upon under the WCI.

The WCI cap-and-trade programme is expected to cover about 90 per cent of GHG emissions in participating American states and Canadian provinces once it is fully implemented in 2015. WCI's proposed sectors and sources coverage is higher than any regional or national market-based GHG reduction mechanism currently in operation.

Scope

All six Kyoto GHGs would be covered under this programme. Starting in 2012, emissions from electricity generation,[8] combustion at industrial and commercial facilities, and GHGs from industrial processes would be covered. The emissions threshold for entities to be covered under the cap is 25,000 metric tonnes of CO_2-equivalents (CO_2e). Many smaller sources, including residential, commercial and industrial fuel combustion, fall below this individual facility threshold; further, transportation fuel will be regulated upstream starting in 2015, the beginning of the second compliance period. Emissions from carbon neutral biomass and biofuels would be excluded from the programme.

Cap and allocation

While the regional WCI cap will be the sum of all the individual partner caps, the programme's overarching goal is to reduce GHG emissions to 15 per cent below 2005 levels by 2020. To do this, the WCI regional goal remains consistent with the state and provincial goals and does not replace the individual goals. The regional cap and all partner caps will decline annually with a straight-line trajectory. The specific individual partner budgets and the combined regional budgets for the years 2012 through 2020 will be set prior to 2012, when the programme begins. The following table lists the goals that are already established in various states.

Each partner will be responsible for allocating its own allowance budget. WCI may work to develop uniform allocation schemes for certain sectors throughout all jurisdictions in order to prevent entities in some jurisdictions from having a competitive advantage over those in others. Subject to applicable laws, each WCI partner will auction at least 10 per cent of allowances from 2012 to 2020 and 25 per cent of allowances in 2020.

Table 5.3 WCI emissions reduction goals in North America states

	Short term (2010–2012)	Medium term (2020)	Long term (2040–2050)
Arizona	Not established	2000 levels by 2020	50% below 2000 by 2040
British Columbia	Not established	33% below 2007 by 2020	Not established
California	2000 levels by 2010	1990 levels by 2020	80% below 1990 by 2050
Manitoba	6% below 1990	Not established	Not established
New Mexico	2000 levels by 2012	10% below 2000 by 2020	75% below 2000 by 2050
Oregon	stop emissions growth	10% below 1990 by 2020	>75% below 1990 by 2050
Washington	Not established	1990 levels by 2020	50% below 1990 by 2050

Penalties, offsets and other cost controls

It is proposed that allowances are to be completely fungible across all WCI jurisdictions, with unlimited banking of allowances permitted. However, borrowing of allowances from future compliance periods is not allowed.

The WCI design document recommends that offsets could be used to satisfy up to 49 per cent of the emissions reductions required by the plan in any particular year. This is equivalent to approximately 1 per cent of the overall cap in 2013, increasing to 7.35 per cent of the cap in 2020. WCI Partners are to encourage offsets located in any WCI jurisdiction, but may also approve projects located anywhere in the US, Canada or Mexico, although offsets will comply with comparably rigorous monitoring and reporting. Furthermore, Kyoto's CDM may be used for compliance, however the conditions surrounding this are yet to be determined.

It is also the ultimate intention that the WCI will link in with other mandatory cap-and-trade programmes in America.

The Midwestern Regional Greenhouse Gas Reduction Accord (MGA, 2008)

Introduction

On 15 November 2007 six states and one Canadian province established the Midwestern Regional Greenhouse Gas Reduction Accord. Under the Accord, members agreed to establish regional GHG reduction targets, including a long-term target of 60–80 per cent below current emissions levels, and develop a multi-sector cap-and-trade system to help achieve the targets. The governors of Illinois, Iowa, Kansas, Michigan, Minnesota and Wisconsin, as well as the Premier of the Canadian Province of Manitoba, signed the Accord as full participants, while the governors of Indiana, Ohio and South Dakota joined the agreement as observers to participate in the development of the cap-and-trade system. The Accord represents the third regional agreement among US states to collectively reduce GHG emissions, and aims to be fully implemented within 30 months.

In early 2009, the Midwest Accord is still in its early stages. According to a recent *Climate Report* (Hight and Silva-Chávez, 2008, p16), programme designers announced that the market design will be finalized after March 2009.

Conclusion

US climate change policy is far more complex and developed than commonly thought in countries that ratified the Kyoto Protocol. The relative absence of US national action on climate policy has prompted initiatives by the Congress, regions, states and even cities. A wide variety of cap-and-trade proposals have been discussed in Congress and many subnational initiatives are under way. These are likely to converge in a long-term, collaborative effort to harmonize national policies to tackle GHG emissions (Peterson and Rose, 2006).

In many cases, national initiatives are far more compelling than a patchwork of local initiatives. As a result, it is expected that lower-level government policy structures such as those developed in the western, midwestern or northeastern states will not preclude but rather advance federal initiatives in the area of climate change (Lutsey and Sperling, 2008).

Reflecting the proposals discussed above, it is predicted that the US will probably use 2005 as the reference year for the system as opposed to 1990, and develop their own project-based (also called baseline and credits) offset system rather than relying solely on UN programmes such as the CDM. The cap's downward movement will be gradual at first, with more radical reductions occurring after 2020.

From the federal bills under discussion during the 110th Congress, we can expect a 2020 target to range anywhere from stabilization at 2006 levels (as found in the Bingaman-Specter bill) to an ambitious 19 per cent below 2005 levels (as in Boxer-Lieberman-Warner). 2050 targets are likely to be somewhere between 70 per cent and 85 per cent below 2005 levels. The new President has announced a national target of 80 per cent in January 2009 (White House, 2009).

Because transportation and domestic fuels account for a significant amount of national emissions, these are likely to be included in any federal cap-and-trade scheme. Petroleum is likely to be regulated upstream with both importers and producers as covered entities. Overall, both entities are likely to be included upstream as suppliers of products that generate emissions as well as downstream as large plants (e.g. refining process).

The allocation system will probably result in a hybrid system that includes free allocation to covered entities as well as auctioning. If banking and borrowing are to be allowed as cost-control instruments, the use of price floors and ceilings is not expected though they are present in a number of proposals (Berendt, 2008).

Current federal legislative proposals, as well as the regional and municipal initiatives, are likely to become more consolidated under the new presidency. Both throughout his campaign and in the weeks following the election, Obama has said that addressing climate change will be a significant focus of his administration, calling for an 80 per cent reduction in emissions by 2050 (against a 2005 baseline) and suggesting that 100 per cent of allowances in a federal cap-and-trade system should be auctioned. Proceeds from this auctioning would achieve a 'double dividend' as they would be funnelled to investment in renewable energy, clean technology upgrades, energy-efficiency enhancement, and assistance for low-income families coping with high energy costs. Finally, the new President has called for 10 per cent of the nation's electricity to be generated from clean sources by 2012, rising to 25 per cent in 2025.

However, the same internal obstacles and clashes that have plagued US climate policy for more than a decade will remain significant over the coming years. These include issues such as ensuring US competitiveness against countries such as China, protecting employment, and guaranteeing a sense of 'fairness' in distribution of reduction responsibilities. Energy security and geopolitics will also continue to play a major role in US climate policy as America strives to lessen dependence on oil from the Middle East, Venezuela and Russia.

While President Obama's Energy and Environment Policy (White House, 2009) sets out a new vision, it will be tempered by these forces that have made it difficult for previous administrations to realize strong action on climate change. Central to the agreement of a national emissions trading scheme is likely to be the management of competitiveness concerns with China. Embedded in many of the bills before the Senate and House are proposals to penalize imports from countries that have not instituted appropriate carbon pricing on their polluting imports, in other words – border tariffs. While at first glance, such proposals may seem to make sense in theory, such schemes should only be pursued with caution. In reality, a vast range of carbon prices already exists across the world as a product of multiple competing policy objectives and economic circumstances. Action that does not adequately take the multiplicity of factors affecting energy prices into account may run the risk of triggering a trade war under the banner of environmentalism.

Notes

1   It is only after 2006 that China, with a population more than four times the size, exceeded US emissions. As we have seen in Chapter 1, US per capita emissions are more than twice the EU average and 15 times that of India. Given their size, comparisons between Chinese and American emissions often take centre stage in climate change debate. The distinction of per capita emissions is also often brought into the debate, as the US has 5 per cent of the world's population relative to China's 22 per cent. Thus targets based on per capita emissions, as opposed to absolute emissions, are favoured by populous developing countries as a more appropriate basis for climate politics.

2   The Corporate Average Fuel Economy (CAFE) standards were enacted by Congress in 1975. These are federal regulations intended to improve the average fuel economy of cars and light trucks (trucks, vans and sport utility vehicles) sold in the US in the wake of the 1973 Oil Embargo. Overall fuel economy for both cars and light trucks in the US market was 26.7 in 2007 (US Department of Transportation, 2008).

3   The United States Climate Action Partnership (USCAP) is a coalition that includes major firms such as Shell, Chrysler and General Electric, and influential NGOs such as the Pew Center on Global Climate Change, the Environmental Defense Fund and the National Resource Defense Council. They are actively asking Congress to establish a mandatory, comprehensive GHG cap-and-trade system with a goal of reducing emissions to 60–80 per cent below 2007 levels by 2050.

4   The committee does this both by holding public hearings, to which it invites experts to share their views, and by meeting in private with stakeholder groups.

5   In the House of Representatives the debate is limited by rules established by the majority-led Rules Committee. These rules dictate who can speak and for how long. In the Senate, debate can continue for as long as Senators wish to discuss a proposal or until three fifths of the Senate membership votes to end debate. If this does not occur, a single Senator can block a proposal by 'talking it to death'.

6   The Clean Power Act of 2001 and the Clean Air Planning Act preceded the Climate Stewardship Act, but their scope was limited as they would have capped CO_2 emissions from the power sector only.

7   A filibuster is a form of obstruction in a legislature or other decision-making body. An attempt is made to infinitely extend debate upon a proposal in order to delay the progress or completely prevent a vote on the proposal taking place.

8   Including electricity imported into any WCI Partner jurisdiction.

References

Alliance to Save Energy (2008) Fact Sheet, Summary of Dingell-Boucher Climate Change Discussion Draft, October, Washington DC

Arrandale, T. (2008) 'Carbon goes to market', *Governing* (September), pp26–30

Bang, G., Bretteville Froyn, C., Hovi, J. and Menz, F. (2007) 'The United States and international climate cooperation: International "pull" versus domestic "push"', *Energy Policy*, vol 35, pp1282–1291

Berendt, C. (2008) 'Gazing into the crystal ball', *Trading Carbon*, vol 2, no 9, pp30–32, November

Broder, J. M. and Connelly, M. (2007) 'Public remains split on response to warming', *The New York Times*, 27 April

California Air Resources Board (2008) Draft AB 32 Scoping Plan Document, June

CDP (2008) www.cdproject.net, accessed 6 November 2008

Christiansen, A. C. (2003) 'Convergence or divergence? Status and prospects for US climate strategy', *Climate Policy*, vol 3, no 3, pp343–358

Clinton, W. J. and Gore, A. (1993) The Climate Change Action Plan, October, www.gcrio.org/USCCAP/toc.html, accessed 6 November 2008

Feldman, L. and Raufer, R. K. (1987) *Emissions Trading and Acid Rain: Implementing a Market Approach to Pollution Control*, Rowman & Littlefield, Totowa, NJ

Hight, C. and Silva-Chávez, G. (2008) 'Change in the air: The foundations of the coming American carbon market', *Climate Report*, no 15, October

Jordan, M. (2007) 'Gore accepts Nobel Prize with call for bold action', *Washington Post*, 11 December, pA14

Lisowski, M. (2002) 'The emperor's new clothes: Redressing the Kyoto Protocol', *Climate Policy*, vol 2, no 3, pp161–177

Lutsey, N. and Sperling, D. (2008) 'America's bottom-up climate change mitigation policy', *Energy Policy*, vol 36, pp673–685

MGA (2008) www.midwesterngovernors.org, accessed 10 November 2008

Peterson, T. and Rose, A. (2006) 'Reducing conflicts between climate policy and energy policy in the US: The important role of the States', *Energy Policy*, vol 34, pp619–631

Pew Center on Global Climate Change (2008a) 'Economy-wide Cap-and-Trade Proposals in the 110th Congress Includes Legislation Introduced as of October 20, 2008', www.pewclimate.org/docUploads/110thCapTradeProposals10–15–08.pdf, accessed 6 November 2008

Pew Center on Global Climate Change (2008b) 'Climate Change 101: Cap and Trade', www.pewclimate.org/docUploads/Cap-Trade-101–02–2008.pdf, accessed 10 November 2008

Rabe, B. G. (2004) *Statehouse and Greenhouse: The Emerging Politics of American Climate Change Policy*, Brookings Institution Press, Washington DC

Rabe, B. G. (2008) 'Regionalism and global climate change policy: Revisiting multistate collaboration as an intergovernmental management tool', in T. J. Conlen and P. L. Pozner (eds) *Intergovernmental Management for the 21st Century*, Brookings Institution Press, Washington DC, pp176–208

RGGI (2008) Fact sheet, www.rggi.org/docs/RGGI_Executive_Summary.pdf, accessed 10 November 2008

Rosenzweig, R., Youngman, R. and Nelson, E. (2008) 'Next Stop USA: The progress so far', *Trading Carbon*, vol 2, no 8, pp16–18, October

Trading Carbon (2008) 'Power companies dominate RGGI auction', *Trading Carbon*, vol 2, no 9, p4, November

US Department of Transportation (2008) 'Revised summary of fuel economy performance', January 15

US House of Representatives (2007a) The Olver-Gilchrest Climate Stewardship Act, 110th Congress, H.R. 620

US House of Representatives (2007b) The Waxman Safe Climate Act, 110th Congress, H.R. 1590

US House of Representatives (2008a) The Markey Investing in Climate Action and Protection Act, 110th Congress, H.R. 6186

US House of Representatives (2008b) The Doggett Climate MATTERS Act, 110th Congress, H.R. 6316

US House of Representatives (2008c) Dingell-Boucher Discussion Draft, 10/7/2008

US Senate (2007a) McCain-Lieberman Climate Stewardship and Innovation Act, 110th Congress, S. 280

US Senate (2007b) The Sanders-Boxer Global Warming Pollution Reduction Act, 110th Congress, S. 309

US Senate (2007c) Kerry-Snowe Global Warming Reduction Act, 110th Congress, S. 485

US Senate (2007d) Bingaman-Specter Low Carbon Economy Act, 110th Congress, S. 1766

US Senate (2007e) Lieberman-Warner Climate Security Act, 110th Congress, S. 2191

US Senate (2008) Boxer-Lieberman-Warner Climate Security Act, 110th Congress, S. 3036 (Substitute amendment to S. 2191)

Van Vuuren, D., den Elzen, M. and Berk, M. (2002) 'An evaluation of the level of ambition and implications of the Bush Climate Change Initiative', *Climate Policy*, vol 2, no 4, pp293–301

Western Climate Initiative (2008) Design Recommendations for the WCI Regional Cap-and-Trade Program, September 23

White House (2009) 'Energy and the environment',
www.whitehouse.gov/agenda/energy_and_environment, accessed 30 January 2009

White House Office of Management and Budget (2008) Statement of Administration Policy,
June 2, www.whitehouse.gov/omb/legislative/sap/110–2/saps3036-s.pdf

Chapter 6

Emissions Trading in Australia

Introduction

It is somewhat surprising that with its long history and experience of using property-rights approaches to managing natural resources such as water, Australia is a relative newcomer on the global stage of emissions trading. Perhaps this can be best explained by the generous targets and special provisions relating to land-clearing negotiated under the Kyoto Protocol, which mean that Australia will probably meet its international targets until 2012, with little need for strong policy action at the national level.

The picture at the domestic level, however, is very different. CO_2 emissions from stationary energy sources are growing at an alarming rate, having increased by 50 per cent over the period 1990–2006 with little sign of slowing. Emissions from transport are up 30 per cent. The only major source of emissions reductions are from a decline in the rate of land-clearing for agricultural production, of which there are many co-benefits, such as biodiversity protection.

So while Australia sits comfortably within its Kyoto targets, actual environmental performance in the key emitting sectors is a serious concern. On one level this raises difficult questions for the international community's efforts to reduce greenhouse gas emissions – if a rich country with strong institutions and a flexible dynamic economy cannot tame its CO_2 emissions, what hope is there in countries such as China and India?

Looking forward, in 2007, following what may have been the world's first election fought around the issue of climate change, there is now strong bipartisan support for emissions trading and curbing domestic emissions in the stationary energy and transport sectors. Given the scale of the challenge this suggests a big future for carbon markets in Australia.

This chapter provides an introduction to the politics of climate change and emissions trading in Australia, before moving onto discussing the experience with the New South Wales emissions trading scheme and the proposed national level scheme to be brought in by 2010. With Australia currently at a turning point in the political and economic landscape relating to climate change, now is a crucial time for business and policy makers to understand and shape the risks and opportunities that this transformation of the economy demands.

The first 'climate change election'

The November 2007 Australian general election heralded a dramatic shift in Australia's climate policy. Held just weeks before the 13th Conference of Parties in Bali, a newly elected Labour Party ousted the incumbent Liberal-National Coalition in Government and immediately ratified the Kyoto Protocol.[1] Second, the new government sought to fast-track the institutions of a formal CO_2 market by bringing forward the implementation date for a national emissions trading scheme from 2012 to 2010 and committing Australia to a long-term target of a 60 per cent reduction in emissions relative to 2000 by 2050.

As shown in Figure 6.1, climate change and the environment was only one of several factors important to voters in the November 2007 election. However, it took centre stage in the political discourse between Prime Minister, John Howard, and the Leader of the Opposition, Kevin Rudd. In terms of its significance to voters and the political capital invested in it by political agents (evidenced by the steady climb of its relative importance) it was perhaps the most decisive issue of the campaign, rising around 13 points to 70, compared to the other big issue of the campaign, industrial relations, which rose around 25 points to just over 50.[2]

Prior to November 2007 emissions trading policy had followed a course closely aligned with the United States. Both countries refused to ratify the Kyoto Protocol or introduce a formal cap on domestic emissions, leaving the way open for state-based emissions trading markets to develop in an ad hoc manner and voluntary emissions markets to emerge in response to growing public concern.

At the core of the Liberal-National (Howard) Government was the position that Australia would commit to achieving its Kyoto Target of 108 per cent of 1990 emissions during the period 2008–2012 but that it would not ratify the Protocol until the meaningful participation of major developing countries such as China and India was achieved.

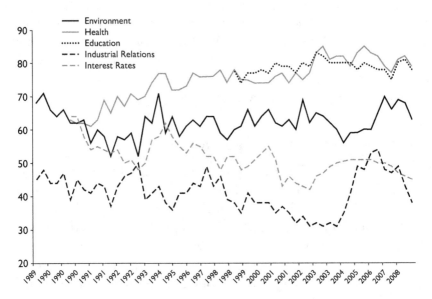

Source: Newspoll database (2008) 'Importance of federal issues' and 'Best party to handle federal issues', extracted November 2008 from www.newspoll.com.au

Figure 6.1 The evolution of the importance of federal issues in Australia

This policy was supported by a number of domestic measures such as a Mandatory Renewable Energy Target; the Greenhouse Challenge; Generator Efficiency Standards; and the Ozone Protection and Synthetic Greenhouse Gas Management Act (2003). Internationally, Australia focused efforts on establishing the Asia–Pacific Partnership on Clean Development and Climate, which set out a framework for clean technology transfer between Australia, the US, China, India, Japan, Canada and the Philippines,[3] and established a programme focused on slowing deforestation in Indonesia.

In addition to Australia's 108 per cent target, at Kyoto in 1997 the then Environment Minister, Senator Robert Hill, had negotiated the inclusion of emissions from land clearing (deforestation) in the base year ('the Australia clause'). As can be seen in Figure 6.2 below, this clause is critical for Australia's ability to meet its 108 per cent target. This is because since 1990 emissions from land clearing have declined sharply due to a combination of new federal and state regulatory native vegetation controls.[4, 5]

Indeed, as can be seen from Figures 6.2 and 6.3, emissions savings from land use constitute the only substantial emissions reductions over the 16 years to 2006, falling by 54 per cent. All other major categories of emissions have risen strongly in Australia since 1990 with stationary energy emissions rising the fastest by almost 50 per cent.

Despite this highly contingent sectoral emissions profile, the government viewed that it could retain the moral high ground by staying within the, albeit generous, target negotiated under the Kyoto Protocol in Kyoto in 1997.

In the post-11 September diplomatic environment, during the 2002–2003 national debate on emissions trading and Kyoto ratification, Australia was able to stand firmly alongside its US ally while rebutting disappointed Europeans with the assertion that the EU was in no position to criticize, given that Australia would meet its Kyoto target and most European states would not. It is also worth noting that in addition to the strong personal relationship between Prime Minister Howard and President Bush, at the time Australia was negotiating a long-desired Free Trade Agreement with the US, which was finally agreed and brought into effect in 2004.[6]

While it is difficult to point to any one causal factor explaining the government's decision not to ratify the Kyoto Protocol, especially given that Kyoto was unlikely to impose any immediate additional cost on the

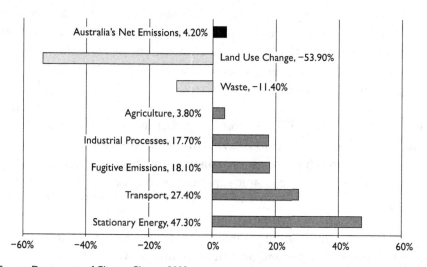

Source: Department of Climate Change, 2008

Figure 6.2 Percentage change in emissions 1990–2006

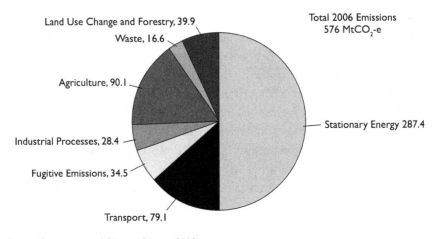

Source: Department of Climate Change, 2008

Figure 6.3 Composition of Australian greenhouse gas emissions

economy, these factors go some way to explaining the optics of the decision-making process that led to the decision.[7, 8] From the Howard Government's perspective, the decision to ratify or not ratify seems to have been regarded as a symbolic one. However, over the year leading up to the election (see Figure 6.4), a combination of international criticism and pressure made it increasingly difficult for the government to maintain the credibility of this position.

In October 2006 the British Government released *The Economics of Climate Change* (known as the Stern Review, HM Treasury, 2006). This report seems to have been as much intended as a political and diplomatic staging post to launch a vigorous international public relations campaign as it was a serious attempt at the most comprehensive and rigorous economic analysis of climate change to date. As discussed in Chapter 2, by making explicit his approach to the ethics of discounting, Stern arrived at a benefit-cost calculus that gave economic support to strong early action on climate change, favouring emissions trading over carbon taxation. Stern also attempted to reframe climate change as an opportunity for business and a boost for the economy, rather than the standard opinion that emissions controls would cost jobs and prevent economic growth.

In March 2007, amid much media interest, Nicholas Stern visited Australia to present his report to both John Howard and Kevin Rudd. As a

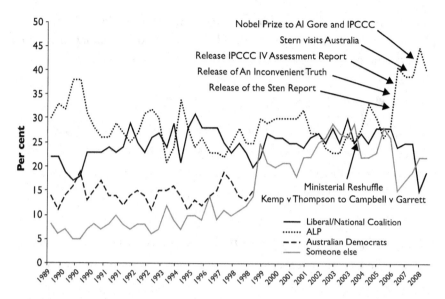

Source: Authors, based on Newspoll

Figure 6.4 Labour benefits from increased international pressure
on climate change

visiting academic, he was less constrained than British officials would have
been in criticizing the government position on Kyoto:

> More and more countries round the world are prepared to move on the
> basis of their own responsibilities and their judgement of their own
> responsibilities in the light that others are also moving. That gains
> momentum and if some countries peel off then that momentum is seriously
> damaged. (ABC, 2007)[9]

On 2 February 2007 the United Nations Intergovernmental Panel on
Climate Change (IPCC) handed down its Fourth Assessment Report
(IPCC, 2007) in Paris. This coincided with the first sitting week of the
year in the Federal Parliament and provided yet further impetus to
growing momentum on the climate change issue. On the first sitting day
of parliamentary session a Matter of Public Importance was called by the
Leader of the Opposition, Mr Rudd, on the challenges of climate change

and water scarcity. In his address to Parliament he made it clear that he planned to frame the election around sound economic management *and* climate change:

> This year we will see a battle for ideas for the nation's future... The battleground on which we are going to engage this fight is one which centres around our [the Labour Party's] two sets of values regarding the way we want to shape this country's future... We have to build long-term prosperity without throwing the fair out the back door and we have to build long-term prosperity and take action on climate change and water. (Parliamentary Hansard, 2007, p49)[10]

Quoting directly from the IPCC Report he went on to criticize what he characterized as the government's overly sceptical approach to the issue:

> The understanding of anthropogenic warming and cooling influences on climate has improved since the Third Assessment Report, leading to very high confidence that the globally averaged net effect of human activities since 1750 has been one of warming... Going to the footnote, what is 'very high confidence' defined as? 'Very high confidence' means ... at least a 9 out of 10 chance of being correct... (Parliamentary Hansard, 2007, p51)

Then Environment Minister Malcolm Turnbull responded with the government's long-held position that the Kyoto Protocol was not the best instrument to address the problem and room must be given to climate sceptics:

> The response to climate change is a complex one. It requires an open mind, and it requires practical measures. What the opposition is giving us now is some kind of cramped political theology. Nobody is allowed to doubt. Sceptics are to be banned. Anybody with an open mind is to be banned. (Parliamentary Hansard, 2007, p19)[11]

> We all recognise that ratifying the Kyoto protocol by itself will not result in Australia emitting any less greenhouse gases because we are already on track to meet our Kyoto target. It will not have, in and of itself, any effect on the greenhouse gases in the atmosphere. (Parliamentary Hansard, 2007, p52)

Another major element in the intensifying international campaign for greater cooperation on climate change came with the release of Al Gore's movie documentary *An Inconvenient Truth* late in 2006. This film was a worldwide phenomenon leading to a Nobel Peace Prize for Mr Gore in conjunction with the International Panel on Climate Change. In addition to the film running for the year leading up to the election, the Nobel prize award was announced just one month before the November 2007 election, again elevating the issue and damaging the government for its perceived scepticism at a crucial time.

This view is supported by research undertaken by Nielsen for Oxford University's Environmental Change Institute showing that in Australia the film had a significant impact on public perceptions (Nielsen Environmental Change Institute, 2007). Survey data showed that half of the people who saw the film said it changed their mind on the issue, with 54, 74, 87 and 91 per cent for the age groups under 25, 25–39, 40–55 and 55+ respectively saying it would change their habits.

Figure 6.4 shows how Labour was able to use these mutually reinforcing and repeated messages to gradually move from being regarded as equally able to handle the environment to establishing a dominant and election-winning lead over the Howard Government.

In recognition of the growing electoral threat that climate change posed to the government, Prime Minister Howard established a group to report to him on the establishment of a new Australian Emissions Trading Scheme in December 2006. In January 2007 he also appointed the Liberal Party's rising star Malcolm Turnbull to shore up the environment portfolio, to ensure a competition with Labour's celebrity environment front man, Peter Garrett.[12, 13]

The Emissions Task Group had for its terms of reference:

Australia enjoys major competitive advantages through the possession of large reserves of fossil fuels and uranium. In assessing Australia's further contribution to reducing greenhouse gas emissions, these advantages must be preserved.

Against this background the Task Group will be asked to advise on the nature and design of a workable global emissions trading system in which Australia would be able to participate. (Howard, 2007)[14]

In May, six months before the election, the Task Group handed down its report and the government announced that it would move to implement an emissions trading scheme in 2012. However, the government could not shake a perception of being overly sceptical of climate change – a position, as we can see in the figures above, that had lost resonance with the public. Electoral momentum continued against the government and they were defeated by Labour's landslide victory in November 2007.

This combination of elevated public concern around the environment (Figure 6.1), increased international pressure and the ability of Labour to harness these concerns (Figure 6.4) support the view that the November 2007 election was indeed the first election to be fought and won around climate change. This is significant as it is a concrete example of how the weight of public opinion on climate change can foster greater international cooperation. As a classic example of social coordination around managing a global public good, international norm building is fundamental if nations are to put aside short-term national self-interest in favour of the longer term gains that cooperation on CO_2 mitigation offers. This coordination relies on solving the problems of collective action and the ascension of the free rider at international level.

The 2007 Australian election showed (at least in the context of a liberal democratic state such as Australia) that this was possible by exerting the weight of international and moral pressure and without recourse to trade restrictions or other punitive measures.

Australian experience with tradable emissions markets

The section above traced the political evolution of a national cap-and-trade scheme for Australia. The rest of this chapter will outline its practical experience with emissions trading. First, the New South Wales (NSW) Greenhouse Gas Reduction Scheme (GGAS) will be examined alongside the Federal Government's Renewable Energy Certificate Program. These two programmes are examples of base line and credit emissions trading schemes and have been running for several years.[15]

On its implementation, the new national Carbon Pollution Reduction Scheme (CPRS) will be a cap-and-trade scheme that will supersede and absorb the NSW GGAS. Many of the key elements of CPRS were first foreshadowed in a Green Paper released by the Federal Government in July 2008. This served as an exposure draft for a White Paper released in December 2008, which sets out a draft of the legislation that is to establish the scheme. The final section of this chapter will provide an overview and discussion of the key issues for the proposed future scheme.

The New South Wales Greenhouse Gas Reduction Scheme

Launched in 2003, the NSW GGAS scheme was one of the world's first mandatory emissions trading schemes. It operates by allowing accredited parties to create carbon allowance certificates or credits, each of which represents a reduction in emissions compared to a baseline such as average practice or some other metric.[16] These certificates are created by 'accredited abatement certificate providers' and form the basis of the supply side of the carbon market. Each GGAS certificate represents 1 tonne of CO_2 mitigation.

On the demand side, electricity retailers and other large users of electricity, called 'benchmark participants', have an obligatory requirement to offset part of the emissions associated with the electricity they sell or use. If they fail to meet their benchmark, participants in the scheme are required to pay a penalty of AUS$12 per tonne of CO_2 not abated. They can offset their emissions by either purchasing GGAS offset credit certificates (produced by the accredited providers), claiming credits generated from the Commonwealth Government's Mandatory Renewable Energy Target or by generating emissions savings in-house through accredited energy-efficiency measures.

While the NSW Department of Water and Energy oversees the policy framework of GGAS, the scheme is administered by an Independent Pricing and Regulatory Tribunal (IPART), which controls the accreditation and monitoring of abatement certificate providers and ensures that benchmark participants comply with their emissions reduction obligations. To ensure the integrity and validity of the CO_2 reduction permits generated, IPART has also established an audit panel to assist with the management of the system. A GGAS registry manages the creation, transfer of ownership and final surrender of the abatement certificates.[17] The registry does not provide a trading function. Figure 6.5 below illustrates the structure of GGAS and its key participants.

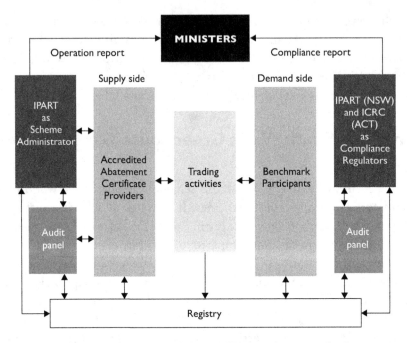

Source: Department of Climate Change (2008) State and Territory Greenhouse Gas Emissions

Figure 6.5 The structure of GGAS and key participants

GGAS scope and NSW greenhouse gas target

GGAS operates in NSW and the Australian Capital Territory. Together these states comprise around 28 per cent of Australian GHG emissions (see Figure 6.6). However, GGAS is limited primarily to the stationary energy sector and a few large energy consumers.

The NSW State Government had set a state-wide electricity sector target for reducing GHG emissions to 7.27 tonnes of CO_2e per capita by 2007, which it claims is '5 per cent below the Kyoto Protocol baseline year' of 1989–1990 (for the sector). However, care should be taken interpreting this per capita, sectoral target. Per capita emissions have declined as the population in NSW has risen from roughly 2.9 million residents in 1990 to 3.4 million in 2006 (ABS, 2008). In absolute terms emissions from stationary energy have risen strongly over the Kyoto period from 59 to $78MtCO_2e$ (see Figure 6.7).

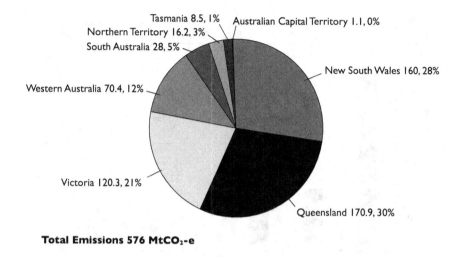

Tasmania 8.5, 1%   Australian Capital Territory 1.1, 0%
Northern Territory 16.2, 3%
South Australia 28, 5%
New South Wales 160, 28%
Western Australia 70.4, 12%
Victoria 120.3, 21%
Queensland 170.9, 30%

Total Emissions 576 MtCO₂-e

Source: IPRT, 2008

Figure 6.6 State emissions of greenhouse gas pollution, 2006

This approach of linking the demand for abatement permits to NSW population has been identified as a serious design flaw of the scheme (Passey et al, 2008, p3013). The authors note that in the long term to 2050 (assuming conservative rates of population growth and current policy paremeters) the CO_2 emissions allowable under GGAS would actually increase to over 9 per cent above 2003 levels. However, this would be veiled by declining emissions per capita due to population growth rather than actual CO_2 reduction.

In 2007, there were 40 benchmark participants in GGAS (IPRT, 2008). This included all 26 licensed electricity retailers, one market client who takes electricity directly from the NSW grid, three generators of electricity and 11 large users of electricity who voluntarily participate in GGAS (see Annex 6.1 for the full list of mandatory and elective GGAS participants).

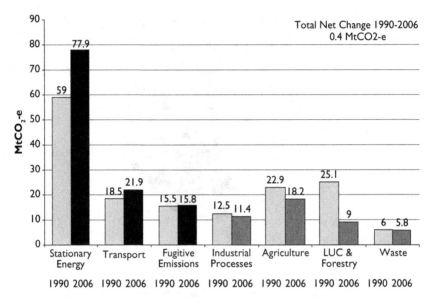

Source: Department of Climate Change, 2008

Figure 6.7 NSW change in sectoral emissions 1990–2006

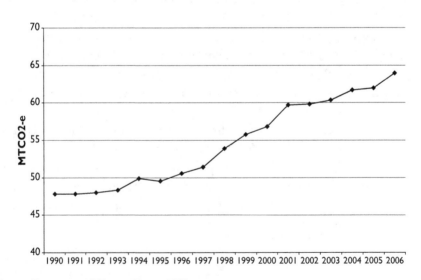

Source: Department of Climate Change, 2008

Figure 6.8 Change in energy industry emissions 1990–2006

GGAS baseline

As previously mentioned, the measure for this baseline and credit scheme is calculated according to a mandatory per capita electricity sector GHG target for NSW of 7.27 tonnes CO_2e. GGAS then compares this emissions target to an approximation of actual emissions from the NSW electricity sector in a given year. The difference between these two estimates is calculated and allocated to benchmark participants based on their respective market shares of NSW electricity sales.

Each benchmark participant is required to self-assess its required emission reduction level based on several parameters released by the regulator, and which are held constant for the entire year. The parameters are:

- the pool coefficient (0.941 tonnes CO_2e per MWh for 2007);
- total state electricity demand (70,595GWh for 2007);
- total state population (6,896,800 for 2007);
- electricity sector benchmark (50,139,736 tonnes CO_2e for 2007).

To calculate its individual benchmark the participant uses the following formula:

Equation 1: *Firm level benchmark calculation*

[1]

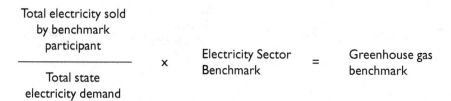

$$\frac{\text{Total electricity sold by benchmark participant}}{\text{Total state electricity demand}} \times \text{Electricity Sector Benchmark} = \text{Greenhouse gas benchmark}$$

The first part of the equation determines the participant's share of total NSW electricity sales. This is then multiplied by the overall NSW electricity benchmark in order to determine the participant's share of the greenhouse gas target. To calculate whether they are liable to pay a penalty at the end of the compliance year GGAS participants must calculate their attributable emissions and compare this with their greenhouse gas benchmark.

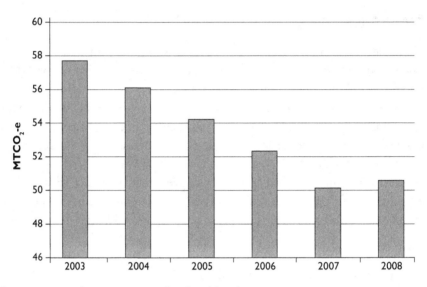

Source: www.greenhousegas.nsw.gov.au/benchmark/key_factors.asp

Figure 6.9 NSW GGAS Energy Sector Emissions Benchmark

Equation 2: *Emissions liability calculation*

[2]

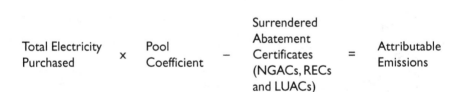

The total electricity purchased is the amount of electricity bought by the participant from NSW power generators. This is then multiplied by the average emissions intensity of power generation in NSW before abatement (the pool coefficient), which is calculated as the simple average of the five previous years' pool values, lagged by two years to smooth the figure.[18] The product of these two parameters gives the emissions liability. To determine whether this puts the participant over or under its benchmark the number of abatement certificates purchased must be considered. This yields the attributable emissions for the benchmark participant; these must be lower than the greenhouse gas benchmark should the participant wish to avoid the $12 per tonne fine for unabated CO_2.

Over the life of GGAS the Electricity Sector Benchmark has tightened from $57.8MtCO_2e$ in 2003 to 50.6 in 2008 (See Figure 6.9). It is through comparing Figures 6.8 and 6.9 that the environmental effectiveness of GGAS can be assessed.

The declining benchmark shows how since its inception in 2003 GGAS is now delivering around $8MtCO_2e$ of emissions savings each year. However, there is a trend of increasing emissions from energy industries: these have risen by approximately $17MtCO_2e$ since 1990 or by approximately $4MtCO_2e$ over the period 2003–2006. This suggests that, while GGAS has been successful in stimulating offsets to CO_2 emissions from stationary energy, it has not significantly changed the underlying structure of emissions in this sector away from fossil fuels.

To examine where the emissions reductions have occurred, we now turn to the three sources of abatement certificates available to benchmark participants to offset their emissions.

Abatement certificate providers

Under GGAS there are three types of abatement certificates that can be used to assist benchmark participants achieve their emissions baseline. These are:

* transferable NSW Greenhouse Gas Abatement Certificates (NGACs);
* non-transferable Large User Abatement Certificates (LUACs); and
* Renewable Energy Certificates (RECs) generated under the Federal Government's Mandatory Renewable Energy Program.

NGAC and LUAC certificates represent 1 tonne of CO_2e that would have otherwise been released into the atmosphere. These certificates can only be produced by accredited Abatement Certificate Providers (ACPs). At the end of 2007 there were 204 such organizations creating certificates under four categories of Abatement Certificate Rules.

NGAC abatement certificates may be generated from:

* Low or reduced emissions generation. To qualify for the generation of credits in this category, generators must demonstrate that they are

producing electricity at a level lower than the NSW pool coefficient or prove that they have implemented an energy efficiency measure that has lowered the emissions intensity of generation.[19]

- Electricity demand side abatement. Credits from demand side abatement are actions on the customer side that reduce electricity consumption. For example, this could involve changes to processes, control, maintenance of plant or equipment, the installation of energy-efficient appliances such as new showerheads or improving the efficiency of on-site power generation not sold onto the grid.
- Carbon sequestration through forestry. This element of GGAS recognizes the role of forests in sequestering carbon. To qualify, forestry projects must:
  - take place in planted forests that are located in NSW;
  - comply with the requirements of the Kyoto Protocol; and
  - have the carbon sequestration right registered on its title under the Conveyancing Act 1919 (NSW).

LUACs (non-tradable) certificates may be generated by:

- The abatement of on-site greenhouse gas emissions (from industrial processes) not directly related to the consumption of electricity. To qualify, entities must meet the definition of being a 'large user', which requires the LUAC creator to be a benchmark participant that uses more than 100GWh per year in NSW. LUACs can only be used by the customer that created them as a means to manage their own benchmark.

The incentive for the creation of NGACs and LUACs is driven by the price for these certificates, which is determined through the interplay of demand (set through the NSW benchmark) and supply (set by the Abatement Certificate Providers). All abatement certificates must be registered within six months of the end of the calendar year in which the abatement activity occurred.

GGAS also gives benchmark participants credit for any Renewable Energy Certificates (RECs) they submit under the Commonwealth Mandatory Renewable Energy Target Scheme, with the provision that credits claimed in this respect are limited to renewable electricity sales in NSW. An REC and a NGAC cannot be created for the same activity (i.e. if a REC is created for 1MWh of output, an NGAC cannot be created with respect to that output). However, if the renewable energy project is also reducing methane emissions, it is possible to create NGACs for the methane emissions that are being avoided (IPRT, 2008, p75).[20]

In practice, because RECs trade at a much higher price than NGACs, the number of RECs converted has been limited. In total 5,894,139 RECs have been counted towards compliance in this way (see Figure 6.10).

Although there are various types of certificates, all certificates in Figure 6.10 represent the abatement of 1 tonne of CO_2e and are priced equally on the market. The creation of abatement certificates from low or reduced emissions generation accounts for the majority of certificates with 68 per cent of the 68,987,471 certificates created over the course of the programme's history. At a project level these certificates came from improved management of 'waste coal mine gas', followed by improved management of landfill gases and the increased use of natural gas in electricity generation. For the demand side abatement, the majority of projects involved residential energy-efficiency actions such as the installation of energy efficient showerheads.

2007 also saw the emergence of the voluntary acquisition of NGACs as a way for individuals and firms outside the mandated scope of the scheme to

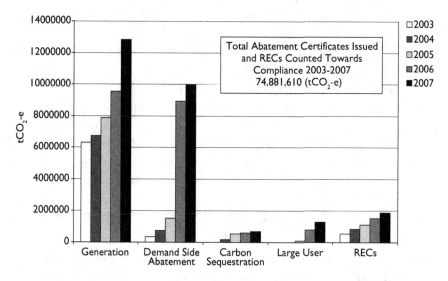

Source: IPRT, 2008

Figure 6.10 Supply of NSW abatement certificates and RECs used

manage their carbon emissions with a total of 49,898 certificates being acquired for this purpose.

Box 6.1 The Commonwealth Mandatory Renewable Energy Target (MRET) Scheme[21]

One of the major policy changes following the November 2007 election of the Rudd Government in Australia was the lifting of MRET from 9,500GWh to 45,000GWh by 2020. This is part of a broader policy to source 20 per cent of electricity production from renewable sources by 2020.

When it was introduced in 2001 along with a 2 per cent target, it was the world's first *mandatory* (as opposed to aspirational) renewable energy target (Kent and Mercer, 2004).

MRET operates as a baseline and credit emissions trading scheme through the creation of Renewable Energy Certificates (RECs). Each REC represents 1MWh of renewable energy generated. RECs can be created when solar hot water heaters are installed or when renewable energy is produced by small generation units or by power stations.

All electricity retailers and wholesalers (called liable parties) are required to purchase RECs in proportion to the amount of electricity they sell onto the national market. In 2005, for example, the target was 1.64 per cent of energy sold. Therefore a liable party purchasing 100,000MWh of electricity in 2005 would have to surrender 1640 RECs to fully discharge their MRET liability for that year.

Other initiatives that have been introduced to support MRET include: an Aus$500 million fund to provide finance for the development, commercialization and and deployment of renewable technologies; $150 million for solar and clean energy research; and around $500 million for a Solar Cities, National Solar Schools and Green Precincts initiatives.

Under GGAS, as with all baseline and credit schemes, the supply of abatement credits is determined by the generators of the abatement certificates themselves, rather than by the regulator. One risk with this approach is that it can lead to uncertainty in the supply of credits. In 2007, for example, the successful creation of a large number of credits (see Figure 6.10) resulted in a large fall in price of certificates (see Figure 6.11).

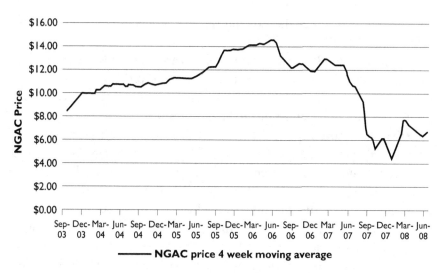

NGAC price 4 week moving average

Source: The Green Room, see www.nges.com.au

Figure 6.11 Trends in the NGAC spot price

Independent assessment of GGAS

As discussed in Chapter 2, fundamental to the successful operation of any emissions trading scheme is that the property rights created are robust and transferable. This presents a considerable challenge in practice. Abatement certificates, while commonly all denominated in terms of 1 tonne of CO_2e (actual or abated), are actually created by a range of different rules relating to different GHGs, across different sectors and, within sectors, across different activities. Thus the integrity of the rules or institutions that support the emissions trading system are of fundamental importance. In the context of baseline and credit schemes such as GGAS, this means the issue of additionality must take centre stage if regulators, businesses and individuals are to be sure that emissions trading delivers what it promises – lower emissions achieved at least cost.

Fundamental to baseline and credit schemes, the concept of additionality requires first that abatement projects lead to real emissions reductions over what would have occurred anyway. Second, that the project investment would not have been economically feasible without the creation of the carbon credits and, third, that the project is additional to what is required under the existing set of policy and regulatory settings (UNFCCC, 2007).

Passey et al (2008) recently evaluated GGAS against these criteria. They found flaws in the institutional structure of the programme such that a significant proportion of the tradable abatement certificates created may not correspond to the emissions reductions claimed.

Perhaps the most important design flaw identified results from the use of what is called the Relative Intensity Rule, which originates as a result of tying the creation of abatement certificates to the NSW Pool Coefficient (average emissions intensity of NSW electricity generation). To see how this emissions intensity rule has undermined the institutional integrity of the CO_2 property right, Passey follows the CO_2 emissions from newly commissioned coal power plants.

Problems arise because any new energy production can create NGACs provided its generation has an emissions intensity lower than the NSW Pool Coefficient. This could even apply if the power plants' actual emissions were increasing. The following text box is taken from Passey's article evaluating the GGAS scheme.

Box 6.2 The trouble with emissions intensity rules

Between 2002/03 and 2005/06, demand in the Australian national electricity market increased 19.7 per cent (NEMMCO, 2006). The 445MW Tarong North coal-fired power station in Queensland started operation in August 2003 and created 118,981 NGACs for the 2003, 2004 and 2005 compliance years, while at the same time emitting an estimated 3.1 million tonnes of CO_2e per year. The 840MW Millmerran power station's two coal-fired generating units started operation in 2002 and 2003 respectively, and have so far created 171,177 NGACs for the 2003, 2004 and 2005 compliance years. These are supercritical steam-cycle units of a similar size to the Tarong generator and so would have emitted approximately 6 million tonnes of CO_2e per year. Both Tarong North and Millmerran power stations have created NGACs and so, according to the scheme's rules, have reduced per-capita emissions since the GGAS began. Ironically, the more electricity (and therefore emissions) they produce, the larger the number of NGACs they can create.

The second fundamental design flaw, according to Passey et al (2008), is that while each NGAC corresponds in principle to 1 tonne CO_2 abated (i.e. the absence of emissions) in practice this is extremely difficult to measure. This is because it is impossible to independently verify something that might have occurred but ultimately did not occur. One study examining this aspect of additionality in eastern European countries for demand side CO_2 abatement projects found that there was a ± 35 per cent uncertainty in the level of emissions (Parkinson et al, 2001). This is a common problem in all baseline and credit schemes and has been a major source of criticism of them (Hepburn, 2007).

An Australian emissions trading cap-and-trade scheme: The Carbon Pollution Reduction Scheme (CPRS)

As mentioned above, the Australian Government has committed to commencing a national level cap-and-trade scheme called the Carbon Pollution Reduction Scheme (CPRS) by 2010. This section will outline the essential elements of the proposed scheme including the impact of likely emissions caps, the scope of the scheme, reporting and compliance arrangements, the allocation and auctioning of permits in the context of international competitiveness, and finally the degree of international linking that will be permitted under the scheme.

The cap

The setting of the CPRS cap for the period 2010 to 2014–2015 will not occur until around March 2010, just months before the planned commencement of the scheme on 1 July of that year (White Paper, 2008). In contrast to the 1990 base year of the EU ETS and the Kyoto Protocol, the cap is to be set relative to the year 2000. It will be influenced by the Government's medium term national target, which was set in the White Paper as a minimum of a 5 per cent reduction of national emissions by 2020 relative to 2000. In absolute terms, this amounts to a reduction of 27.6MtCO₂e from the 2000 base-year value of 552.8MtCO₂e. If the emission reductions from land clearing are factored in, this does not represent much a difference from Australian emissions in 1990 of 552.6MtCO₂e. So in fact if 1990 had been chosen as a base year this quantum of emissions reductions would still have been around 5 per cent.

In the event of a 'global agreement under which all major economies commit to substantially restrain emissions …' the Government also signalled it was willing to adopt up to a 15 per cent target (an absolute reduction of $82.9MtCO_2e$).

The White Paper outlines that the 2020, 5 per cent target will translate into the following indicative national emissions trajectory:

- in 2010–11, 109 per cent of 2000 levels ($602.6MtCO_2e$);
- in 2011–12, 108 per cent of 2000 levels ($597.0MtCO_2e$); and
- in 2012–13, 107 per cent of 2000 levels ($591.1MtCO_2e$).

These trajectories cover all emissions in the economy, however, the CPRS will only cover around 75 per cent of Australia's emissions and involve mandatory obligations for around 1000 entities (White Paper, 2008). While the CPRS cap itself has not been announced it is reasonable to deduce from the indicative trajectories published in the White Paper that up until 2012 it will not impose any additional quantitative requirement than what was roughly negotiated under the Kyoto Protocol.

With regard to the alignment of the CPRS cap with international commitments, it is the preferred position that the scheme cap not be adjusted in the event that it is incompatible with internationally negotiated national targets (Green Paper, 2008, p187); rather, any obligations would be met by the government buying international emissions credits. This provision is intended to provide certainty to CPRS participants. It also shifts the risk of targets negotiated internationally away from the private sector to the public, as the Australian Government would be expected to meet any gap by purchasing credits on international carbon markets.

It is proposed that CPRS caps be set over a minimum period of five years at any one time and be extended by one year, each year to maintain a five-year window of certainty.

All sectors proposed to be covered by the scheme will be required to account for their all their CO_2 emissions to a high degree of certainty. Other sectors, such as emissions from land use, land use change, forestry and agriculture will be more difficult to accurately measure. It is the intention to

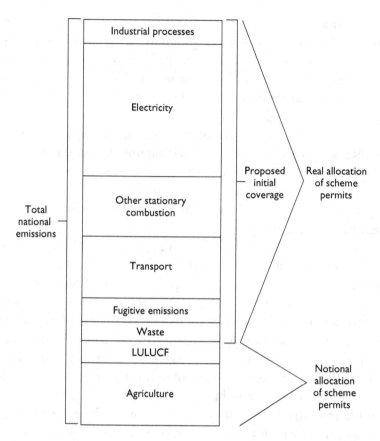

Source: Green Paper, 2008, p176

Figure 6.12 CPRS scope

gradually bring these sectors into the scheme as reporting improves (Green Paper, 2008, p176).

Point of obligation

Ideally, in order to ensure that the incidence of the carbon price falls on the actors most closely related to the production of emissions, it is theoretically optimal to apply the obligations of the scheme at the point where emissions are physically produced. This creates a 'direct obligation' that provides the clearest signal to encourage mitigation among those involved in the polluting behaviour. This direct obligation works particularly well for large, fixed sources of emissions. However, in some sectors such as transport, the direct point of obligation can involve many small actors (car owners) where the practical transaction costs of implementing a carbon trading scheme would be extremely high.

For example, the carbon accounting threshold to warrant inclusion in the CPRS is 25,000 tonnes of CO_2e per annum. A typical individual in a developed country may emit around 10–20 tonnes CO_2e each year. The argument to not include these small users in carbon trading stems from this low quantity of emissions relative to the effort it would take each person to engage with the scheme.

In these cases, the point of obligation can be more effectively placed at another point along the supply chain away from the actual physical source of emissions – a system of 'indirect obligation'. The CPRS intends to adopt this kind of system in the transport sector by placing obligations on upstream suppliers of fuel such as oil refiners. These suppliers would then have to pass on the carbon price imposed by the scheme to downstream consumers. In the medium to long term, higher fuel costs for petrol and diesel would then encourage the use of more efficient cars and the development of new low-carbon technologies.

For the agricultural sector, it is proposed to make the point of obligation not at the farmer level but downstream on large purchasers of agricultural produce. The logic behind this approach is that in this sector a large and diffuse number of farmers sell into highly concentrated markets. The much smaller number of abattoirs, wholesalers, supermarkets and export cooperatives could be made the point of obligation, with permits introduced to reflect the carbon intensity of different agricultural management practices. In theory, the costs of these permits could then be passed down to consumers and overseas importers of Australian farm produce, with higher prices charged for more carbon-intensive food and fibres to reflect the carbon price (Green Paper, 2008, p97). In practice, however, given the extremely competitive nature of Australian agricultural markets and their high exposure to international competition, this could also result in declining market share or profitability of many types of farming, with limited environmental gain unless similar actions are taken by other countries.

Box 6.3 Managing the political risks of higher prices at the pump

Traditionally, petrol prices and fuel taxation are two of the most politically combustible areas of government policy. Every year at Christmas and Easter, as families plan long-distance interstate travel, a high-stakes game is played out between fuel consumers, retailers, politicians and the competition watchdog – the Australian Competition and Consumer Commission (ACCC). Retailers, keen to push up prices at a time of high demand in order to maximize profits, raise petrol prices at the pump. This, inevitably, creates consumer outrage and calls for politicians to do something, such as lower fuel taxes. Australia already has the fourth cheapest petrol in the OECD, and politicians typically refer angry motorists to the ACCC, who may or may not find retailers are colluding unlawfully. In such an environment, it is very difficult for politicians to increase fuel taxes without risking a damaging voter backlash. Raising fuel prices, however, is what the government is planning to do by including the transport sector in the CPRS.

To manage this risk, the Australian Government is proposing to cut fuel taxes for the first three years of the scheme, thus counterbalancing the price rises it will impose under the CPRS. The intention behind this behaviour-neutral strategy is that it will give consumers time to plan ahead for the full implications of the CPRS, for example to buy a new fuel-efficient car. For this strategy to work, future price rises will need to be clearly communicated so that motorists can factor them into their expectations.

The CPRS in the context of Australia's rapidly growing emissions

Given Australia's rapidly growing emissions trends, it is likely that the CPRS will create a large carbon market. This can be simply illustrated by looking at the stationary energy sector, which comprises around half of total Australian emissions (Figure 6.3), and where emissions have risen by almost 50 per cent over the Kyoto period (Figure 6.2) as a result of heavy reliance on coal power generation.

This means that Australia's relatively modest emission targets need to be put in context with rapidly rising energy sector emissions. In 2006 (the most recent year of data) Australia's emissions from stationary energy were 400.9MtCO$_2$e and growing at a rate of around 2 per cent, or 8MtCO$_2$e, each year. To put these emissions cuts into perspective, the 445MW Tarong North power plant in Queensland produces 3.2MtCO$_2$e each year (Passey et al, 2008, p3011).[22] This means achieving any cuts from this baseline, or even stabilizing absolute emissions will see strong demand for emission permits.

Reporting and compliance

As discussed above, defining a practical point of obligation is a critical aspect of implementing the CPRS. This may or may not be the actual point of emissions, although ideally it would be the point of pollution, especially for large emitters. Once the point of obligation is identified it becomes obligatory for the entity involved to rigorously account for and manage its CO$_2$ emissions under the scheme.

There are several options for how this accounting and emissions assurance is done. The robustness of the different methods is of critical importance for establishing a workable scheme, built on a system of well-defined property rights that can interact with broader carbon markets. For instance, a scheme that creates CO$_2$ baselines and credits that are not robust or do not align accurately with the reality of actual emissions will lack environmental effectiveness and not be able to be integrated with other markets.

Under the CPRS it is proposed that the point of obligation will generally fall on entities with operational control over the covered facilities or activities. Where multiple entities exercise a degree of control, then a single responsible entity will be required to register and meet CPRS obligations (Green Paper, 2008, p196).

Four methodological approaches to measuring emissions (Green Paper, 2008, p198) have been put forward by the government. These are shown in Box 6.4.

Box 6.4 Methodological approaches to measuring emissions under the CPRS

Method 1: National Greenhouse Accounts default method

This method is the most abstracted from actual physical CO_2 measurement. It assumes emissions factors and applies them to various activities as set out by UN Framework Convention on Climate Change guidelines. The scale of the activity is compared to the emissions factors and an estimate of CO_2 emissions is obtained. These emissions factors are determined by the Department of Climate Change using the Australian Greenhouse Emissions Information System. Entity-level reporting under this methodology is least likely to reflect actual emissions; however, it has the advantage of being easy and cheap to apply.

Method 2: A facility-specific method using industry sampling and listed Australian or international standards or equivalent for analysing fuels and raw materials

Method 2 enables participants to undertake additional measurements – for example, the quantities of fuels consumed at a particular facility – in order to gain more accurate facility-specific measurements. Furthermore it draws on the large body of Australian and international documentary standards prepared by standards organizations to provide benchmarks for procedures for analysing the properties of fuels being combusted.

Method 3: A facility-specific method using Australian or international standards or equivalent for sampling and analysing fuels and raw materials

Method 3 is very similar to Method 2, except that it requires entities to comply with Australian or equivalent documentary standards for sampling (of fuels or raw materials) and documentary standards for analysing fuels.

Method 4: Direct monitoring of emissions systems, on either a continuous or periodic basis

Rather than inferring CO_2 emissions by analysing or making assumptions about the chemical properties of fuel inputs (or in some cases products) this method aims to directly measure the GHG emissions arising from an activity. This approach can provide a high level of accuracy depending on the type of emissions process; however, it is also costly and data-intensive. As with methods 2 and 3 a substantial body of documentary procedures underpins the methodology for this measurement approach.

In determining which method is to be used under the scheme, the Australian government has had to weigh up the advantages of more accurate measurement approaches against the costs of implementing them. On the one hand, accurate measurement increases the environmental effectiveness of the scheme, its integrity and also promotes equity by ensuring that each polluter faces the carbon costs that most truly reflect their emissions profile. However, on the other hand rigorous methodologies, such as direct measurement of CO_2, are costly to implement.[23]

In the Government's Green Paper (2008, p203) the preferred position is to set minimum reporting standards according to the class of emission source. This is to take account of the existing and potential measurement and reporting capacity within specific entities. For example, facility specific reporting (methods 2–4) are already extensively used for reporting emissions from electricity generation and perfluorocarbons (from aluminium smelting) and fugitive emissions from underground coal mines. For this reason, the minimum standard of applying methods 2–4 will apply for these three sources of emissions (White Paper, 2008). Entities with other sources of emissions will be able to choose from methods 1–4 when measuring their emissions, for at least the first two years of the scheme. Emission sources in this class include: non-electricity uses of coal and gas, open-cast coal mines and emissions from solid waste.

In the transport sector, it is proposed that fuel suppliers will be required to account for the emissions generated from fuels not sold to participants already directly covered by the scheme. It is proposed that these reporting arrangements will build on reporting procedures already in place as part of the fuel excise and customs duty systems.

Assurance of emissions reporting

As already emphasized in the discussion of the NSW scheme, the success or failure of any emissions trading scheme depends on the integrity and credibility of the property rights created. If economic agents perceive that they will be able to avoid facing a carbon price by way of masking their true emissions behind opaque carbon accounting standards, then property rights are poorly defined. This means that although emissions reductions may appear on paper and credits created, in reality these credits may not actually be supported by the CO_2 reductions claimed. Independent emissions assurance schemes are therefore an important feature to include in emissions trading design.

As with reporting, there are two tensions with the quality assurance of emissions data. A strong level of assurance would require emissions reports to be verified by an independent third party before their submission, such as in the EU ETS. This provides greater integrity but can be costly for participants. An alternative approach would be to employ a system of self-assurance, supported by targeted retrospective audits by the government (similar to self-assessment taxation).

For the CPRS, the government will adopt a system of third-party assessment for entities with emissions over 125,000 tonnes of CO_2e and a system of self-assessment backed up by government audits for smaller polluters (Green Paper, 2008, p210).[24]

The CPRS registry

A national registry will be created to track the ownership of eligible compliance permits issued under the CPRS and to manage their surrender. This registry will also be responsible for the recording and management of Australia's Kyoto Units (Assigned Amount Units, Removal Units, Emission Reduction Units and Certified Emission Reductions).

Liable entities, permit brokers and members of the public will be able to use an on line interface to the registry to hold, transfer, surrender and view public information on the CPRS. The registry will coordinate several of the key actions required of participants under the CPRS including:

- the opening of an account to participate in the emissions trading market;
- the receipt of permits purchased at primary auctions or via free allocation;
- the registration of permits and Kyoto units acquired on the secondary market; and
- the surrender of eligible permits where obligations are due under the scheme.

Compliance and enforcement

The CPRS places four key obligations on organizations that come under its scope:

- to register for the reporting regime;
- to lodge accurate emissions reports, in accordance with the prescribed methods;
- to lodge emissions reports on time; and
- to surrender sufficient permits to balance emissions.

Entities under the scope of the scheme will be expected to voluntarily comply with these obligations; if they do not they can become liable for administrative penalties, escalating to civil and criminal penalties based on the seriousness of the breach. It is also likely that participants will be required to make up for any unmet surrender of permits in subsequent years in addition to any penalties applied.

An emissions trading regulator is to be established and is likely to have the powers to request information, inspect books and facilities, and to have access to sites covered by the CPRS. It is also expected that the regulator will work with other agencies to protect against illegal collusion or the creation of artificial transactions under the scheme in order to manipulate the price of carbon permits.

Managing the costs of emissions reductions under the CPRS

A recent Treasury report presented an extremely optimistic view of the costs of implementing mitigation strategies to achieve the 2050 target of a 60 per cent cut in emissions. Modelling broad policies at a macroeconomic level, it concluded that Australia's GDP will slow by around 0.1 per cent each year in the policy scenario (requiring cuts) relative to the reference scenario (business as usual) (Treasury, 2008, p137).

Furthermore, by isolating the effect of carbon pricing on the economy, Treasury found that the economy would actually *benefit* by 0.1 per cent of GDP as a result of carbon pricing (Treasury, 2008, p138).

However, Treasury found that while mitigation policies impose small aggregate costs, carbon pricing policies result in a structural shift in the economy away from high-carbon infrastructure and technologies towards low-carbon ones. This transformation results in a significant shift in income and employment between sectors. These results are shown in detail in Annex 6.2 to this chapter with selected sectors highlighted in Figure 6.13 below.

As expected, emissions-intensive sectors are the most negatively impacted by the implementation of the emissions trading scheme including coal-fired electricity generation (–68 per cent), aluminium production (–56 per cent), oil refining (–45 per cent) and coal mining (–38 per cent). Counterbalancing these negative effects on national output there is extremely rapid growth in the renewable energy sector (+1535 per cent), forestry (+585 per cent) and an expansion in low-emissions intensity manufacturing (21 per cent) and gas power generation (+7 per cent).

While not modelling the economic effects of the CPRS itself, the White Paper details how the energy sector will receive significant support in the initial years of the scheme as a strongly affected sector (2008, pxxxviii). Under the Electricity Sector Adjustment Scheme, the government has

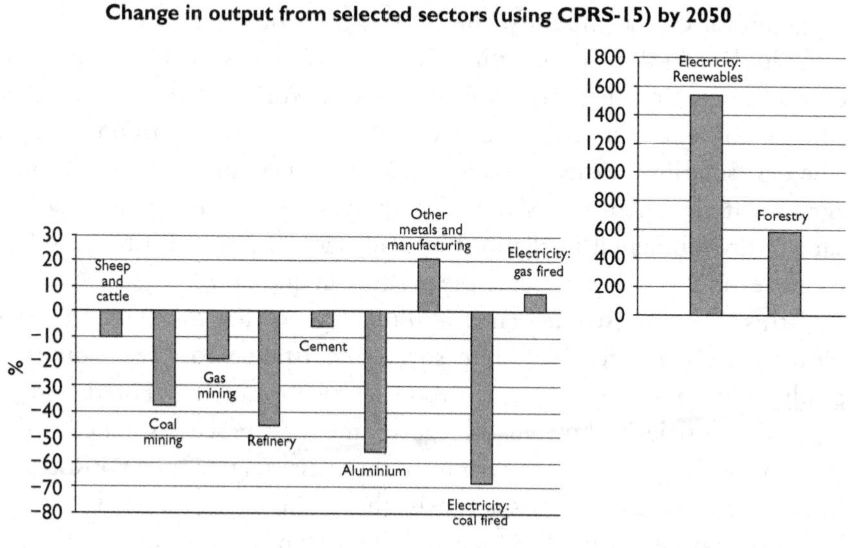

Change in output from selected sectors (using CPRS-15) by 2050

Note: See Annex 6.2 for further detail.

Figure 6.13 Sectoral impact of a likely emissions trading scenario

signalled it intends to provide assistance of around $3.9 billion to the most emissions-intensive coal-fired generators based on an initial carbon price of around AUS$25 per tonne. Assistance will be determined in relation to the historic energy output of the power station between 1 July 2004 and 30 June 2007, and the extent to which the generator's emissions intensity exceeds the 'threshold' level of emissions intensity of 0.86 tCO_2e/MWh generated, which is the average emissions intensity of all fossil-fuel based generation.

Emissions-intensive trade-exposed industries

In many cases, the carbon-intensive industries that face higher costs due to the price of carbon will be able to pass on the costs of the CPRS in the price of their final product and ultimately on to consumers. To the extent that these price rises are not mitigated by the assistance to coal generators discussed above, consumer demand for carbon-intensive energy may then change as individuals switch towards cheaper low-carbon substitutes.

However, industries facing the new carbon price may be exposed to international competition from similar firms overseas not facing a carbon constraint. In this case, assuming perfect competition and reasonable geographical capital mobility, the introduction of the carbon price may result in the relocation of polluting activities to a non-regulated market. For example, aluminium production may move from Australia to another country in Southeast Asia. This concern is referred to as carbon leakage. The best solution to this problem would be to negotiate an international agreement that neutralizes these competitiveness concerns by putting similar environmental regulations in place globally, or at least in the key countries and sectors producing the product in question.

If this is not possible, then it is often argued that the trade-exposed industries should receive some sort of assistance to keep domestic production going and prevent carbon leakage occurring. For the trade exposed industries in Australia, the government proposed assistance in the form of the free allocation of permits in the initial stages of the CPRS.

Three other broad policies also exist that could achieve a similar result. These are: border tariff adjustments on imports of the emissions-intensive goods, the exemption of trade exposed entities under the scheme, and the provision of compensation in cash.

It is noted in the Green Paper (2008, p292) that in a market-based economy the relative prices of commodities and production change regularly, often due to the interference of governments. For example, health and safety and other labour laws have affected the competitiveness of Australia's labour-intensive trade-related industries such as footwear, textiles and clothing. This has seen the profitability of many firms fall in the face of lower product prices from countries with laxer laws, and production move to countries such as China. In these cases, assistance is not usually provided to keep firms in production as these labour regulations reflect the priorities and values of the government and the community generally. The result of Australia's labour and health and safety laws has been a structural change in the economy away from labour-intensive goods.

Given other pre-existing government intervention, why should carbon-intensive industries receive special treatment? The answer to this question will ultimately be resolved through the political economy of auctioning permits as various interest groups vie for their share of economic rent. As discussed in earlier chapters, the creation of the property rights in emissions trading schemes can create billions of dollars of new assets. Who owns these assets and how they are distributed – to taxpayers or to carbon-intensive industry – is one of the key issues facing policy makers in designing the CPRS.

Auctioning of Australian carbon pollution permits

The government has already warned that while a proportion of permits will be allocated via free allocation to trade-exposed emissions-intensive industry, allocation will move progressively towards 100 per cent auctioning (White Paper, 2008, pixvi). Auctioning can provide an important early signal to market participants about the price of carbon, especially while the secondary market for permits is immature. This is because a competitive and transparent bidding process between liable entities (the demand side) will provide an indication of the tightness of the emissions cap (on the supply side).

Under the CPRS, the Australian Government intends to distribute the available permits earmarked for auctioning through 12 auctions every year. This approach aims to optimize the provision of timely carbon-price information to participants while the scheme is still immature, and to manage the impact of auctioning on business cash flows. The intention is to allow the market more room to absorb the permits over the course of the year, also potentially optimizing revenue for government. At least one of these auctions will be held after the end of the relevant reporting period, but before the surrender date to give participants the opportunity to best manage their carbon allocation, particularly at the start of the scheme (White Paper, 2008, pixvi).

An indicative auction timetable was set out in the Green Paper (2008, p269). It is intended that future 'vintages' of property rights to the atmosphere will be allocated many years in advance once the scheme is operational (see Figure 6.14).

There are two types of auction process under consideration for the CPRS: the *ascending clock* methodology where the auctioneer announces a price and the bidders indicate the quantity of permits they are prepared to buy at that price. If demand exceeds the supply of quotas, then the auctioneer raises the price in the next round and bidders resubmit their bids. This continues until the quantity of permits on offer equals or is greater than demand. The second method is a *sealed bid* process, where the

Financial year / Quarter ending	Financial Years																					
	2009-2010				2009-2010				2009-2010				2009-2010				2009-2010				2014-15	
	Sept	Dec	Mar	Jun	Sept	Dec	Mar	Jun	Sept	Dec	Mar	Jun	Sept	Dec	Mar	Jun	Sept	Dec	Mar	Jun	Sept	Dec
Vintage 2010-2011	1/4	1/8	1/8	1/8	1/8	1/8			1/8													
Vintage 2011-2012	1/4	1/8	1/8						1/8	1/8	1/8	1/8	1/8									
Vintage 2012-2013	1/8				1/8				1/8				1/8	1/8	1/8	1/8	1/8					
Vintage 2013-2014					1/8				1/8				1/8				1/8	1/8	1/8	1/8	1/8	
Vintage 2014-2015									1/8				1/8				1/8				1/8	1/8
Vintage 2015-2016 (Transitional period)													1/8				1/8				1/8	
Vintage 2016-2017																	1/8				1/8	
Vintage 2017-2018																					1/8	

Source: Green Paper, 2008, p269

Figure 6.14 Proposed Australian carbon rights auction schedule

auctioneer announces the number of permits to be sold and the liable parties submit bids that only the auctioneer sees. The auctioneer can then decide to charge the price offered by the lowest successful bidder (uniform price), or the price the bidders actually submitted (pay-as-bid).

The government intends to use the ascending clock process as this has greater transparency, revealing the demand schedule for prices to the market as part of the process (White Paper, 2008, pixvii). Furthermore, as entities in carbon-intensive trade-exposed sectors will receive free allocation, it is also intended that they will permitted to participate in the primary allocation market through a double-sided auction process (Green Paper, 2008, p273). This will allow them to unlock the value of their allocation or sell any surplus credits. However, it is noted in the Green Paper that allowing double-sided auctioning may undermine the development of the secondary emissions market.

International linking and the CPRS

The fundamental tenet of emissions trading – that emissions reductions occur where it costs least to produce them – means that the broader the scope and coverage of the scheme, the greater its potential benefit. This is one rationale for the international linking of carbon markets. The Green Paper sets out that Australia's emissions targets such as the 50 per cent reduction on 2000 levels by 2020 and the 60 per cent cut by 2050 are to be interpreted as net targets. This means that any carbon reductions imported from overseas via the purchase of carbon credits count towards meeting the target, and any export of credits from Australia count against meeting the target. The CPRS is being designed in such a way that it will be compatible with other emissions trading schemes, such as the Kyoto Protocol, the EU ETS, the New Zealand emissions trading scheme and with an eye to integrating with US schemes.

As a small country, with a tiny proportion of emissions relative to other markets such as the EU and the US, the Australian CPRS is unlikely to have a significant effect on the international price of carbon credits. This means that under unrestricted international linking, the CPRS permit price would be set by international factors outside the government's control. There was a shift in approach between the Green and White Papers away from restricted trading towards an unrestricted international linking model.

Under the White Paper, there will be no quantitative limit on eligible international credits (2008, pixix).

The Green Paper (2008, p223) outlines a framework for the consideration of international linking; this is outlined in Box 6.5 below.

Box 6.5 A framework for international linking

In general terms, links with other schemes can be described as either:

Direct: where units from scheme A can be used for compliance in scheme B (e.g. emissions credits from the EU ETS used for compliance under the CPRS).

Indirect: where scheme A and B have no direct link but both accept units from scheme C, creating an indirect pricing link between them (e.g. if both the Australian scheme and the European scheme recognized units created under the Kyoto Protocol).

In addition links can either be:

Unilateral: where units from system A can be used in system B, but not vice versa.

Bilateral: where governments responsible for schemes A and B agree to accept units from each other's schemes.

Even though the CPRS will create emissions units based on rules unique to the Australian emissions trading market, covered entities will be able to buy and trade eligible Kyoto units. By allowing relatively unrestricted access to international carbon markets polluters will have access to a safety-valve or cap on the domestic price of emissions at the ruling international price for emissions.

Allowing Kyoto units in the CPRS also encourages the development of the international carbon market and the participation of developing countries in mitigation efforts. However, as described below, not all units from Kyoto's flexible mechanisms are to be treated equally.

Certified Emissions Reductions and Emissions Reduction Units to have limited inclusion

Imposing restrictions on the use of CDM credits (CERs) would have the effect of allowing the price of CPRS credits to decouple from the international carbon price. This has both positive and negative implications. The benefits from decoupling include affording the government greater control over its domestic emissions price. This could be important especially while the future of the Kyoto Protocol is uncertain. Second, as the CDM is a baseline and credit scheme, the supply of permits under the CDM is not controlled by governments, but by carbon credit project developers. A final source of uncertainty is the concern about additionality (environmental integrity) that comes with some baseline and credit projects such as the CDM.

To account for these problems, the Australian Government is intending to limit the use of CERs by excluding 'those [CERs] that have associated contingent obligations and high administrative costs: currently, temporary certified emissions reductions and long-term certified emissions reductions from forestry-based projects' (White Paper, 2008, pixx). Joint Implementation project credits (ERUs) are to be included on similar terms to CDM project credits insofar as they can be imported by participants to meet their commitments.[25]

However, the government intends to prohibit Australian entities to host Joint Implementation projects in sectors that are covered by the CPRS (Green Paper, 2008, p347). Under the Joint Implementation provisions of the Kyoto Protocol, companies in Australia would be able to generate emissions credits (ERUs) for sale on international markets. The ERUs could then be used by another country to meet their targets. However, to issue ERUs Australia must cancel an equivalent number of its allocated AAUs to avoid double-counting the emissions reduction. This makes it more difficult for Australia to meet its target. Disallowing JI projects in CPRS-covered sectors is likely to be opposed by many low-carbon technology companies, as it is set to limit their ability to sell credits on the international market – an advantage that has often been used as a way to market Australia's involvement in the Kyoto Protocol.

Assigned Amount Units (AAUs) to be excluded

The Australian Government has also decided against allowing participants in the CPRS to access Assigned Amount Units (AAUs) under the Kyoto Protocol. These are the units in which a country's emissions cap is denominated. The problem with AAUs is that there is currently an oversupply of them on world markets as a result of 'unexpected events' (e.g. the collapse of Russian heavy industries following the transition away from communism in the former USSR), and this has led to what has become known as 'hot air'.

This hot air is underscored by a massive oversupply of AAUs relative to demand. The World Bank estimates the compliance shortfall for Kyoto Parties at about 3.3 billion tonnes CO_2e. However, the supply of AAUs has the potential to deliver around 7.1 billion tonnes CO_2e onto the international carbon market (World Bank, 2007). If this were to occur, the carbon price would effectively collapse to zero.

Finally, the government has also stated that Removal Units (RMUs) will be allowed for compliance purposes under the scheme but not beyond 2012–2013.

Other linking mechanisms

There are other emissions credit markets outside the scope of the Kyoto Protocol that it may be desirable to link with the CPRS. For example, emissions credits generated in the US, voluntary carbon markets, and credits from schemes currently not recognized, such as from Reduced Emissions from Avoided Deforestation projects.

However, a problem with units from such schemes is that if imported they will not currently count towards Australia's internationally agreed emissions targets. Thus, credits not translatable into Kyoto units will not be recognized under the CPRS. However, this position (notably for emissions reductions from deforestation) will be reviewed after the post-2012 international framework is agreed (White Paper, 2008).

The sale and transfer of Australian generated credits to international markets

The export of CPRS certificates overseas would have the effect of pushing up the domestic price for CPRS certificates, and also increasing the quantity of domestic abatement required to meet domestic and international targets. While recognizing the general desirability of allowing the export of CPRS credits to international markets, because of concerns of its effect on permit price stability the government proposes not to allow Australian permits to be converted into Kyoto units for export.

Conclusion

This chapter discusses the politics of climate change in Australia that led to the bipartisan support for a national-level emissions trading scheme in 2007. This is significant as it is one of the most concrete examples of the international norm that is strengthening around the climate change issue. As a example of global coordination, the manifestation of this norm will be essential if nations are to put aside short-term national interests in favour of the longer-term gains offered by greater cooperation in this area of policy. That this problem can be resolved through the democratic process rather than using trade sanctions or other punitive measures offers hope that solutions can be found without sparking damaging conflicts.

Early experience with emissions trading in Australia with the NSW Greenhouse Gas Reduction scheme offered mixed results but valuable lessons. While successful in developing carbon market institutions and providing incentives to carbon offset providers, the NSW experience high-lights the importance of good trading scheme design to environmental effectiveness. For instance, the use of carbon intensity rules, rather than absolute carbon emissions as the basis for the production of permits, has meant that emissions certificates can be created even while emissions from the covered plant *increase*.

The important lesson here is that implementing an emissions trading scheme does not guarantee the lowering of emissions. Much depends on how the system is designed and there can be great heterogeneity in the carbon permits created, even though they may be denominated in the perhaps misleadingly simple unit of 1 tonne of CO_2 abated. Different carbon trading schemes have different rules and different levels of quality assurance.

This point is further reinforced in the Green and White Papers that outline the proposed national scheme. The cap of the scheme is unlikely to impose restrictions much greater than what are Australia's current commit-ments under the Kyoto Protocol. However, covering around 70 per cent of national emissions, it will play a significant role in helping to meet the government's medium term target of a 5 per cent reduction in emissions by 2020 relative to 2000. Significantly the CPRS is to include the transport sector from the outset, which extends it beyond the scope of other schemes such as the EU ETS.

Following Europe's lead, it is the intention of the Australian Government to use the free allocation of permits to emissions-intensive trade-exposed sectors in order to reduce the impact of the new carbon price on firms' profitability. This is despite the recognition of alternative (more environmentally effective) mechanisms to manage the problem of carbon leakage. Perhaps more concerning for the environmental integrity of the scheme is the AUS$3.9 billion package to support the most polluting of coal generators 'adapt' to the scheme.

A study by the Commonwealth Treasury suggested that although there would be structural adjustment within sectors, the macroeconomic costs of implementing the government's long-term 2050 target of a 60 per cent cut in emissions were negligible. Indeed, Treasury models showed that a carbon price would actually slightly boost economic growth. Given the scale of the transformation required in the Australian economy some economists might caution that these models underpinned by optimistic assumptions could run the risk of lulling business, the community and politicians into a false sense of security around the scale of the challenge. This is particularly pertinent for Australia, given that it may be argued that it was the generous targets negotiated at Kyoto that have potentially contributed to delayed action in curbing rapid emissions growth in the energy sector.

Finally the chapter discussed the international linking of the CPRS in the context of the global carbon market. The CPRS will allow unrestricted access to certain Kyoto units that will effectively set a price ceiling for emission permits at the international price. However, because of the problem of 'hot air', Australia will exclude the use of Assigned Amount Units in the scheme. This highlights the problem of integrating heterogeneous schemes: linking requires nations to adopt similar systems, particularly in terms of carbon measurement and quality assurance. Where carbon permits are robust and accurately reflect the emissions they purport to represent, those permits should be more valuable. Where the additionality of the emissions reductions is questionable, then these permits may be discounted or excluded from emissions trading schemes.

Australia faces considerable challenges in curbing the strong growth emissions, particularly in its energy sector. However, for carbon markets, this problem also heralds the beginning of a new, large and globally integrated carbon market.

Notes

1   On 3 December 2007.

2   On a scale where 0 is unimportant and 100 is extremely important to voters.

3   See www.asiapacificpartnership.org/

4   Australia is one of the few developed countries with large-scale deforestation still occurring.

5   Such as the Environment Protection and Biodiversity Act (2003) and various state-based native vegetation controls.

6   This relationship was cemented during the visit of Prime Minister Howard to the US and the White House during September 2001, symbolized by his appearance in press conferences alongside the President shortly after the terrorist attacks in New York and Washington on 11 September. 'A friendship forged in the fire of war', according to President Bush (ABC, September 2008).

7   As Australia was expected stay within its Kyoto target of 108 per cent of emissions.

8   For a critical examination of the role of the fossil-fuel industry in lobbying on the Kyoto Protocol, see Pearse, 2007; http: //www.guypearse.com/. For another critical discussion of the evolution of climate policy in Australia, see Hamilton, 2001.

9   Australian Broadcasting Corporation (28 March 2007) See www.abc.net.au/news/stories/2007/03/28/1883733.htm

10   See Parliamentary Hansard, 6 February, www.aph.gov.au/hansard/reps/dailys/dr060207.pdf

11   See Parliamentary Hansard, 6 February, www.aph.gov.au/hansard/reps/dailys/dr060207.pdf

12   Now Leader of the Opposition for the Liberal Party.

13   Formally lead singer in the band 'Midnight Oil'.

14   www.pandora.nla.gov.au/pan/10052/20070321–0000/www.pm.gov.au/media/Release/2006/media_Release2293.html

15   See Chapter 2 for a discussion on the difference between baseline and credit and cap-and-trade emissions trading schemes.

16   The legislative framework for the scheme is set out by Part 8A of the Electricity Supply Act 1995, the Electricity Supply (General) Regulation 2001, and five Greenhouse Gas Benchmark Rules made by the NSW Minister for Energy. Mirror legislation exists in the Australian Capital Territory (ACT) in the Electricity (Greenhouse Gas Emissions) Act 2004 (ACT).

17   www.ggas-registry.nsw.gov.au. LogicaCMG operate the registry.

18   For example, a drought will reduce the quantity of electricity generated by hydropower, which increases the energy intensity of the NSW electricity sector, which increases the pool coefficient.

19   See Greenhouse Gas Benchmark Rule (Generation) No. 2 of 2003.

20   This, as pointed out in Passey et al (2008), raises additionality concerns.

21   See www.orer.gov.au for further information.

22   There are around 100 major power generation facilities in Australia.

23   The EU, for example, has addressed this tension by requiring entities with high levels of emissions to adopt more accurate methodologies than those with lower emissions. What it means in practice is that not all 'emission rights' are defined in the same way.

24   However, the government will review this in light of developments relating to international linking and the compliance burden likely to be placed on smaller entities.

25   Originating from projects in developed rather than developing countries.

References

Australian Broadcasting Corporation (2008) 'The Howard Years', Video documentary, ABC, Canberra

Australian Bureau of Statistics (2008) Australian Demographic Statistics (3101.0)

Department of Climate Change (2008) National Greenhouse Gas Inventory 1990–2006, www.climatechange.gov.au/inventory/2006/index.html

Green Paper (2008) *The Carbon Pollution Reduction Scheme*, Department of Climate Change, Commonwealth of Australia

Hamilton, C. (2001) *Running from the Storm*, University of New South Wales Press, Sydney

Hepburn, C. (2007) 'Carbon trading: A review of the Kyoto mechanisms', *Annual Review of Environmental Resources*, vol 32, pp375–393

HM Treasury (2006) *Stern Review on the Economics of Climate Change*, HM Treasury, London, www.hm_treasury.gov.uk/sternreview_index.htm

Howard, J. (2007) 'Terms of reference for the Prime Minister's Emissions Task Group', National Library of Australia, Canberra

IPCC (2007) *International Panel to the Convention on Climate Change, Fourth Assessment Report*, Synthesis Report, IPCC, Geneva

IPRT (2008) 'Compliance and Operation of the NSW Greenhouse Gas Reduction Scheme during 2007', Report to Minister

Kent, A. and Mercer, D. (2004) 'The Australian Mandatory Renewable Energy Target (MRET): An assessment', *Energy Policy*, vol 34, no 9, pp1046–1062

NEMMCO (2006) *The National Electricity Market Management Company Annual Report 2006*, NEMMCO

Nielsen Environmental Change Institute (2007) *Climate Change and Influential Spokespeople*, University of Oxford, Oxford, http://lk.nielsen.com/documents/ClimateChampionsReportJuly07.pdf

Parkinson, S., Begg, K., Bailey, P. and Jackson, T. (2001) 'Accounting for flexibility against uncertain baselines: Lessons from case studies in the eastern European energy sector', *Climate Policy*, vol 1, pp55–73

Parliamentary Hansard (2007) 'Matter of public importance', 6 February, Parliament of Australia

Passey, R., MacGill, I. and Outhred, H. (2008) 'The governance challenge for implementing effective market-based climate policies: A case study of the New South Wales Greenhouse Gas Reduction Scheme', *Energy Policy* 36, pp3009–3018

Pearse, G. (2007) *High and Dry*, Penguin Viking, Melbourne

Treasury (2008) 'Australia's low pollution future: The economics of climate change mitigation', Commonwealth of Australia

UNFCCC (2007) 'Tool for the demonstration and assessment of additionality', (Version 03), CDM-Executive Board, UNFCCC/CCNUCC

White Paper (2008) 'Carbon pollution reduction scheme', Department of Climate Change, Commonwealth of Australia, Canberra

World Bank (2007) 'State and trends in the carbon market 2007', Washington DC

Annex 6.1 NSW benchmark participants and status

Surrendered sufficient certificates to meet 2007 benchmark	Did not directly purchase or sell enough electricity in NSW to require the surrender of certificates for 2007	Failed to meet their greenhouse gas benchmark requirements for 2007
Mandatory Participants		
ActewAGL Retail	Citipower	Momentum Energy Ltd
AGL Sales (Queensland)	Cogent	
AGL Sales	Dodo Power and Gas	
Aurora Energy	Eraring Electricity	
Australian Power and Gas	ERM Power Retail	
Country Energy	GridX Power	
Delta Energy	NSW Electricity	
Energy Australia	Powercor	
Energy One Limited	Sun Retail	
Independent Electricity Retail Solutions		
Integral Energy		
Jackgreen International		
Macquarie Generation		
Origin Energy		
Powerdirect Australia		
Red Energy		
Tomato Aluminium		
TRUenergy		
TRUenergy Yallourn		
Elective Participants		
Amcor Packaging	n/a	n/a
Bluescope Steel		
Boral Ltd		
Carter Holt Harvey Australia		
Hydro Aluminium Kurri Kurri		
Norske Skog Paper Mills		
OneSteel NSW		
OneSteel Trading		
Orica Australia		
Visy Holdings		
Xstrata Coal Australia		
Total: 30	Total: 9	Total: 1

Annex 6.2 *Change in output by sector by 2050*

Industry	Change from reference scenario				Change from 2008
	CPRS –5	CPRS –15	Garnaut –10	Garnaut –25	CPRS –5
	Per cent	Per cent	Per cent	Per cent	Per cent
Sheep and cattle	–6.7	–10.2	–6.2	–12.7	88
Dairy cattle	3.9	2.9	4.3	7.9	116
Other animals	2.2	1.7	1.8	4.6	144
Grains	1.5	0.9	1.8	1.7	120
Other agriculture	–0.2	–1.0	0.3	–2.4	211
Agricultural services and fisheries	2.1	2.7	2.4	17.1	189
Forestry	150.1	584.5	166.2	874.9	484
Coal mining	–30.1	–38.0	–25.8	–42.4	66
Oil	–0.4	–0.6	–0.4	–0.6	–75
Gas mining	–17.0	–19.6	–16.5	–21.7	59
Iron ore mining	5.1	6.2	7.5	4.5	234
Non-ferrous ore mining	–5.6	–7.5	–3.8	–9.4	93
Other mining	0.0	–0.7	3.2	–1.8	120
Meat products	–4.8	–7.7	–4.5	–6.9	134
Other food	5.7	5.1	6.2	11.5	140
Textiles, clothing and footwear	5.3	2.8	4.2	–2.4	33
Wood products	8.8	11.9	8.3	10.5	124
Paper products	3.1	2.6	2.9	2.3	87
Printing	1.2	0.8	1.0	0.2	139
Refinery	–37.7	–45.3	–35.0	–52.2	88
Chemicals	1.6	3.8	2.2	6.4	–7
Rubber and plastic products	2.2	2.2	2.5	3.2	39
Non-metal construction products	4.2	6.1	4.6	7.8	92
Cement	–6.0	–6.4	–5.9	–6.9	106
Iron and steel	0.7	–0.2	1.1	–0.6	12
Alumina	–16.8	–24.2	–15.2	–21.3	73
Aluminium	–45.2	–56.3	–48.9	–61.9	–7
Other metals manufacturing	21.1	20.9	22.8	33.5	–71
Metal products	–2.5	–2.8	–2.7	–3.0	54
Motor vehicles and parts	7.8	7.9	7.3	7.3	45
Other manufacturing	5.7	5.1	5.6	4.2	55

Annex 6.2 *Continued*

| Industry | Change from reference scenario | | | | Change from 2008 |
| | CPRS −5 | CPRS −15 | Garnaut −10 | Garnaut −25 | CPRS −5 |
	Per cent	Per cent	Per cent	Per cent	Per cent
Electricity: coal-fired	−71.5	−68.3	−56.3	−65.9	−38
Electricity: gas-fired	12.0	6.8	−1.2	−33.8	132
Electricity: hydro	24.6	−0.6	9.2	31.1	71
Electricity: other	1735.4	1534.8	1302.6	1692.5	2960
Electricity supply	−12.8	−17.4	−13.6	−18.1	71
Gas supply	−2.8	−5.0	−3.2	−8.2	107
Water supply	−2.8	−3.6	−3.1	−4.2	100
Construction	−6.4	−7.6	−6.5	−8.9	145
Trade	−1.8	−1.8	−1.8	−1.1	158
Accommodation and hotels	−3.8	−5.3	−4.4	−7.7	187
Road transport: passenger	−3.4	−5.6	−4.1	−8.5	245
Road transport: freight	−0.5	0.8	−0.3	1.8	189
Rail transport: passenger	10.4	9.5	9.9	6.7	359
Rail transport: freight	−0.1	−1.5	1.2	−4.0	222
Water transport	−1.8	−2.5	−1.6	−2.5	174
Air transport	−1.1	−3.4	−1.7	−7.0	592
Communication services	−3.1	−3.6	−3.4	−4.0	321
Financial services	−1.1	−1.4	−1.3	−1.8	242
Business services	−0.8	−1.2	−0.8	−1.6	327
Ownership of dwellings	−4.2	−5.0	−4.4	−5.2	161
Public services	−0.8	−1.2	−0.9	−1.7	229
Other services	−4.2	−4.8	−4.5	−5.5	170

Chapter 7

Other Emerging Mandatory Schemes

The New Zealand Emissions Trading Scheme

The political context

If Australia proved an example of how the politics of a nation rapidly switch in support of climate change policies, the election of the centre-right National Government of John Key on 8 November 2008 in New Zealand provides a counterpoint. The Nationals secured 45 per cent of the national vote, up from 39 per cent in the 2005 election, compared with the Labour Party's 34 per cent, down from 41 per cent in 2005.

On coming into office, the Nationals suspended the implementation of what was to be the first national emissions trading scheme outside the EU and launched a comprehensive review of New Zealand's climate change policies. This was driven, in part, by an agreement with the libertarian ACT party, which prefers an emissions tax. However, despite the fundamental review under way, the new Prime Minister said he was still confident that an emissions trading scheme would be brought into law by September 2009 and be up and running by 2010. What his party was seeking to achieve through the review was 'more balance' in the debate, particularly regarding managing the costs of the scheme to business.[1]

In addition to the review of the New Zealand Emissions Trading Scheme (NZ ETS) the incoming government also lifted a ban that had been placed on any new build of fossil-fuel power generation, halted the phasing out of old incandescent light bulbs and distanced itself from an unfunded $1 billion Labour promise to insulate homes. However, on a more positive note, the new government is investigating alternative initiatives, such as an exemption of road user charges for electric vehicles, is committed to a 50 per cent reduction target on emissions by 2050 and reaffirmed New Zealand's intention to honour its Kyoto obligations.[2]

At the international climate negotiations in Poznań, Poland in December 2008 the new Minister for Climate Change, Nick Smith, said that it was wrong for New Zealand to be claiming to be a world leader on climate change while over the past nine years it had the third worst increase in emissions worldwide.

Figure 7.1 shows how New Zealand has significantly failed to meet its Kyoto target, which was set at the level of 1990 emissions. This has left the government liable to purchase emissions credits off international markets, making the National government's affirmation of New Zealand's Kyoto commitments a substantial commitment.

New Zealand's emissions path has two key elements. The first is an underlying trend driven by steady growth in the agricultural, transport and non-transport energy sectors. In calculating the business as usual scenario, this emissions path is assumed to grow at about 1 per cent per annum through to 2045. The second element is a forestry trend as the forests that were planted in the 1990s are due to be harvested in the 2020s

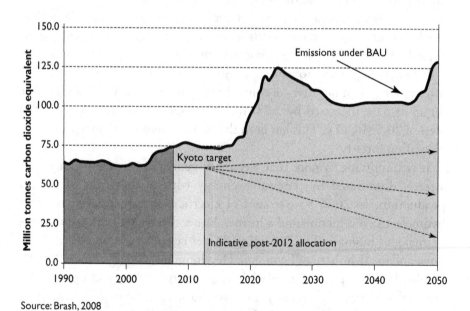

Source: Brash, 2008

Figure 7.1 New Zealand experiences third highest emissions growth worldwide (1999–2008)

and 2030s, accounting for an abrupt acceleration of emissions as they are harvested and deceleration while new forests are planted (New Zealand Government, 2007b).

In 1990, New Zealand's total greenhouse gas emissions were equivalent to $61.9MtCO_2e$, increasing by 15.9 or 25.6 per cent to $77.86MtCO_2e$ in 2006. Net emissions, including the effects of forest sinks, were $41.44MtCO_2e$ in 1990, increasing $13.679MtCO_2e$ to $55.199MtCO_2e$ in 2006, or by 33 per cent. As Figure 7.2 shows, the key sectors were energy, which grew the fastest over this period, with 45 per cent growth driven by increased fossil-fuel use in transport, heating and power generation, and agriculture, which grew by 16 per cent due to expanded cattle and livestock herds. Globally, New Zealand's emissions are small, representing around 0.2 to 0.3 per cent of total anthropogenic emissions.

New Zealand (along with Australia) is also fairly unique among developed countries with its high proportion of emissions from agriculture ($37.7MtCO_2e$), which makes up 48.4 per cent of total emissions (Figure 7.3). In other advanced economies, average agriculture emissions are around 12 per cent of the total. These emissions are largely in the form of nitrous oxide from animal excreta, fertilizer use and methane from livestock. For instance, the use of nitrogenous fertilizers has increased sixfold since 1990 (Ministry for the Environment, 2008).

It is also important to note that emissions from land-use change and forestry have been negative for some time, acting as an emissions sink. Net removals have increased by $2.24MtCO_2e$ (10.9 per cent) since the 1990 level of $20.5MtCO_2e$. This has been the result of significant investments in plantation forestry.

It is important to note that electricity generation in New Zealand is already dominated by renewable energy with 66 per cent of overall production. In 2006 55 per cent of electricity production came from hydroelectric production and a further 11 per cent came from wind, geothermal and biomass. The remaining 34 per cent came from coal and gas power plants (Ministry of Economic Development, 2007).

This large proportion of electricity generation from hydropower has meant that there is significant year-to-year variation in the use of fossil fuels for electricity generation, depending on the seasonal volume of hydropower available. Under the previous government, New Zealand had set the following targets (Ministry for the Environment, 2008):

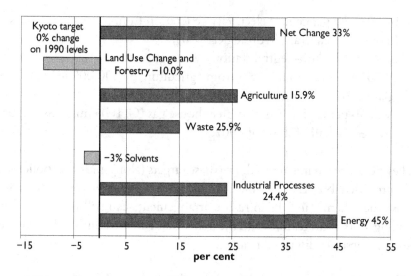

Source: NZ Greenhouse Gas Inventory 1990–2006, Ministry for the Environment, 2008

Figure 7.2 Sector-by-sector change in New Zealand emissions

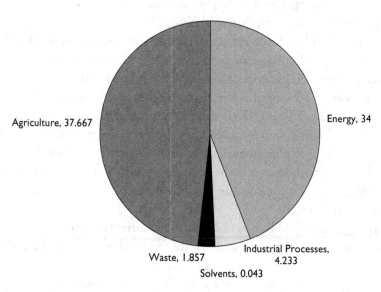

Note: Units = $MtCO_2e$.
Source: NZ Greenhouse Gas Inventory 1990–2006, Ministry for the Environment, 2008

Figure 7.3 Composition of New Zealand emissions

- by 2025 90 per cent of electricity generation from renewable sources (based on an average hydrological year);
- by 2030 a carbon-neutral stationary energy sector;
- by 2013 to reduce emissions from agriculture by 300,000 tonnes, relative to the business as usual baseline;
- by 2040 per capita transport greenhouse gas (GHG) emissions will be reduced by half of those of 2007.

A key policy mechanism to achieve these targets (alongside other policies) is the proposed NZ ETS. While it is likely that the new government will revise the scheme, insight to future arrangements can still be gained from looking at its main features and the issues that emerged during the scheme's design. These are discussed below.

Key elements of the proposed New Zealand Emissions Trading Scheme

The legislation underpinning the NZ ETS achieved parliamentary assent on 25 September 2008.[3] While this legislation is under review it still provides the initial framework for how the NZ ETS will develop. The analysis below is based on this legislation.

The NZ ETS has the objective to reduce New Zealand's emissions in line with international obligations as set out in the first commitment period of the Kyoto Protocol. However, as its scope is restricted in the short term it has limited scope to achieve this objective and other policies will be important.

A New Zealand Unit (NZU) will be the primary domestic unit of trade, which is equivalent to 1 tonne of CO_2. For the first commitment period, NZUs will be fully comparable to, and backed by, Kyoto units. The compliance period, known as the 'true-up' period, is also in line with international targets. This means the first phase of the NZ ETS is likely to run up until 2012 as well.

The legislation involves an obligation on participants to hold NZUs that match the emissions for which they are responsible. A limited number of NZUs will be issued each year, and the scheme will operate within the global cap on emissions set by the Kyoto Protocol (New Zealand Government, 2007a).

The legislation looks to allocate emissions permits via a process of free allocation and auctioning, depending on the ability of participants to pass on costs to consumers, and exposure to international competition. To be consistent with the Kyoto Protocol, this means in the first period that the government would only be able to issue NZUs in line with the number of AAUs available to it under the Protocol (or buy additional permits on the international carbon market).

At the end of the compliance period, participants will have to return to the government NZUs equal to their emissions. In the event that their emissions exceed the number of NZUs they received in the initial allocation, they will have to make up the difference by purchasing eligible credits on international carbon markets.

The proposed ETS system is therefore closely integrated with international carbon markets, with both the government and participants able to buy and sell (convert) NZUs overseas for Kyoto units. The NZ ETS may also provide for direct linking to other markets, should this be deemed consistent with maintaining the scheme's environmental integrity and goals. Given that the number of NZUs in the context of international carbon markets is very small, the price of NZUs is likely to closely follow international carbon prices. International linking will therefore, in effect, create a price cap on NZUs. However, it will also expose New Zealand to uncertainties in carbon prices as a result of unpredictable decisions in other countries and expose the domestic carbon price to uncertainties as international negotiations develop.

While there is a general principle that the NZ ETS will not impose limits on the volume of Kyoto units that can enter the scheme, the responsible minister has the ability to place restrictions on the entry of classes or subclasses of Kyoto units. For example, CERs from nuclear projects may not be allowed and some provision may be made regarding 'greened' AAUs, reflecting concerns over Russian 'hot air'.

The cap

The emissions cap for the NZ ETS is taken directly from national targets negotiated under international agreements. In the context of the Kyoto Protocol, this means that New Zealand has a cap on total emissions of 0 per cent change in emissions over the period 2008–2012 relative to 1990. This means that New Zealand must have emissions averaging $61.9 MtCO_2e$ over 2008–2012 or buy credits on international markets to make up any deficit to comply with international law.

Under a 'most likely' emissions scenario, which reflects policies in place as of April 2007, New Zealand's net position is projected to be a deficit of 45.53MtCO$_2$e over the first commitment period of the Kyoto Protocol (Ministry for the Environment, 2007). This deficit will need to be met through the purchase of emission credits on international markets.

Banking and borrowing of NZUs

The legislation underpinning the NZ ETS allows for the banking and borrowing of permits. NZUs may be banked across each compliance period, with the restriction that AAUs banked from the Kyoto Protocol commitment period can be used for compliance in the NZ ETS only after 2012.

Limited borrowing of NZUs may occur between periods through the release of the next year's permits before acquittal time. These NZUs could then be used for acquittal as soon as they are released.

Scope

The NZ ETS is intended to be as broad as possible, covering all the key emitting sectors of the New Zealand economy and to be as closely linked as possible with the flexible mechanisms of the Kyoto Protocol. This is in order to maximize the benefits of least cost emissions reduction trading offers.

A timetable for sectors to enter the scheme is set out in Table 7.1 below.

Table 7.1 *Proposed time frame for sector entry into NZ ETS*

Sector	Voluntary Reporting	Mandatory Reporting	Full Obligations
Forestry (pre-1990) and forestry removal activities (post-1989)	–	–	2008
Liquid fossil fuels (and opt-in for jet fuel)	2009	2010	2011
Stationary energy (and opt-in for purchasers of natural gas)	–	–	2010
Industrial processes	–	–	2010
Synthetic gases	2011	2012	2013
Agriculture	2011	2012	2013
Waste	2011	2012	2013

Source: New Zealand Government, 2007a

This staged implementation means that the NZ ETS will not fully distribute the cost of New Zealand's Kyoto obligations to emitters during the first commitment period. This is especially significant in the case of agriculture, which has large emissions. This means that sectors not included as of 2012 will have their emissions costs paid for by default by the government, most likely by the purchase of Kyoto units.

Point of obligation

As a general principle, the point of obligation in the NZ scheme is planned to be set in order to minimize the number of participants. For example, individual motorists will not be required to participate, but upstream entities such as fuel refineries will. In the agricultural sector, the government has signalled a preference for a processor/company point of obligation. Schedule 3 of the Climate Change Response Act 2002 sets out the activities and thresholds for participation.[4]

Allocation of emissions units

As a general principle, the proposed NZ ETS combines the use of free allocation for trade exposed participants, which are less able to pass on the increased costs of the scheme, and has limited auctioning for those sectors that do not face these costs. The proposed allocation plan was set out by the previous New Zealand Government (2007a):

In the forestry sector, free allocation is proposed to be provided for deforestation activities undertaken between 2008 and 2012 up to $21MtCO_2e$ plus a small amount of free allocation for weed control (e.g. wilding pine). From 2013 an additional $34MtCO_2e$ is planned to be provided in free allocation for plantation forestry.

For the agricultural sector and for industrial polluters free allocation will be provided for 90 per cent of 2005 emissions. This will be phased out according to a linear formula by the year 2025.

New emissions sources that begin emitting during the operation of the NZ ETS are not set to have access to the free allocation of permits, and firms that cease to operate will not retain their free allocation rights (a use-it-or-lose-it policy). No free allocation will be provided to participants in the upstream liquid fossil fuel, stationary energy and land-fill sectors.

Impact on business and households

The New Zealand Government has released a Cabinet Paper discussing the NZ ETS, which includes a Regulatory Impact Statement for the proposed scheme (New Zealand Government, 2007b). In this statement the government estimates that New Zealand emissions (excluding emissions from deforestation) are expected to be around 30 per cent above 1990 levels by 2010. The impact of various carbon prices on key components of the New Zealand economy are summarized in Table 7.2; however, it is important to note that the carbon price will not be the mechanism by which New Zealand manages this 30 per cent deficit on 1990-level emissions.

Once the scheme with its full scope is up and running in the post-Kyoto environment, assuming New Zealand has new internationally negotiated targets, the carbon price will emerge through the interplay between the New Zealand and global carbon market. As New Zealand's emissions are small relative to world markets, this will mean the carbon price in New Zealand would be the international carbon price, as New Zealand demand is unlikely to significantly push up global emissions credit prices.

The results of the modelling underpinning Table 7.2 shows how an emissions price impacts different sectors. The largest impact will be on wholesale coal prices, up 67 per cent in the moderate carbon price scenario relative to gas, which increases by 18 per cent. Petrol prices increase by 4 per cent, inducing an expected 0.6 per cent decrease in emissions.

Under the moderate price scenario of a carbon tax of NZ\$25/tCO_2e, the scheme results in retail electricity prices rising by about 10 per cent and the maintenance of emissions from electricity generation at about (2007) levels in 2020.

Most households and businesses are likely to face increased costs under the NZ ETS. Some businesses will be able to pass these costs onto consumers, while others, due to the competitive nature of their sector, will not. This is the basis for the government's industry assistance plan and the free allocation of emissions permits.

For households the main impact of the NZ ETS will be in the form of increased electricity and fuel prices. For example, a carbon price of around NZ\$25 will result in a petrol price increase of around 7 cents a litre from 2011 and an increase in electricity prices of about 5 per cent from 2010. The prices of secondary goods will also probably increase because of higher freight and other charges. To manage these effects the government proposes providing electricity rebates and financial assistance to families who receive benefits.

In the agricultural sector around two thirds of GHG emissions come from methane from livestock and dairy and the rest from the application of nitrogen-based fertilizers. In the short run the analysis in the New Zealand Cabinet Paper suggested that it would be very difficult to reduce agricultural emissions through a carbon price. Furthermore, with approximately 30,000 pastoral farmers who are largely price takers selling into concentrated markets, it is suggested that the ETS effects would be borne by farm profits. The estimated reduction in the payout to farmers as a result of ETS prices is shown in Table 7.2. It has been suggested that due to farmers' limited ability to pass on costs, agriculture will be compensated by the allocation of free permits under ETS.

The forestry sector is of key importance for New Zealand in managing its emissions. Forestry can either be a source of significant emissions reductions or increasing emissions, depending on what incentive structures are put in place. It is for this reason that forestry has been the first sector to be included in the NZ ETS, with the first tranche of credits due to be earned during 2008. Since the election of the new government and the suspension of the NZ ETS, forestry's participation has been subject to considerable uncertainty. For every 12 months that deforestation remains outside the NZ ETS, the previous government calculated that increased emissions of around $12–24MtCO_2e$ are likely to occur at a cost to the government of NZ$180–360 million (New Zealand Government, 2007b).

While the forestry sector was officially the first participant in the NZ ETS, commencing on 1 January 2009, participants are yet to receive their allocation of NZUs. The previous Labour government proposed that participation will be compulsory for pre-1990 forests, but voluntary for post-1990 forests (for areas greater than 2ha). This was to allow owners of post-1990 forests to choose whether to enter the ETS and pay for their NZUs but receive the benefits of the relevant sink credits. Forestry also was to differ from the other sectors in that it has a two-year compliance period opposed to one year for the other sectors.

Under the previous government's approach forestry was to be allocated a total of 55 million NZUs, of which 21 million were to be eligible for use during 2008–2012, with another 21 million in the period 2013–2018 and

Table 7.2 *Indicative price changes on the economy of a carbon price*

Price changes due to an ETS (assuming no compensation or free allocation)	NZ$15/tCO$_2$e	Emission price scenario NZ$25/tCO$_2$e	NZ$50/tCO$_2$e
Households			
Average increase in household expenditure (per annum)	$100–$200	$170–$330	$330–$660
Approximate percentage of total household expenditure	0.3%–0.5%	0.5%–0.8%	1%–1.6%
Liquid fuels (transport)			
Petrol c/litre GST incl. (% increase over current price)	3.7c (2.5%)	6.1c (4%)	12.2c (8%)
Diesel c/litre GST incl. (% increase over current price)	4c (4%)	6.7c (7%)	13.3c (14%)
Transport sector emissions reductions in the medium term (relative to BAU)	0.3%	0.6%	1.1%
Electricity			
Wholesale c/kWh (% increase over BAU)	0.7c (9%)	1.4c (19%)	2.9c (37%)
Retail c/kWh GST incl. (% increase over BAU)	1c (5%)	2c (10%)	4c (20%)
Long-term (2020 and beyond) electricity generation emissions levels	Emissions at about current levels: improvement over BAU around 6.5MtCO$_2$ p.a.		1990 levels: about 3.5MtCO$_2$ p.a.

Other fossil fuels

Wholesale gas $/GJ	$0.8 (11%)	$1.4 (18%)	$2.6 (35%)
Retail gas $/GJ (GST incl.)	$0.9 (2%)	$1.7 (4%)	$2.8 (6.5%)
Wholesale coal $/GJ	$1.5 (40%)	$2.5 (67%)	$4.9 (134%)

Agriculture (methane and nitrous oxide emissions only)

Dairy: reduction in payout if facing full cost (relative to payout of $4.56kg/ms)	-3.5%	-5.9%	-11.8%
Beef: reduction in payout if facing full cost (relative to current payout)	-6.3%	-10.4%	-20.9%
Sheepmeat: reduction in payout if facing full cost (relative to current payout)	-10.1%	-16.9%	-33.8%
Venison: reduction in payout if facing full cost (relative to current payout)	-12.8%	-21.4%	-42.8%

Note: GST = goods and services tax.
Source: New Zealand Government, 2007b

the final 13 million after 2018. However, the new National Government is reviewing the allocation plan and pushed back the date for allocating permits until later in 2009.

Conclusion

This section has outlined the structure of New Zealand emissions, the political context of climate change and the likely shape and impact of the emissions trading scheme that was proposed by the previous government. With a Kyoto target of stabilizing emissions at 1990 levels, but with net emissions in 2006 33 per cent above this level, New Zealand is likely to be a significant purchaser of carbon credits on international markets. In February 2009, the government is reported to have estimated the costs of complying with its Kyoto target at approximately NZ\$531 million or US\$273 million based on offset costs of around €10 per tonne (Point Carbon, 2009a).

While the November 2008 change in government has signalled a more conservative approach to emissions trading, the NZ ETS still officially commenced on 1 January 2008 with coverage of the forestry sector as the sole participant. While it is expected that the new government will seek to reduce the cost of the scheme to business, few expect that the change in government will see a major shift in policy away from emissions trading.

Emissions trading in Japan

Introduction

As one of the world's most significant economies and a bridge between western and eastern economies, it is fitting that the historical Japanese city Kyoto was host in 1997 to the summit that gave the UNFCCC's protocol its name. In 2007 Japan was ranked the third most powerful national economy (in terms of GDP) by the International Monetary Fund behind the United States and China. However, it was only fifth in terms of world emissions, with Russia and India moving up the order of polluters in front of it. This reflects the fact that Japan is one of the most technologically advanced and energy efficient countries in the world. These qualities are a double-edged sword for Japan as on one hand, it is a great source of clean technology innovation, but on the other, the scope for achieving easy, inexpensive emission cuts is low. This has contributed to making Japan a leading purchaser of both Assigned Amount Units, mainly from central and eastern Europe, and Clean Development Mechanism credits from developing countries.

Domestically, however, Japan has been reluctant to implement a mandatory emissions trading scheme, preferring to pursue an evolutionary voluntary approach with several different schemes emerging in recent years. Japan's influential industry group, Nippon Keidanren, has opposed the introduction of a European-style cap-and-trade scheme for fear it will damage Japan's already fragile economic situation (Ohta et al, 2008). Keidanren has also introduced their own voluntary action plan, with a range of voluntary industry and sector specific emissions targets that should assist the government in meeting its targets. The Japanese Ministry of the Environment also launched a voluntary emissions trading system (JVETS) in 2005 and an Integrated Emissions Trading Market in October 2008. These aim to facilitate exposure to emissions trading and build institutional capacity within industry. However environmental groups remain sceptical of voluntary targets, which often use emissions intensity rules and have less rigorous transparency and accountability back to government and the public (Kiko, 2008).

This section will discuss the political context of the climate change debate in Japan and the structure of Japanese emissions alongside the main emission trading experiments. It is a common practice of the Japanese Government to implement rules on a small scale or voluntary basis in order to gain experience and social acceptance before making such rules compulsory (Ohta et al, 2008). Observers are therefore closely watching the voluntary schemes that are emerging, such as JVETS and the Unified Emissions Trading Market, alongside the first mandatory Japanese cap-and-trade scheme in Tokyo, set to be implemented in 2010.

Political context

As host nation to the development of the protocol to the United Nations Framework Convention on Climate Change in 1997, climate change has taken a special place in Japanese politics. Prior to the Kyoto Protocol, Japan had only very limited experience with multilateral environmental treaties and foreign policy had always tracked closely with that of the United States (Kameyama, 2004, p71). When Japan finally ratified the Protocol in June 2002, agreeing to reduce emissions by 6 per cent relative to 1990, it signalled a shift in policy on both these counts.

Domestically, the tensions in arriving at Japan's target were played out between the relevant government ministries (Takeuchi, 1998; Tanabe, 1999) and the main environmental and industry groups. The Ministry for Foreign Affairs suggested that a target of a 6.6 per cent reduction on 1990 levels was realistic and would help establish Japan as a leader in Asia on environmental matters. The Ministry of International Trade and Industry was concerned at the impact this would have on energy supply and industry costs, particularly given Japan's already relatively efficient system, and argued the best that could be achieved would be to stabilize emissions at 1990 levels. The Environment Ministry employed various economic models to assess the realistic contribution Japan could make to avoid dangerous climate change and argued that, if sufficient additional measures were adopted, a reduction of between 6 and 8 per cent was achievable. The summit in Kyoto also encouraged the rise of a new influential environmental NGO, the Kiko Climate Network, to raise awareness on climate change. In international negotiations, Japan was particularly keen to secure the participation of the United States, and argued strongly for differentiated targets between Annex I countries to support that objective. This contributed to the key nations of the EU, the United States and Japan adopting emissions reduction targets in Kyoto of 8, 7 and 6 per cent respectively.

Following Kyoto in 1997, the Japanese Government established the Global Warming Prevention Headquarters, which endeavoured to bring together the relevant ministries (Government of Japan, 2002). This office articulated a detailed plan, 'Guidelines of Measures to Prevent Global Warming'. These suggested that the 6 per cent target could be achieved through emission reductions of 2.5 per cent in the industrial sector (from increased energy efficiency and use of low-carbon energy), 3.7 per cent from land use and land use change, while emissions from hydrofluorocarbons would be limited to a 2 per cent increase. The remaining 1.8 per cent would be met through the purchase of credits using the flexible mechanisms of the Kyoto Protocol.

The structure of Japanese emissions is presented in Figures 7.4 and 7.5. From this it can be seen that between 1990 and 2006 net emissions have increased by approximately 6 per cent, with the strongest rises in the energy and waste sectors.[5]

With 55 reactors, nuclear power supplies around 30 per cent of Japan's electricity needs. However, nuclear energy is currently only used at around

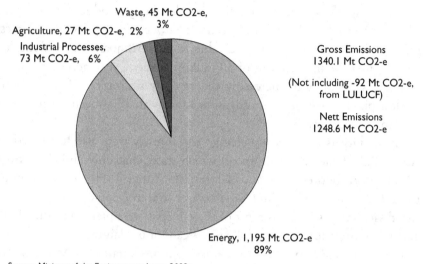

Source: Ministry of the Environment, Japan, 2008c

Figure 7.4 Composition of Japanese Emissions in 2006

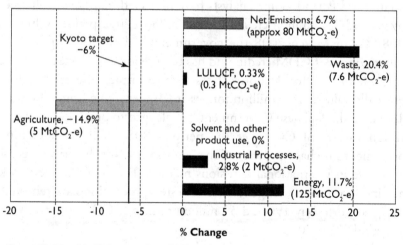

Source: Ministry of the Environment, Japan, 2008c

Figure 7.5 Change in Japanese greenhouse gas emissions 1990–2006

61 per cent of capacity. For example, electricity production at Tokyo Electric Power Co's Kashiwazaki-Kariwa power plant, the world's largest nuclear plant, was halted in 2007 due to an earthquake. This alone has resulted in a rise in emissions of 30 million tonnes a year, according to the company's calculation. Increasing the capacity utilization of the nation's nuclear plants is therefore a mitigation strategy that has been suggested by the Japanese Government.

Japan's targets for land-use change and forestry were also hampered by Article 3.3 of the Kyoto Protocol, which states that only emissions from afforestation, reforestation and deforestation since 1990 can be counted towards Kyoto targets. With 66 per cent of land in Japan covered by forest, this disadvantages Japan as most of these forests were planted in the 1950s and 1960s, therefore carbon sink credits cannot be claimed.

Instead of reducing net emissions by approximately $67MtCO_2e$ per annum or 6 per cent below 1990 levels, Japan's net emissions have actually risen by around $80MtCO_2e$ per annum or about 6 per cent. Japan intends to meet this shortfall by buying international emission credits.

The Japanese government has now put in place agreements on AAU trading and Joint Implementation with the governments of Hungary, Ukraine and Poland. Some analysts have predicted that Japan will seek to buy around 587 million credits for the 2008 to 2012 period (Ohta et al, 2008). As of March 2008 the government had already acquired 23.1 million tonnes of CDM credits and has been reported to have set a budget of ¥30.8 billion for carbon offsets. For example, one transaction is reportedly valued at 30 million tonnes at €10 per tonne from Ukraine. In all, to date the Japanese Government has pledged to purchase around 100 million tonnes of CO_2 over the period 2008–2012. In addition to government purchase of international emission credits the private sector is also active in international emissions markets. For example, the two key emitting sectors of power generation and steel production have reported to have pledged to buy 190 and 59 million tonnes of CO_2 respectively, over the period 2008–2012.

Looking forward, the government has set out a long-term goal for emissions to be at 80 per cent of 1990 levels by 2050. In 2009, the government will also announce a medium-term 2020 emissions target that will frame Japanese post-Kyoto negotiations. A government committee is currently considering a range of targets from 6 per cent above to 20 per cent below

1990 levels. The Prime Minister of Japan mentioned in 2008 that a 14 per cent cut on 1990 levels should be possible if Japan increased by 50 per cent the proportion of nuclear and renewable energy generation and replaced half of all cars with 'next generation' technology.

> ## Box 7.1 Next generation cars in Japan
>
> The Prime Minister of Japan has pledged that by 2020, 50 per cent of all cars sold will be non-petrol and also aims to convert all of Japan Post's fleet of 21,000 vehicles to electric cars. Discount rates are to be offered on parking, insurance and loans for electric vehicles (EV) and 'model districts' are being created to compete with each other for funding to install EV infrastructure. Several car manufacturers will be releasing plug-in hybrid cars in 2009 including Subaru, Toyota and Mitsubishi. These are vehicles that use an electric battery for approximately the first 100km of travel, with the option of a combustion engine petrol tank for longer journeys. Tokyo electric power has announced that it has developed a recharging device which gives a 5-minute 40km charge and a 10-minute 60km recharge (Oxford Analytica, 2009).

At present perhaps the major initiative to reduce emissions has been the Keidanren Voluntary Action Plan on the Environment, which was laid down in 1997 by Nippon Keidanren, Japan's main business group and is a major plank of the government's Kyoto Protocol Achievement Plan (Government of Japan, 2005). Its primary goal is, 'to endeavour to reduce CO_2 emissions from the industrial and energy converting sectors [fuel combustion] in fiscal year 2010 to below the level of fiscal year 1990'. Each industry group sets its own target, which can be an absolute emissions goal or energy intensity target. For example, the power generation sector has a voluntary target to reduce emissions from 0.45kg CO_2 to 0.34kg CO_2 per kilowatt hour or around 100 million tonnes a year.

In its 2007 self-evaluation report Keidanren states that in 2005, 35 industries were participating in the programme, which together represented 508$MtCO_2$e in the base year of 1990. It is claimed that this accounted for approximately 44 per cent of Japan's total emissions in 1990 and around 83 per cent of the total amount of CO_2 emitted by Japan's industrial and energy conversion sectors. The results of the programme, according to Keidanren, show that in 2005 fiscal year these industries were responsible for 505.07MtCO$_2$e, or a decline of 0.6 per cent relative to 1990 levels, making it the sixth consecutive year the target has been achieved (Keidanren, 2006). Furthermore, Keidanren state that if the effect of the worsening of CO$_2$ intensity of electricity from the long-term shut-down of nuclear power plants is excluded, CO$_2$ emissions in 2005 would have been approximately 497.8MtCO$_2$e, a fall of around 2 per cent compared with 1990.

However, each of the 35 industries selects their own targets such as gross CO$_2$ emissions, CO$_2$ emissions per unit, energy consumption and energy efficiency. The Keidanren plan endeavours to bundle these targets together into its one goal – the stabilization of GHG emissions in 2010 at 1990 levels. The Kiko Climate Network has reviewed the effectiveness of this plan and questioned the Keidanren's self-evaluation and concluded that rather than being a success, it may have held back more effective policies such as carbon trading or taxation (Kiko, 2008).

What can be observed quite clearly is that there seems to be a disparity between the results of the Keidanren self-assessment, which has emissions as stable (for around the 44 per cent of total Japanese emissions it covers), and the 6 per cent increase reported in the Japanese national GHG accounts.

Box 7.2 Japan's Top Runner approach

The Japanese Ministry of Economy, Trade and Industry created the Top Runner programme in 1998 as part of the New Energy Conservation Law for improving energy efficiency in energy using products (Bunse et al, 2007). The project targets 21 product groups including cars, air conditioners, lighting, consumer electronics, gas heaters and cookers and heavy vehicles. Each product category is divided into further subgroups and an energy-efficiency target is set for each group. Instead of setting a minimum energy performance standard, the current highest energy efficiency rate of the products in each subgroup is taken as a standard (the 'Top Runner'). This standard must then be reached within a certain time frame, and standards are continuously updated.

Evidence suggests that the Top Runner programme has been effective in promoting energy-efficiency targets (Bunse et al, 2007). For example, the energy efficiency of video tape recorders improved by 73.6 per cent between 1997 and 2003, 15 per cent above original expectations and personal computers achieved their Top Runner standard well before their 2002 target year. The programme is particularly notable as it focuses on the positive incentives of being the 'Top Runner' rather than the more negative incentives imposed by minimum energy-efficiency requirements common in the EU and America. However, as noted by the researchers at the Wuppertal Institute, despite these successes, total emissions in the relevant sectors are still increasing (Bunse et al, 2007). Policy makers should therefore be cautious about overemphasizing energy-efficiency measures at the expense of losing focus on achieving absolute emissions reductions.

While industry may have been generally opposed to implementing a mandatory emissions trading scheme, it is very much aware that Japan must keep pace with regulatory development overseas to avoid possible trade sanctions or other disadvantages. This has given rise to the emergence of several emission trading experiments as Japan seeks to gain experience with these new institutions for environmental management. These experiments are discussed below.

The Japanese Voluntary Emissions Trading Scheme

The Japanese Voluntary Emissions Trading Scheme (JVETS) was introduced in April 2005 under the auspices of the Ministry of the Environment. JVETS has around 150 participants including businesses from the steel, paper and pulp, ceramics, glass, car and chemical industries. Participation is open to private companies and entities that the Ministry deems appropriate. The stated aims of JVETS are to accumulate knowledge and experience in a domestic emissions trading scheme and to learn how to manage such a scheme with regards to the quality and accuracy of emissions data (Ministry of the Environment, Japan, 2008a).

So far, there have been three rounds of JVETS that have run concurrently. In the first there were 31 participants, in the second there were 58 and in the third 61. The sectoral distribution of participants is shown in Figure 7.6 below.

JVETS employs three methods to achieve its goal of cost-effective and real emissions reductions (Kunihiko, 2005). Firstly, under JVETS, businesses are

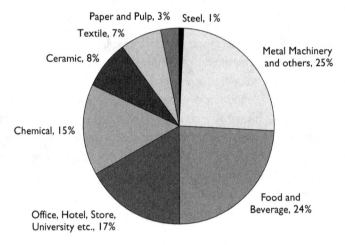

Paper and Pulp, 3%   Steel, 1%
Textile, 7%
Ceramic, 8%
Metal Machinery and others, 25%
Chemical, 15%
Office, Hotel, Store, University etc., 17%
Food and Beverage, 24%

Source: Ministry of the Environment, Japan, 2008c

Figure 7.6 Industrial share of JVETS

asked to apply for subsidies to implement energy-efficiency schemes. The Ministry of the Environment then awards subsidies to the most cost-effective plans. Subsidies can only account for up to a third of total project cost. In exchange, firms also commit to a voluntary emissions reduction target or cap. In the case of non-compliance, participants must return the subsidy. The third element of JVETS is emissions trading. This allows participants to manage the risks of over and underachievement against their cap through selling and buying permits.

Figure 7.7 outlines the operational structure of JVETS. The first step for participants is to prepare and tender their emissions cap and reduction plan to the Ministry of the Environment. This involves the identification of the geographic boundary of the site and emission sources and monitoring (metering) points, and articulation of measurement responsibility within the firm. Examples of emissions sources include: metered power-receiving equipment, incinerators, boilers, gas turbine generators, on-site service stations for forklifts, liquified petroleum gas (LPG) cylinders, waste incinerators, glass manufacturing furnaces and freezers (using dry ice). The Ministry of the Environment then selects successful participants and a 'competent authority' reviews the monitoring plans. Plans are then

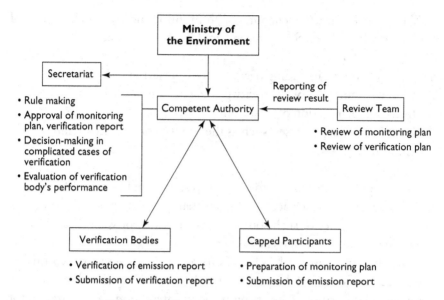

Figure 7.7 Operational structure of JVETS

implemented with each capped participant recording their emissions data and submitting it in an annual report to a 'verification body'. The base year for which emissions are benchmarked is taken as the average emissions for the previous three years. Participants are required to have allowances (called JPAs and jCERs) covering their verified emissions either from implementing efficiency measures, or from buying surplus emissions permits from another participant. The final step is for the 'competent authority' to approve the final verified annual reports.

Emissions measurement is done according to a bottom-up procedure involving the following identities:

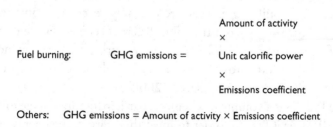

Figure 7.8 Formulae for calculating emissions

While participants are encouraged to monitor and record all sources of GHG emissions, JVETS only recognizes CO_2 from four activities:

1 from fuel usage, including heat and transportation;
2 from consumption of electricity generated from fossil fuels;
3 from the incineration of waste; and
4 from industrial processes, such as the production of cement and ammonia.

Firms do not have to account for emissions sources of less than 10 tonnes of CO_2 per annum or which account for less than 0.1 per cent of the firm's total emissions. Examples of such sources could include hot water heaters, CO_2 fire extinguishers and emergency generators.

An important feature of JVETS is its adoption of standardized quality assurance protocols. JVETS participants, 'validation organizations' and the 'competent authorities' all must comply with International Organization for Standardization (ISO) standards.[6] These include:

● ISO 14064–1: Organizational GHG Inventories Documentation, Monitoring and Reporting;
● ISO 14064–2: GHG Project documentation, Baseline Setting, Monitoring and Reporting (for relevance, completeness, consistency, accuracy and transparency);
● ISO 14064–3: Validation and Verification Process (for level of assurance, objectives, criteria and uncertainty); and
● ISO 14065: Requirements for validation or verification bodies (governance, impartiality and competence).

ISOs are considered to be an important element of Japan's emissions trading capacity building as they are one way to ensure consistency and quality assurance across countries and different schemes. One of the challenges of implementing JVETS has been ensuring the competence of the verifier, and ISO standards provide a framework to address this challenge (Ministry of the Environment, Japan, 2008b).

While JVETS is a voluntary scheme, if participants are unable to retire the required JPAs or jCERs in order to meet their target, the energy-efficiency subsidies they received should be returned.

The integrated or unified market for emissions trading

The decision to establish an 'integrated domestic market for emissions trading' was made by the Japanese Cabinet as part of its Action Plan for Creating a Low Carbon Society on 29 July 2008 (Government of Japan, 2008). This new approach is called the Integrated Market for Emissions Trading as it brings together initiatives such as the Keidanren Voluntary Action Plan for carbon emissions reductions and JVETS. It encourages participants to account for emissions, set reduction targets, and allows trading of permits, if necessary.

As of 13 December 2008 the Integrated Market had 446 participants, including the 120 existing JVETS participants covering around 50 per cent of Japanese emissions (see Table 7.3).

The government also states that 1052 companies and organizations (including these participants) have joined a 'Trail Emissions Trading Conference', which will be a public—private forum for discussing the development of the scheme (Ministry of the Environment, 2008a). The scheme includes target-setting participants, trading participants (who only trade in allowances) and providers of offsets in the Domestic Credits Scheme.

Under the Integrated Market each target-setting participant must verify their baseline emissions and then set an emissions target similar to the rigorous monitoring and reporting requirements under JVETS. However, unlike JVETS participants, organizations do not automatically receive an energy-efficiency subsidy.

The key features of the Integrated Market have been set out by the Ministry of the Environment (2008b) and have been discussed by researchers at Baker and McKenzie (Ohta et al, 2008). The scheme covers all CO_2 emissions generated from energy consumption. Target-holding participants can be an individual facility, a company or a group of companies. Emissions targets can either be for the total amount of emissions in a year or an emissions intensity goal such as emissions per unit of product produced. It is intended that participants should set targets in a way that achieves the goals set out in the Keidanren Voluntary Action Plan for their sector. Targets can be set for one or more years starting from 1 April to 31 March each year over the period 2008–2012 and participants must report results by mid-December after each accounting year. Participants receive yearly emission allowances, up to the size of their cap, either at the beginning or at the end of

Table 7.3 *Participants in the Unified Emission Trading Scheme*

Industrial sector	Number of participants
Electricity	9
Oil refinery	8
Gas	4
Steel	74
Chemical	41
Paper	12
Cement	11
Electric appliances	16
Automobile manufacturing	58
Rubber	21
Trading companies, convenience stores	13
Aviation, Construction, Transportation, Residence	7
Industrial waste disposal	1
Other industrial sectors	53
Other office sectors	13
Participants in JVETS	120
Participants with targets	**446**
Trading participants	**50**
Other Participants	**5**
Total participants	**501**

Source: Ministry of the Environment, Japan 2008b

the target year. If they receive it at the beginning, they can sell up to 10 per cent of their allocated emissions in anticipation of exceeding their targeted reductions. This option is not available to emissions intensity target-holding participants who can only receive allowances after the target year has ended.

Banking and borrowing of emissions permits is permitted between years and the government has signalled that it will intervene in the market to stop price changes due to 'over-speculation' by traders.

Aside from their own mitigation efforts, participants can use three flexible mechanisms to assist them in achieving emissions goals. These include:

1 other entities' allowances issued by (certified) emissions reductions exceeding their targets;
2 domestic CDM credits; and
3 Kyoto mechanism credits.

This introduces the second important feature of the Unified Market – the creation of a domestic offset market. Domestic credits are created by small and medium-sized businesses who are not participants in the Keidanren Voluntary Action Plan or JVETS participants. These enterprises can undertake certified emission reduction projects, including forestry biomass according to the Kyoto Protocol Target Achievement Plan (Government of Japan, 2005). Under this system, emission offset credits are produced through a partnership of domestic credit providers and large corporations who provide funds, technology or other assistance. Projects must be registered, approved and accredited with the Domestic Credit Accreditation Committee and verified by an independent third party. This process uses standardized emissions reduction documentation consistent with specific technologies in order to keep it as simple as possible while ensuring system integrity and additionality.

As the Unified Market is not a mandatory scheme there are no formal penalties for not achieving targets. However, once a target is set it may hold a high degree of informal impetus as a tacit agreement with government and society at large.

The Tokyo Cap and Trade Scheme

The first EU-style cap-and-trade scheme to be launched in Japan is to be the Tokyo Emissions Trading Scheme, to be introduced on 1 April 2010. The Tokyo Metropolitan Prefecture is responsible for around 5 per cent of Japanese emissions. Under the scheme participants will have mandatory emission reduction obligations. These can be met through achieving actual reductions, or purchasing credits on the carbon market.

While the plan is still in development, some details have been reported by Point Carbon (2009b). Under the plan, the industrial sector will have to cut emissions by 6 per cent between 2010 and 2014 from a baseline using the average of the previous three years' emissions. Office buildings, hotels and other commercial facilities will have an 8 per cent reduction target over the same period. The metropolitan government plans to increase the target cuts to 17 per cent for the next stage of the scheme, which runs from 2015 to 2019.

The Tokyo Metropolitan Government has used local planning laws to place emissions obligation on 'large offices'.[7] The government estimates that it will have around 1300 such businesses involved in the scheme. A 'large office' is defined as an office using energy of 1500 kilolitres or more of crude oil per year. Sanctions for non-compliance will include an administrative order to reduce the amount of the shortfall, multiplied by 1.3. If the facilities fail to comply with this order, the metropolitan government can buy permits on the offending party's behalf and claim the cost from the non-complying entity (Ohta et al, 2008). The scheme will take advantage of emissions trading as a supplemental mechanism to achieving greenhouse gas emissions. It is proposed that participants will be able to use credits generated from mitigation projects in Japanese small and medium enterprises under the so-called 'domestic CDM'.

While only accounting for around 5 per cent or less of total Japanese emissions, the Tokyo Mandatory Emissions Trading Scheme will be watched closely by the national government and industry groups, particularly with regards to the costs it imposes on business. It follows the path taken in California and Australia, where smaller scale emission trading schemes were implemented before more comprehensive ones. It thus sets an important precedent in the evolution of Japanese emissions trading.

Conclusion

Despite one of the most energy-efficient economies and largest and most effective voluntary initiatives in the world, in 2006 Japanese emissions were about 6 per cent above 1990 levels. With a Kyoto target of 6 per cent below 1990 levels, this implies in 2006 Japan was around 11–12 per cent in excess of its target. This will mean that in order to comply with its international commitments, Japan is likely to have to source emissions credits on the international market. This most probably will involve the purchase of so-called 'hot air' from the former communist nations of Central and Eastern Europe in the form of AAUs and also the use of CDM credits from developing or emerging countries.

Despite the arguable success of the Keidanren's Voluntary Action Plan, of stabilizing CO_2 at 1990 levels over 44 per cent of total Japanese emissions, Japanese emissions as a whole continue to rise. The Japanese have been particularly cautious about introducing a European-style cap-and-trade scheme. Instead Japan has endeavoured to establish the institutional capacity to account for and trade CO_2 through JVETS and the Unified Emissions Trading Market while avoiding placing mandatory caps on sectors or businesses. One important feature in favour of the voluntary approach particular to Japan, is the strong relationship of trust that traditionally exists between industry and government. With respects to significant environmental regulation, two previous initiatives – the regulation of Hazardous Air Pollutants and Volatile Organic Compounds – were both also based on voluntary agreements with industry. This suggests both government and industry favour the use of voluntary initiatives where possible. However, such standards, even if environmentally effective, are not likely to result in least cost mitigation. This is where emissions trading can be seen to be making an important contribution even within the distinct Japanese regulatory culture. Here we have seen the merging of voluntary self-regulation with emissions trading in the JVETS and Integrated Market.

Notes

1   For more information, see *New Zealand Herald*, www.nzherald.co.nz/nz/news/article.cfm?c_id=1&objectid=10543330, accessed 9 March 2009.
2   For more information, see the National Environment Policy 2008. www.national.org.nz/files/2008/environment%20policy.pdf, accessed 9 March 2009
3   Climate Change Response (Emissions Trading) Amendment Act 2008. For more information, see www.climatechange.govt.nz/emissions-trading-scheme
4   For more information, see www.legislation.govt.nz
5   The Kyoto Protocol baseline comprises data from fiscal year 1990 for CO_2, CH_4, N_2O and from fiscal year 1995 for HFCs, PFCs and SF_6. Note that data on these later three gases were not available in earlier years, actually technically lowering 1990 emissions. If these technically lower emissions are taken as a base then Japanese emissions look to have risen by around 11 per cent, however, this is merely an accounting anomaly.
6   For further information see www.iso.org
7   Law Concerning Maintenance of the Environment for Protection and Health and Safety of Tokyo Residents.

References

Brash, D. (2008) 'The NZ ETS: An overview', 30 October 2008

Bunse, M., Irrek, W., Herrndorf, M., Machiba, T., Kuhndt., M. (2007) 'Top Runner approach', Wuppertal Institute, UNEP Collaborating Centre on Sustainable Consumption and Production, September 2005, 2007, Wuppertal

Government of Japan (2002) 'Japan's third national communication to the United Nations Framework Convention on Climate Change', Submitted to the UNFCCC Secretariat, Tokyo

Government of Japan (2005) 'Kyoto Protocol Target Achievement Plan', Tokyo, www.kantei.go.jp/foreign/policy/kyoto/050428plan_e.pdf, accessed 9 March 2009

Government of Japan (2008) 'Action Plan for Achieving a Low Carbon Society', Cabinet Decision, Tokyo, www.kantei.go.jp/foreign/policy/ondanka/final080729.pdf, accessed 9 March 2009

Kameyama, Y. (2004) 'Evaluation and future of the Kyoto Protocol: Japan's perspective', *International Review for Environmental Strategies*, vol 5, no 1, pp71–82

Keidranren (2006) 'Results of the fiscal 2006 follow-up to the Keidanren Voluntary Action Plan on the Environment (summary – section on global warming measures, performance in fiscal year 2005)', Nippon Keidanren, Tokyo

Kiko Climate Network (2008) 'Fact Sheet of the Keidanren Voluntary Action Plan', Kiko Network

Kunihiko, S. (2005) 'Japanese Voluntary Emissions Trading Scheme – Overview and analysis', INECE Workshop To Identify Linkage Issues, 17–18 November, American University's Washington College of Law, Washington DC

Ministry for the Environment (2007) 'Projected Balance of Emissions Units During the First Commitment Period of the Kyoto Protocol', Ministry for the Environment, Wellington, www.mfe.govt.nz

Ministry for the Environment (2008) www.climatechange.govt.nz/reducing-our-emissions/the-path-ahead.html, accessed 9 March 2009

Ministry of Economic Development (2007) 'New Zealand energy data file', Ministry of Economic Development, New Zealand

Ministry of the Environment (Japan) (2007) 'JVETS Monitoring and reporting guidelines, Version 1.0 17 February 2007', Ministry of the Environment' Tokyo

Ministry of the Environment (Japan) (2008a) 'Experimental introduction of an integrated domestic market for emissions trading, result of an intensive recruitment (Oct. 21 - Dec 12)', Ministry of the Environment, Tokyo

Ministry of the Environment (Japan) (2008b) 'Experimental introduction of an integrated domestic market for emissions trading, Global Warming Prevention Headquarters', Decision on October 21, Ministry of the Environment, Tokyo

Ministry of the Environment, Japan (2008c) 'National Greenhouse Gas Inventory Report of Japan', Greenhouse Gas Inventory Office of Japan (GIO), National Institute for Environmental Studies, Ibaraki, Japan

Muramatsu, H. (2007) 'Climate change policy in Japan', presentation given by the Mission of Japan to the EU, Brussels

New Zealand Government (2007a) 'Framework for a New Zealand Emissions Trading Scheme'

New Zealand Government (2007b) 'A New Zealand Emissions Trading Scheme: Key Messages and Strategic Issues', Cabinet Policy Committee

Ninomiya, Y. (2008) 'Japanese Voluntary Emissions Trading Scheme (JVETS) monitoring, reporting, verification system, ICAP 1st Carbon Forum, 19 May 2008', Ministry of the Environment, Japan

Ohta, H., Hiraishi, T. and Ticehurst, E. (2008) 'New trade initiatives', *International Financial Law Review*, London, www.iflr.com/Article.aspx?ArticleID=2075190

Oxford Analytica (2009) 'Crisis bodes well for electric car', *Daily Brief*, Oxford

Point Carbon (2009a) 'Carbon market Australia-New Zealand', *Point Carbon*, vol 2, no 4, p27

Point Carbon (2009b) 'Tokyo sets cap for emissions trading', *Point Carbon*, Hisane Masaki, Tokyo

Takeuchi, K. (1998) 'Chikyu Ondanka no Seijigaku' [The Politics of Global Warming] Asahi Sensho, Tokyo

Tanabe, T. (1999) 'Chikyu Ondanka to Kankyo Gaiko' [Global Warming and Environmental Diplomacy] Jijitsushinshn, Tokyo

Chapter 8

Voluntary Offsetting Market

Introduction

While this book is primarily focused on mandatory compliance or emissions trading schemes, no analysis of the carbon markets would be complete without covering the voluntary offsetting market. Voluntary offsetting began before the Kyoto Protocol and had some influence on the makings of the CDM. However, the CDM system has itself allowed for a better understanding of offsetting activity and forced the voluntary sector in turn to become more professional.

This chapter sets out the context within which this market was established. It goes on to describe the principles behind voluntary offsetting, the type of projects, the market size and the type of buyers. This is followed by a section that summarizes the issues associated with voluntary offsetting. We conclude with a consideration of regulatory initiatives. We consider the impact of these new rules on the voluntary market.

Origins

The term 'offsetting' is often used to encompass all voluntary approaches to compensating (internalizing or neutralizing) the climate impact of GHG emissions from a specific activity.

According to Mission Climat (of the Caisse des Dépôts), the first company to use offsetting was the US power company AES Corporation (Bellassen and Leguet, 2007). In 1989 this company decided to finance an agro-forestry project in Guatemala by investing $2 million in the planting of 50 million trees. The goal was to offset emissions resulting from a new power plant built by the group in Connecticut.

With the recognition and institutionalization of this principle within the framework of the Kyoto flexibility mechanisms, voluntary offsetting has witnessed a tremendous growth over the past five years. Although the size of the market is still very small – about 42 million credits sold in 2007 for just over $258 million – the growth potential is high. For instance, in 2006 the turnover of the sector was only $58 million (Hamilton et al, 2008). It should be noted that even though the voluntary carbon markets function outside the compliance market, a significant share of the offsets sold in the voluntary markets are sourced from CDM projects.

Principle

The principle of offsetting is reasonably straightforward. First, an offset provider estimates a polluter's emissions (or more precisely their carbon footprint, as indirect emissions from electricity or the use of public transport are also accounted for). For individuals it is usually a rough estimate made using an online calculator. For larger organizations this requires a carbon audit, for example using the GHG Protocol, the Bilan Carbone™ method developed by ADEME or Defra's Company Reporting Guidelines (see Chapter 1). In the case of flight offsets, the destination is specified and the calculator automatically estimates the emissions. These calculators use emissions factors that rely on a set of assumptions including the high altitude pollution multiplier effect (although the science of the multiplier effect as applied to aviation emissions is still uncertain, see Chapter 1) and the air passenger occupancy rate or the type of aircraft. These different methods mean emissions estimates to be offset often vary from one provider to another. The offset provider then proposes to offset these emissions at a certain price per tonne. This price also varies significantly depending on the type of project in which the offsetting company invests. For example, projects in renewable energy or energy efficiency are generally more expensive and considered more reliable than forestry projects. Indeed, the type of credits (and thus the associated guarantees of additionality, permanence, traceability and compliance with other specific criteria) is the dominant determinant of the offsets' price.

Type of projects

The credits come primarily from five types of projects: forestry, renewable energy, destruction of fluorinated gases, and energy efficiency projects related to waste management or recovery of methane. A feature of voluntary

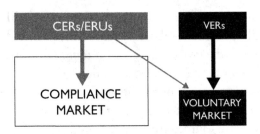

Figure 8.1 Carbon offsets in the compliance and voluntary markets

offsetting projects is that they are often small scale. For instance, a project in energy efficiency could be related to the insulation of a school or the replacement of an inefficient diesel motor. More than one third of the offset credits sold come from forestry projects or other sink projects. Renewable energy projects only represent a third of the credits sold. Credits issued from the destruction of fluorinated gases, often regarded as generating little benefit in terms of sustainable development, accounted for 20 per cent of the credits sold in the voluntary market in 2006. In 2007 F-gases projects accounted only for 2 per cent of the credits sold on the voluntary market and due to sustainability concerns this is likely to fall further. The geographical origins are also wider than in the mandatory compliance market, with

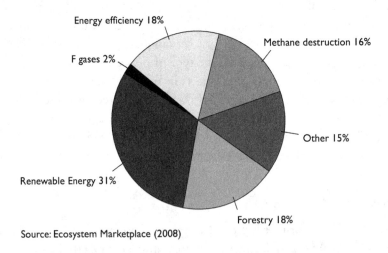

Source: Ecosystem Marketplace (2008)

Figure 8.2 Type of offsets projects in 2007

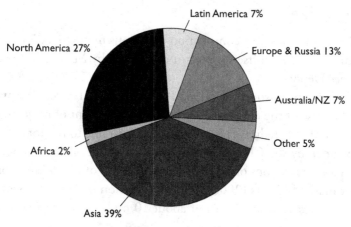

Source: Ecosystem Marketplace (2008)

Figure 8.3 Geographical origins

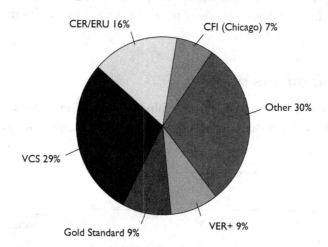

Note: VCS = Voluntary Carbon Standard; CFI = Carbon Finance Instrument
Source: Caisse des Dépôts

Figure 8.4 Type of offsets credits

credits generated both in Europe[1] and North America. However, Africa is still underrepresented, as for the CDM. CERs (and ERUs) accounted for 16 per cent of the credits used voluntarily in 2007.

Market size

The chart below shows a compilation of various market studies predicting the future size of the offsetting sector conducted by Mission Climat of the Caisse des Dépôts.

The most optimistic projection, $1GtCO_2e$ in 2010, seems unrealistic, largely because of the time needed for the development of projects and the limited supply of credits. This volume is comparable to the total emissions to be avoided by the CDM between 2008 and 2012. It is also about 3 per cent of global emissions of GHG or almost a third of EU27 emissions. The high estimate of Harris (2006) (about 50 million offsets credits in 2010), which includes a linear growth of about 10 million credits a year, may be more realistic.

Another factor to consider is the expected regulation of the sector. Future regulations could act as a filter, and some actors now selling credits that do not comply with the criteria defined under the CDM, the Gold Standard or other quality standards may cease to operate or at least reduce their supply of credits as a result.

Carbon offsets buyers

If we look at the demand side in the voluntary offsetting sector, we find that companies account directly for most of the market activity (or indirectly by

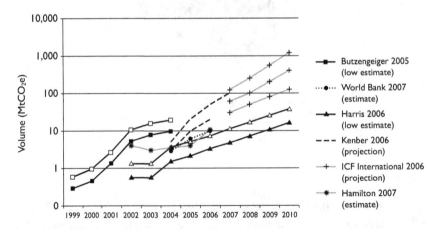

Figure 8.5 Estimates and projections of the market volume of offsetting credits

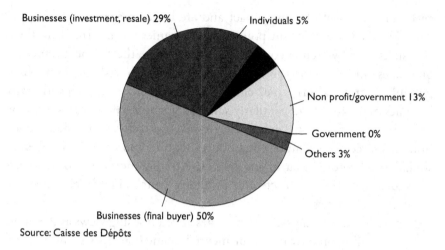

Businesses (investment, resale) 29%   Individuals 5%

Non profit/government 13%

Government 0%

Others 3%

Businesses (final buyer) 50%

Source: Caisse des Dépôts

Figure 8.6 Profile of buyers of offset credits

internalizing the offsetting price in their products). In 2006, purchases of offsets by individuals accounted for about 17 per cent of the market.

Within the corporate world, banking is a major customer. In December 2004 HSBC decided to become the first carbon-neutral bank. Large events have also offset their emissions, for example, the Olympic Games in Salt Lake City in 2002, the World Cup in Germany in 2006 and the UNFCCC conference in Bali in 2007.

Issues and critical elements

Purpose of offsetting

One of recurrent criticisms of offsetting is that it does not reduce emissions at source. Some critics believe that such mechanisms distract businesses and citizens from the main objective: reducing emissions. These critics believe that companies or citizens that offset will continue to act as before, simply paying a few more dollars or euros. For them offsetting is a new form of indulgence and avoids structural and behavioural change in the fight against global warming.

For its proponents offsetting plays multiple roles. First, offsetting is a tool to raise awareness and educate individuals and companies about their climate impact. Though offsetting, individuals and businesses become aware of their own climate impact and are better prepared to act on it. Also, by putting a price on pollution, companies are internalizing their emissions costs, which encourages them to reduce them. For instance, if one takes into account the offsetting cost for a short-haul flight, it is possible that an alternative, cleaner choice such as high-speed train becomes more attractive. Similarly some companies, knowing the costs of offsetting their emissions, may decide to invest directly in emission reductions at source, for example when budgeting for a more efficient boiler. It should also be noted that in any case offsetting money seeks to subsidize emissions reductions projects and promotes sustainable development in developing countries.

In practice, offsetting can embody these two opposing views at the same time, depending on how it is implemented. Some operators spend a lot of time on the audit and reduction stages, while others ignore this step. Some choose their projects carefully ensuring that they have no adverse effects and are genuinely additional, while others issue credits from existing activities (e.g. hydroelectric installations) or as yet incomplete projects (or before project starts, based on assumptions). Thus whether offsetting should be considered as positive or negative from a climate perspective can be very contingent.

Calculation of emissions to be offset

One of the issues regarding voluntary offsetting is that there are no official standards for calculating emissions. While there are guidelines to allow countries that have ratified Kyoto or companies involved in the EU ETS to estimate their emissions accurately, no such rules are defined in voluntary offsetting. If some offsets providers are more scientifically up to date or more accountable and use the latest available IPCC emissions factors, others use inaccurate figures, sometimes in good faith, due to a lack of knowledge.

For example, to estimate emissions from electricity companies it is necessary to know the name of the power supplier and its carbon intensity (usually expressed in gCO_2/kWh delivered to the network). Often offsetting providers use an average rate that is not always representative of the actual context.

These inaccuracies can be even greater when a company calculates its global carbon emissions. A company carbon footprint varies according to the chosen scope. Assumptions also have to be made about the greenhouse gases included (i.e. CO_2 or the six GHGs recognized by Kyoto?), the geographical area (e.g. should travel abroad be taken into account?), the company boundaries (inclusion or exclusion of subsidiaries). These problems explain why CO_2 emissions vary from one carbon audit to another and why independent or accredited consultants are often contracted.

Verification

Verification is a central element of project-based offsets. Avoided emissions need to be verified by an independent third party who can provide assurance on the calculation. Currently Certified Emissions Reductions issued under the CDM and Verified Emissions Reductions (VERs, sometimes also describe as Voluntary Emissions Reductions) assessed under the Gold Standard and the Voluntary Carbon Standard give perhaps the greatest assurance on the quality of the offset projects. Other standards, such as the Verified Emissions Reduction+[2] or the Voluntary Offset Standard, are being developed and could play the same role.

Traceability register: In the project cycle

Multiple sales of the same credit is a risk in carbon offsetting. Once a credit has been sold to a customer it should be cancelled. Registries such as the CDM registry and the ITL have so far no equivalent in the voluntary market. To overcome this problem, many operators have their own registers. However, the Gold Standard, Voluntary Carbon Standard, Verified Emissions Reduction+ and Voluntary Offset Standard are developing their registries. Ultimately it may be desirable for sellers of credits to join a common registry in order to guarantee the cancellation of sold credits and avoid the risk of fraud and double-issuing.

Another problem is related to the stage in the project cycle. Some operators do not hesitate to sell non-existent VERs (or even CERs) credits. Indeed, because it is cheaper to buy future CERs or VERs before they are verified or certified, some operators invest only in this type of project and sell these credits to their customers. Some of these VERs/CERs projects might never be validated but the credits have already been sold. By behaving like this offset providers pass to customers the risks of validation, often without warning them. Moreover, such a practice also raises the question of the timing of emissions and offsetting. Ideally emissions should be offset by reductions that have already been verified/certified, not with projects that are likely to deliver emissions reductions in the future.

Forestry projects

These projects are considered more controversial than energy or waste projects (e.g. methane recovery in landfills), mainly because of the greater uncertainty in accounting for avoided emissions and the temporary aspect of carbon sinks (if the trees rot or burn the carbon sink becomes an emission source, thus losing all offset benefits). Nevertheless forestry projects may represent a significant source of income for people living in high deforestation areas. Protecting forests is also a key element in the fight against global warming (Osborne and Kiker, 2005). There is clearly an urgent need for the development of financial mechanisms to encourage owners of primary forests not to exploit them. Here, too, only good quality project governance can give offset buyers the necessary guarantees.

Projects in Annex B countries and double-counting issues

Offsetting projects in so-called Annex B countries (most industrialized nations and some economies in transition (see above)) can also lead to the double-counting of emissions reductions. Indeed, if a project reduces emissions in the EU (e.g. insulation of a school in London), the state (in this case the UK) will save AAUs that it will be able to sell on the market to allow another country to emit more. Under the JI system ERUs are generated only after the cancellation of an equivalent amount of AAUs, so that the reduction is not counted twice, however, there is no such mechanism to avoid double counting voluntary offsets.

Regulatory initiatives

Carbon offsets are becoming increasingly commonplace, and the volumes in the voluntary carbon market are growing rapidly. However, customers are still often confused by the complexity of the market. With 1 avoided tonne of CO_2 selling for anything between €5 and €40, and with allegations exposing misconduct by some offset providers in the press, it is not easy for customers to know if they are getting value for money. Clearly, there is a need for further improvement in credibility in the voluntary carbon offsetting market, so that customers gain confidence in the offsetting schemes they are using.

Recent developments in the UK and France, two countries where the voluntary carbon market is growing rapidly, show how governments can intervene to address those problems.

Entrepreneurs in the carbon offsetting sector are facing the same dilemmas as organic food suppliers or fair trade companies. On the one hand, they wish to deliver the best quality products that give strong guarantees and promote sustainable development, but on the other hand their costs and therefore prices must remain reasonable. Single words or phrases – whether 'organic', 'fair trade' or 'carbon neutral' – can cover varying degrees of effort and are open to abuse. In the case of organic food, given the interests at stake, the use of the word has been subject to EU regulation since 1991, whereas fair trade certification remains in the hands of the voluntary sector.

In February 2008 the French environmental agency, ADEME, and the UK environment ministry, Defra, published their responses to the lack of standardization in the sector. New regulations were initiated in early 2007 and in each case a consultation process was conducted involving the offset providers themselves. Companies and individuals are often attracted towards officially recognized offset providers – and, as a result, these government initiatives have influence the market and are likely to influence the price of carbon offsets.

Numerous differences exist between the British 'Code of best practice for carbon offset providers' and the French 'Charter of voluntary offset greenhouse gases' (Defra, 2008; ADEME, 2008). The British Code recognizes Kyoto-compliant credits from the CDM or JI projects or EU allowances (EUAs) from the EU Emissions Trading Scheme. It will wait until 'industry has reached a consensus on a standard and it has been fully operational for six months' before confirming whether credits approved under this voluntary offset standard can be included in the government code.

Defra restricts the application of the code to EUAs, CERs and ERUs, and excludes VERs. This proposal, made public in early 2007 has been controversial. Following numerous complaints from stakeholders, the Secretary of State for the Environment, Hilary Benn, annexed an open letter to the draft code, where he states that 'VER market can add value … by bringing forward innovative projects which can be tried and tested before entering the compliance market'.

According to the British Government, good quality offsets should comply with the following principles: They should be additional to business as usual and address problems of leakage. The reduction activity should not simply displace emissions; GHG reductions should not be double-counted, preferably through use of a registry. Reductions should be permanent; and offsets should be transparent and independently verified and certified (i.e. with ex-post certification).

The Defra code promotes the use of 'Defra's Company Reporting Guidelines' and encourages the use of a radiative factor of 1.9 for aviation emissions (Defra, 2007). Offset providers seeking accreditation by Defra must complete an online application form and pay an initial fee. The accreditation is product specific and does not concern all the activities of the offset supplier. The fee for adding an offset product to the accreditation database is £4500. The government has appointed AEA Energy & Environment as the accreditation body for the code, with responsibility to regulate and enforce compliance. Failure to meet the requirements while using the Quality Mark may be considered a breach of a contract and would see the provider taken to court. The code was launched in January 2009 by DECC and renamed 'The Government's Quality Assurance Scheme for Carbon Offsetting' (DECC, 2009).

The French Charter preamble states that its aim is to 'progressively assure the quality and accuracy of the voluntary offset system in France', while linking it to existing international initiatives. Article 1 states that the Charter is neither a new standard nor a certification label but a complementary tool to existing initiatives. The main requirements for signatories of the French Charter are that emissions reductions proposed must be 'real, verifiable, additional and permanent'.

The French Charter justifies the use of VER offsets, stating that CDM/JI projects do not necessarily meet the needs of the voluntary market since less than 20 per cent are from renewable energy projects, almost none from the forestry sector, and the majority are located in two countries (China and India).

Interestingly, signatories of the ADEME Charter can either be offset providers or participating organizations and companies claiming 'carbon neutrality'. The rules are similar for both categories and are respectively described in articles 4 and 5 of the charter. Participants who choose to voluntarily offset must 'systematically describe the activities and scope that

Table 8.1 *Comparison of Defra and ADEME initiatives*

Comparison of Defra and ADEME initiatives		
	DEFRA	*ADEME*
Users	Offset sellers	Offset sellers and buyers
Fees	£4500 per product	Free
Benefits	Quality Mark	Quality Mark
Type of credits	EUAs, CERs, ERUs	VERs, CERs, ERUs
Radiative forcing factor for flights	1.9	2
Recommended guidelines for carbon accounting	Defra's Company Reporting Guidelines	ADEME's Bilan Carbone™
Compliance auditor	AEA Energy & Environment	Monitoring Office (ADEME)
Penalties in case of non-compliance	Prosecution	Exclusion

is subject to offsetting'. Those who want to use the expression 'carbon neutral' must associate this claim with emissions reduction actions.

The French Charter encourages the use of the ADEME's Bilan Carbone (carbon footprinting) methodology. This requires the use of a radiative factor of 2 for aviation emissions. Unlike Defra's reporting guidelines, the Bilan Carbone footprinting method promotes the inclusion of indirect emissions (for instance from refining and transport of petroleum products).

To become a registered offset provider under the French Charter organizations can register on a website and provide detail on the projects proposed to meet the requirements. The French Charter includes implementing a Monitoring Office, which will investigate any claimed abuse as well as carry out random spot checks. A breach of the rules defined in the charter will lead to exclusion.

Conclusion

While on the global scale the voluntary market remains small in comparison to the regulatory market, it is growing rapidly and now represents an important stimulus for the development of carbon reduction projects around the world. The voluntary market offers greater flexibility and can be used to encourage project innovation that might not otherwise occur in the compulsory sector. The voluntary status of this activity means that a wide variety of different practices and standards can be found and harmonization is slow. To date, a light approach to government regulation to try to ensure the quality of the offsets while at the same time leaving a maximum amount of flexibility for innovation in the sector is proving to be difficult to balance.

Notes

1   Projects in Europe (or other Kyoto Annex B Parties) create double-counting issues. Carbon reduction projects in Annex B countries would only be credible if the reductions created are not subsequently counted in these countries' Kyoto emission target. Otherwise these reductions are counted twice, once as belonging to the person who (voluntarily) contributed to the project and a second time by the country that would otherwise have had to impose this reduction internally. Only if Annex B countries with emissions reduction obligations withdrew AAUs for all credits created though the voluntary market (VERs) could this option be viable, e.g. JI projects. National emissions from these countries are already under a cap. Emission reductions generated through a voluntary project will generate an excess of AAUs (or avoid the purchase of Kyoto Units). Theoretically projects must be developed in countries without emissions targets (i.e. countries eligible for CDM projects) or be associated with a cancellation of a similar amount of AAUs (as for a JI project) in order to be additional.
2   Managed by the verifier TÜV-SÜD.

References

ADEME (2008) 'Charte de la compensation volontaire des émissions de gaz à effet de serre', www.ecologie.gouv.fr/IMG/pdf/Charte_de_compensation_volontairefinale.pdf, accessed 1 March 2009
Bellassen, V. and Leguet, B. (2007) 'Compenser pour mieux réduire. Le marché de la compensation volontaire', *Note d'étude de la Mission climat de la Caisse des dépôts*, September
Brohé, A. and du Monceau, T. (2008) 'Giving credit to the voluntary offset market', *The Green Economist*, July
DECC (2009) 'The Government's Quality Assurance Scheme for Carbon Offsetting', http://offsetting.defra.gov.uk/cms/assets/Uploads/NewFolder-2/Scheme-Requirements-Document.pdfÿ§, accessed 1 March 2009
Defra (2007) 'Guidelines to Defra's GHG conversion factors for companies reporting', www.defra.gov.uk/environment/business/envrp/pdf/conversion-factors.pdf
Defra (2008) 'Climate Change: Carbon Offsetting, Code of Best Practice', www.defra.gov.uk/environment/climatechange/uk/carbonoffset/codeofpractice.htm, updated 19 February

Hamilton, K., Sjardin, M., Marcello, T. and Xu, G. (2008) 'Forging a Frontier: State of the Voluntary Carbon Markets', 8 May, Ecosystem Marketplace and New Carbon Finance, Washington DC and New York

Harris, E. (2006) 'The voluntary retail carbon market: A review and analysis of the current market and outlook', MSc Thesis at the Imperial College of London, 158pp

Osborne, T. and Kiker, C. (2005) 'Carbon offsets as an economic alternative to large-scale logging: A case study in Guyana', *Ecological Economics*, vol 52, p4

Chapter 9

Conclusion: Carbon Markets in the Age of Uncertainty

The title of this book, *Carbon Markets: An International Business Guide*, takes as its premise that business will play a key role in reducing greenhouse emissions. At the most basic level, carbon markets seek to turn the tables for business on climate change. Rather than seeing industry only as the culprit of environmental damage to be punished through taxes or regulations, carbon markets give business an opportunity to be environmental champions, harnessing the more positive power of innovation and entrepreneurship through the chance to make money from reducing emissions.

We are currently moving through what Harvard economist John Kenneth Galbraith once called the Age of Uncertainty. The flaws of the current financial system – the brain of the capitalist economy that allocates how and where money is spent – are now revealing themselves through the drying up of credit, recession and unemployment. As Galbraith predicted, we are seeing a resurgence in Keynesian policies from governments as they step in with trillion-dollar banking support packages and new spending plans totalling US$2451 billion worldwide (HSBC, 2009). As of March 2009, $429 billion of these funds had been earmarked for 'green initiatives' across countries such as the United States, China and the European Union to Australia, South Korea and Canada. The idea behind this is for governments to temporarily stimulate economic activity and investor confidence at a time when the private sector is in decline. This time of crisis also presents a window of opportunity to change the politics and policies of an era that contributed to such unsustainability. Importantly, and getting to the subject of this book, this must extend beyond the regulation of the financial sector, to also cover improved regulation of our environment, and the pressing risks of dangerous climate change.

As some of the institutions that we have taken for granted disappear and are remoulded around us, business must re-examine not just its commercial position and how it is influenced by society, but also how business itself influences society through its employment of different values and technologies. Despite the crisis, business is being looked to for solutions to sustainability problems ranging from climate change to poverty alleviation and health. Emissions trading is one framework that is being put in place to assist it with this task. In this book we prompt business to make a fresh examination of how it relates to such institutions.

Much more than the acts of buying and selling, markets are the interrelated systems of human interaction by which we organize some important aspects of our lives. Together, these systems constitute the economy. Economics must focus on understanding the nature and governance of these systems if it is to stay relevant. In particular it must adapt to take account of the natural environment it has traditionally treated as limitless and free. Disturbingly, recent events have suggested that the wires under the table connecting the traditional economic levers to be pulled by government are somewhat detached from the real world and have lost their effectiveness at achieving outcomes. This means more rigour and perhaps less ideology is needed in relating policies to desired outcomes.

Emissions trading is an idea born out of the economic theory of property rights (Coase, 1960). In theory, it provides the incentives for continual improvement in environmental outcomes, achieves these at the lowest cost to society and is a new source of government revenue, less politically sensitive than traditional taxation. However, in practice much can go wrong in the implementation of emissions trading. Property rights may be poorly defined through the use of emissions intensity goals, or through greenhouse gas accounting systems that do not accurately reflect actual emissions. Lack of cooperation between jurisdictions reduces the scope of trading, diminishing one of the key advantages of cap-and-trade systems. There may be no cap on emissions at all as in the case of baseline and credit schemes, and this may undermine the environmental integrity of the system. The billions of dollars of revenue generated from the institution of emissions trading is often recycled back to the most polluting firms as 'structural adjustment assistance', diminishing environmental effectiveness, introducing equity and justice problems and slowing the transition to the low-carbon economy. For example, the extent of this last problem in the proposed Australian emissions trading scheme is staggering in its scale.

If these problems are not addressed in the design of emissions trading schemes, we may well be planting the seeds of the next sub-prime crisis, this time in the carbon market. Decisions taken in the design stage of emissions trading schemes will also dictate the level of control governments can exert over the pace and direction of technological change. Defining the scope of the scheme and setting sectoral caps and rules for including offsets can fundamentally alter the scheme outcomes. For example, some schemes exclude carbon credits generated from nuclear energy, or from avoided deforestation, or indeed from entire countries in the case of 'Russian hot air'. In principle it can be argued that this limits the 'market' opportunities in delivering least cost abatement and works against the efficient market envisioned by economic theorists. In practice, carbon markets need to be designed to take into account other policy objectives relevant to sustainable development, so such choices are not simple or avoidable.

While the financial crisis and recession has put many governments on the defensive when it comes to climate change policy, we see current events in a strategic context as representing a structural break in the politics and economics that contribute to sustainability and economic progress. The evidence gathered in this book suggests that, despite the crisis, momentum for improved climate governance is gathering pace. With the implementation of national carbon markets in the US, Australia and New Zealand over the next few years, carbon markets are likely to treble in size. This is irrespective of the outcome of international negotiations in Copenhagen in 2009 on the international framework to succeed the Kyoto Protocol.

COP15 in Copenhagen represents an opportunity for governments around the world to cooperate in the design of their national emission trading schemes in order to maximize the benefits they each can receive from trade in emissions. Cooperation is vital in promoting the environmental integrity of each nation's scheme and to avoid the spectre of carbon leakage into unregulated markets. Achieving this kind of regulatory consistency on a global scale is a colossal task. What is needed is a combination of coordinated systems that can be tailored for national circumstances (DiPiazza et al, 2009). Building on the Kyoto Protocol, the EU ETS and other cap-and-trade programmes planned in the US, Australia or Asia carbon markets need to be broader (i.e. include more sectors and countries), better linked and more ambitious in terms of setting emission targets compatible with the principles of sustainable development.

Carbon pricing at politically feasible levels alone will be insufficient. The scale of the challenge implies a systemic change in the energy sectors that requires huge innovation and investment in a relatively short time. Governments must complement market measures with other policies to stimulate innovation and encourage social change. These will include tough product and building regulations, tax incentives, greater support for private and public sector research and development, boosting low-carbon education and training in schools, technical colleges and universities, active industry policy through subsidies, reducing regulatory hurdles to clean technology infrastructure and increasing community engagement in low-carbon technologies and lifestyles.

While the EU energy and climate change package approved in December 2008, President Obama's Energy and Environment Policy and the Australian and New Zealand commitments to emissions trading are encouraging signs, their implementation will be tempered by the same forces that have made it difficult for all governments to realize strong action on climate change in the past. The management of competitiveness concerns with countries like China and India will be one key issue. In many OECD countries there is an increasing temptation to penalize imports from countries that have not instituted appropriate carbon pricing. While at first glance, such proposals may seem to make sense in theory, such schemes should only be pursued with caution. In reality, a vast range of carbon prices already exists across the world as a product of multiple competing policy objectives and economic circumstances. Action that does not adequately take the multiplicity of factors affecting energy prices into account may run the risk of triggering a trade war under the banner of environmentalism. This highlights the need to boost the environment and climate change as a priority in the World Trade Organization.

Climate change is a crucial challenge facing the international community. Cutting global emissions by at least 50 per cent below 1990 levels by 2050 is now seen as essential to avoid dangerous anthropogenic interference with the climate system. Through deforestation, agriculture and our use of fossil fuels, CO_2 concentration in the atmosphere has reached levels that the Earth has not experienced since the cycle of the ice ages began some 3 million years ago.[1] Most recent scientific research shows that we are approaching the critical threshold where average temperatures are likely to rise by 2°C or more above pre-industrial levels. Beyond an atmospheric concentration of 450ppm CO_2e, it is very likely that a series of climatic shifts will set up a self-sustaining cycle of rapid global warming. This tipping point could stand no more than a decade or two away.

Tackling climate change can become a powerful engine of technological innovation, economic growth and international cooperation. Investments in renewable or other carbon mitigation projects represent new opportunities in uncertain times. Climate policies, of which cap-and-trade schemes often represent a corner stone, are driven by two imperatives: the necessity to adopt a sustainable emission path and the opportunity to invest in sustainable technologies (DB Advisors, 2008). Changing behaviours through incentives for low emitters is a desirable policy that well designed cap-and-trade schemes and regulated carbon markets could help deliver.

The protection of our climate cannot afford the long delays that have followed previous climate initiatives. It wasn't until 2001 in Marrakesh, four years after the Kyoto Protocol was signed that the rules for the CDM were clearly defined, and it was several years later before CDM markets were truly operational. The Green Paper on greenhouse gas emissions trading within the European Union was published in March 2001, it was not until 2005 that the EU ETS pilot phase began. It was only in 2008 with the start of the 2nd phase of the EU ETS that European emissions were effectively constrained. A similar delay between an agreement at Copenhagen and implementation of measures to tackle emissions could undermine confidence in the carbon markets and delay required investments (DiPiazza et al, 2009). It is therefore crucial that countries or regions continue to act at a local level and not wait for international actions that will inevitably need time to be operational and evolve out of national systems. Climate change has been discussed thoroughly since 1992 and emissions are still going up. It is now time for all governments to act concertedly towards achieving emissions reductions.

Recently, Yale Economist William Nordhaus and Climatologist James Hansen argued at a high-level conference on climate change held at Copenhagen University in March 2009 that carbon taxation was the only way to solve the climate crisis. However, significant challenges face a common international tax regime for carbon. Politically, taxes are unpopular, they work on punishing polluters, rather than through the positive incentives of emissions trading. The political reality of implementing carbon taxation was recently exemplified by the electoral defeat of the Canadian Liberal Party to the incumbent Conservative party. The Liberals campaigned heavily on the need for a carbon tax and were successfully attacked by Conservatives, who prefer emissions trading. There is also currently little experience with an international regime of taxation, and countries already have vastly different levels of fuel taxation that would be difficult to reconcile in practice under such an international system. For these reasons we suggest that carbon markets are more likely to succeed as an international climate policy than taxation.

With the sudden and dramatic economic downturn, investors are lacking confidence and governments are dealing with the urgency of the financial crisis. For 2009, this means that stabilizing a shattered banking sector, helping a collapsing automotive industry and thawing a frozen real estate market will be at the top of world leaders' agendas. With these issues in mind, some might argue that 2009 is not a good time to negotiate a post-Kyoto treaty under the UNFCCC. We believe the opposite. Long-term clarity is needed more than ever. A set of clear rules articulated in a global climate treaty, supported by all major economies, could deliver this. The economic downturn should not be seen as an excuse for inaction but as a window for opportunity.

The challenge of climate change is interconnected with many others, such as energy security, biodiversity protection, reliable access to food and water and political stability. Perversely, the regions of the world that are or will be the most severely hit by the consequences of global warming will be those least likely to be able to respond and are least responsible for the problem. If not addressed in the short term, the long-term implications of climate change will irreversibly undermine living standards, prosperity and security across the world (de Vasconcelos and Zaborowski, 2009).

As we move towards Copenhagen at the end of 2009, presaged by the tectonic shifts in economic and political power of 2008, one cannot but sense history in the making. The last time the world community was confronted with challenges of such magnitude in the early decades of the last century it descended into geopolitical turmoil and world war. In addition to wars in Iraq and Afghanistan, in recent years the world community has had to respond to conflagrations in Georgia, Lebanon, the West Bank and Sudan. As a physical phenomenon, climate change is also contributing to the risk of military conflict. This was deemed such a matter of significance that the *Journal of Political Geography* dedicated a special issue to the topic in August 2007. However, climate change may also prove to be a powerful force for peace and cooperation, linking nations together through an international emission trading scheme against a common and deadly external threat.

Notes

1   For more information, see Sir David King, article, *Financial Times*, 30 May 2008. Sir David King is former chief scientific adviser to the UK Government and director of the Smith School for Enterprise and the Environment, Oxford

References

Coase, R. H. (1960), 'The problem of social cost', *Journal of Law and Economics*, vol 3, no 1, pp1–44

DB Advisors (2008) 'Investing in climate change 2009', October 2008, report available at www.dbadvisors.com/climatechange, accessed 9 March 2009

de Vasconcelos, A. and Zaborowski, M. (ed) (2009) 'European perspectives on the new American foreign policy agenda', ISS Report, January 2009, no 04

DiPiazza, S. A., Rogers, J. E., Eldrup, A. and Morrison, R. (2009) 'Tackling emissions growth. The role of markets and government regulation', Thought Leadership Series No1, Copenhagen Climate Council, www.copenhagenclimatecouncil.com/get-informed/thought-leadership-series/tackling-emissions-growth-the-role-of-markets-and-government-regulation.html

HSBC (2009) 'Which country has the greenest bailout?', *Financial Times*, 2 March

Index

Printed in the United States
by Baker & Taylor Publisher Services